PRIVILEGED KILLERS

Karl Schonborn

Suncoast Publishing
Sarasota, Florida

Disclaimer: This is a work of novelized non-fiction. The author used materials including articles, books, news accounts, interviews, diaries, journals, and court documents to tell this story. Some names, institutions, and scenes have been changed to protect the privacy of individuals still living. Although some dialogue may be misremembered, the author made every effort to capture the essence and truth of conversations. Numbered notes describe the sources of specific information. It is hoped that this true-crime account not only points to correctable flaws in the American justice system but also gives readers useful, even lifesaving, information about sociopaths in their midst.

Paperback ISBN: 978-1-7351849-1-3
Hardcover ISBN: 978-1-7351849-2-0
Also available in eBook format
Copyright ©2024 Karl Schonborn
All rights reserved.

Cover Design by Andy Carpenter

 Suncoast Publishing

Suncoast Publishing
Sarasota, Florida
PRINTED IN THE UNITED STATES OF AMERICA

Early Acclaim
for
Privileged Killers

When it comes to crime writers, you've got your wannabes and the genuine articles. Take it from me – I was a prosecutor for a long time, I did this work Schonborn's the real deal. He tells riveting stories of sociopathic killers with nuance, flair, and spot-on precision. *Privileged Killers* goes beyond the 'how' of these savvy criminals and delves deeply and insightfully into the 'why.' "

—**Elie Honig, Fmr Fed/State Prosecutor, CNN Legal analyst. Author of** *Hatchet Man, Untouchable*

"The author's a razor-keen observer, and in this new work he sometimes offers a complex series of events but they always add up, just like a good mystery. Great stuff! Join Schonborn's quest for truth, logic, and understanding in a world that often defies it. You'll love *Privileged Killers* and you'll want to keep it to read again and again."

—**Charles Haid, Award winning Actor/Director, Known for Renko in Hill Street Blues, NYPD Blue, ER, 3rdWatch, Criminal Minds and Murder1**

"Schonborn's true crime page-turner is woven together in a wholly original way. It's part memoir and part true crime. As he takes you on a journey through pivotal events of a generation, he interlaces the famous serial killers who dominated the headlines of those years—along with the unlikely killers and psychopaths who directly touched his life. He experienced some dramatic near misses and, to these, he layers his own insights as one of the great criminologists of our time."

—**Georgette Bennett, PhD, Criminologist, Commentator (NBC News, TED Talk, etc.), Philanthropist, Author of** *Crimewarps* **and** *Religicide*

"By chronicling his own real-life experiences, Schonborn shows how privileged narcissistic and psychopathic individuals often get a mere slap on the wrist, even if they kill people, due to a dysfunctional and imbalanced criminal justice system. Highly recommended!"

—**Scott Bonn, PhD, Criminologist/Professor, News commentator. Author of** *Why We Love Serial Killers,* **"Wicked Deeds"in** *Psychology Today*

"Schonborn's true crime memoir reveals brutal misogyny in the City of Brotherly Love as well as the darkside of sunny California after the sixties' Summer of Love. Turns out the author knew several privileged men who secretly resented the increasing opportunities and ascent of willful women. The successive shocks to Schonborn's sensibilities when each committed murder, changed his perspective on how society should respond to these dangerous men and his effort to reform the criminal justice system."

—**Kip Armstrong, Sociologist, The Penn Commonwealth University**

"Brilliant and terrifying! When police open a trunk, they discover more than the horrific sight of a dead girl. They discover a shocking revelation—the identity of one of the most improbable killers to walk among us.

Schonborn's story of this and other killers is gripping to the last word…and last drop of blood."

—**Sandra Woffington, Author of** *Unveiling* **and** *Wine Valley Mysteries*

"A great true crime read! Schonborn uses a professional criminologist's eye to study four murderers to reveal how privilege and entitlement–coupled with one of the Dark Triad disorders—deceived him and others. Whether a person's type of darkness is narcissism, manipulation, or psychopathy, the author explains its origins and how to handle it on an individual or criminal court level."

—**Peter Vronsky, Criminal Justice Historian, Scholar, Documentarian/Filmmaker, Author of many true crime serial killer studies, including** *Sons of Cain* **and** *American Serial Killers: the Epidemic Years 1951-2020*

SELECTED WORKS BY KARL SCHONBORN

Cleft Heart

Dealing with Violence

Policing Society

Stop, Look, and Listen

Acclaim for
Karl Schonborn's Previous Works

CLEFT HEART, 2014

"A poignant, heartfelt tale of endurance and hope. Schonborn's story is an inspiration to all who endure physical or mental health challenges and those who care about them."
—**U.S. Secretary of State John Kerry**

"There're books written every day that're engaging or charming, and there're those that you'll never forget, or which are life changing. *Cleft Heart* is charmingly life-changing and engagingly unforgettable. Brave, tender, ferocious and smart, it is a book every memoirist will wish they had written. It should be read and shared with people of all ages. It is that good."
—**Grace Hartdegen, Educator**

"Just finished *Cleft Heart* and enjoyed reading it very much. The authormust have been very comfortable in his own skin to have written it."
—**John Schairer, JD, Wisconsin State Public Defender**

"Most of us don't know about living with a disability. And even those with "normal" lives experience bullying, particularly when young. Yet, with a visible disability the taunting and bullying can crush a soul.

We learn so much about this phenomenon from Schonborn's wonderful memoir. It broke my heart to hear the young author suffering through a childhood of scorn and ridicule. Yet he perseveres and has success in life and in love. His family story is also engaging, and his relationship with his parents will haunt me for years. I highly recommend this book."
—**Leonard Edwards, JD, Santa Clara, Ca. Juvenile Court Judge**

POLICING SOCIETY, 2001

"This timely book provides a comprehensive look at police brutality, racial profiling, and zero tolerance—to note only a few topics—in modern-day policing, both in the US and the UK."
—**Heidi Dunkerton, Project Manager, K-H Publishing Co.**

VIOLENCE AND CONFLICT, 1998

"Schonborn was one of the first in the nation to study domestic violence, especially the police response to it. His current book, Violence and Conflict, shows him to be an expert in domestic violence as well as gang, racial, and terrorist violence."
—**Christopher Armstrong, Professor, Bloomsburg University**

"The primary focus of this fine book is domestic violence, street gang violence, bloody encounters with cults and militias, and the riots and disorders that have plagued several American cities of late."
—**The Journal of Adolescence, Fall 1998**

DEALING WITH VIOLENCE, 1975

"*Dealing with Violence* is a comprehensive and pathbreaking work which will contribute to theory as well as practice. Karl Schonborn has a keen analytical mind as evidenced by his research in the areas of peacekeeping and violence-management."
—**William Evan, PhD, Professor, The Wharton School, UPenn**

"This book is a refreshing relief from the barrage of dismal literature on violence. It fosters a sense of hopefulness rather than helplessness in dealing with a critical social malady... This important work should be read by a mass audience."
—**Lewis Yablonsky, PhD, Criminologist, Author of 30 books**

SCREENPLAY

STOP, LOOK AND LISTEN, 1988

"Born with a severe cleft palate and disfiguring hare lip...a young man realizes his boyhood dream of becoming a television news anchor."
—Doug Bruce, Jaffe/Lansing Productions

"Stop, Look and Listen is pretty darn good and covers lots of ground."
—Johnson Burtt, WTA Wallack Talent Agency

DOCUMENTARIES

GANG SIGNS, 1996

"This insightful video explains what to look for if a child or teen is involved with a gang. It explains the five major reasons kids join gangs and explores age groups, slang terms, and gang roles. Best of all, it shows how to reverse the hold gangs have on their members."
—Lana Floyd, Nimco Films, Inc.

"All Parents who suspect gang involvement in their kids' lives should see this video. I'm glad it's at Blockbuster Video now."
—Sidney Rice, Chief of Police, Daly City, California

A TALE OF TWO CITIES: POLICE IN MANCHESTER AND OAKLAND, 2004

"This perceptive documentary looks at similarities in the challenges and responses of police in two different cultures, the UK and the US."
—Elana Joffe, Acquisitions Director for Insight Media and Films Media Group

DEDICATION

To my wife and my siblings,

who were along for the harrowing journey depicted here.

CONTENTS

A Criminologist's Story...xv

PART I – THE UNICORN KILLER

A Detective's Story 1
CHAPTER 1
Ira Interrogates. Eve Enters the Garden.................... 5
CHAPTER 2
Hecklers, Holly, and the Hansons 17
CHAPTER 3
Biting Eve's Apple. Cracking the Zodiac's Code............ 27
CHAPTER 4
Moratorium, Russian Roulette, and Earth Day................34
CHAPTER 5
A Slasher's Story 41
CHAPTER 6
Four Dead in Ohio. Premonitions 43
CHAPTER 7
A Schmoozing Politician and a Boozing Extremist 49
CHAPTER 8
A Serial Killer's Story 59
CHAPTER 9
Terror at a Farmhouse. Berkeley and the Hansons........... 61

PART II – THE PAPER BAG KILLER

CHAPTER 10
The Stalking of a Serial Killer 74
CHAPTER 11
The Making of a Serial Killer 88
CHAPTER 12
Courts, the Insanity Plea, and the Synanon Psychopath........100

PART III – The "PSYCHO"-OLOGIST

CHAPTER 13
Deceitful, Predatory Professor Drell 112
CHAPTER 14
Predator Plays the Court. Zebra Terrorize the Streets.........120
CHAPTER 15
Death at my Doorstep. Dragon Lady.................................... 128
CHAPTER 16
Legal Shenanigans 135
CHAPTER 17
Holly Screams 139
CHAPTER 18
A Unicorn's Story: Cleaning and Scheming 141
CHAPTER 19
Destroying Art and a Relationship..................................... 144
CHAPTER 20
An Executioner's Story 150
CHAPTER 21
The Warehouse Burns. Fire Turns to Ice. 152
CHAPTER 22
Confrontation, Mystery, and an Emotional Desert 162
CHAPTER 23
Shocking News 173
CHAPTER 24
Beauty, the Beast, and Deteriorating Relationships......... 182
CHAPTER 25
Three Psychopaths 191
CHAPTER 26
Einhorn's Defense. Lawson and Lewis. 201
CHAPTER 27
The Making of a Psychopath 208
CHAPTER 28
Burglary, Rape and the Three Mouseketeers 219

PART IV – THE EXECUTIONER

CHAPTER 29
Deceptive Siren. Marriage. 229
CHAPTER 30
Betrayal, Sexual Assault, and a Power Struggle...............238
CHAPTER 31
Kafka in Justice Land. Sleuthing a Psychopath. 246
CHAPTER 32
A Cold, Calculated Crime 255
CHAPTER 33
Brazenness Talks, and a Court Listens 264
CHAPTER 34
Fie on Experts, Plea Bargains, and Psychopaths 271
CHAPTER 35
Arm-Wrestling with the Devil and Parole Officers 279
CHAPTER 36
Blackmail Escalates to Home Invasion....................... 284
CHAPTER 37
Collateral Damage from being Mugged by Reality 295
CHAPTER 38
Bring on the Night Stalker 302

EPILOGUE..309

NOTES..325

BIBLIOGRAPHY 358

ACKNOWLEDGMENTS 363

ABOUT THE AUTHOR 365

A Criminologist's Story

My early life resembled that of a boy in a bubble. If I had any signs of an illness as an infant, surgeons couldn't perform each of the several cleft lip and palate operations I needed. So, my parents isolated me from people, including my two-year-old sister and cousins. This worked until I was in elementary school, when it was harder to keep me away from sick kids and adults. After countless colds and ear infections in our rainy town in the Pacific Northwest, my parents moved our now five-person family to sunny California. The weather bubble in Palo Alto, thirty miles south of San Francisco, improved my health manyfold. And by chance, another bubble enveloped me in the halcyon suburb: insulation from danger and crime.

However, even idyllic Palo Alto couldn't shelter me forever from crime. In April 1955, I heard news about the disappearance of a fellow middle-schooler in nearby Berkeley, across the Bay from S.F. I feared for the life of pretty Stephanie Bryan, who was abducted while taking a shortcut home through the parking lot of the picturesque Claremont Hotel. Local police and the FBI, joined by a hundred other volunteers, feared for Stephanie too as they began one of the largest searches ever for a missing person. The only leads in the case at the time were a witness who saw a girl fighting with a man in a car near the hotel and later, a discarded textbook of Stephanie's in Martinez, twenty minutes away. For more than eight weeks, nothing came of the leads, the search, and the constant media stories.

Then, something blew the case wide open in July. The wife of an accounting student at the University of California (Berkeley) discovered a purse belonging to Stephanie in their basement in the nearby town of Alameda. Authorities then unearthed Stephanie's bra, glasses, and schoolbooks in an unfinished part of the basement. They arrested the woman's husband, Burton Abbott.

An intense investigation into Abbott's life ensued when he started changing his story and alibi. I pictured the worst for Stephanie, as I'd always feared my own death because of all the time I'd spent in hospitals. And though Unitarians had sown the seeds, I soon began to believe that violence, with its harm¬ and negativity, was something to be avoided at all costs. When Stephanie's body was found—tipped off by the discovery of a leg protruding from a shallow grave—near Abbott's cabin three hundred miles north, my heart broke.

In court, prosecutors accused Abbott of being a sexual psychopath. The label was way over my head at the time. But I did wonder why the state argued it was okay to execute, a fancy word for murder, a person convicted of murder. Equally troubling, a follow-up last-minute stay order in 1957 by California's governor didn't reach San Quentin's gas chamber in time. Abbott was already dead.

These memories of mine, and a resulting fascination with state and private violence, persisted with the onrush of real events in my youth and early adult years. I had hoped my participation in nationwide protests during grad school helped in a small way, along with other factors, to end America's state-sponsored violence during the Vietnam War. With a strong belief in nonviolence and a PhD in sociology's subfield of criminology. I began professing, researching, and advocating in the S.F. Bay Area for a less punitive criminal justice system. As someone trained in the social sciences – psychology at Yale, psychiatry at Columbia Med School, and criminology at UPenn — I hoped to turn American cops into the equivalent of less violent, minimally-armed English bobbies. Likewise, I hoped to nudge prison guards into being more humane correctional officers.

However, crimes and events involving different acquaintances, friends, and even loved ones of mine shook up my beliefs and career goals. Besides being privileged, all the people responsible for these wrongdoings possessed antisocial personalities that psychologists consider dark, and sometimes malevolent, disorders. When these are extremely narcissistic, manipulative, or psychopathic, they're part of what psychologists call the Dark Triad, a trio of antisocial personalities. In addition to displaying *similar* dark, socially-aversive traits, these personality types each possess traits *unique* to their own disorder. Psychopaths stand out though among the Dark Triad. Besides disregarding others' rights and manipulating masterfully, they usually lack remorse or guilt, even when they commit violence.

I wrote this true crime memoir in part to share not only the preparation, aspirations, and everyday work of criminologists, but also to show how the harsh realities of a few heinous crimes can crash down on some people. (My family and I might as well have been noted as victims in some of my friends and acquaintances' police reports.) So, just as I look for insights regarding the meaning of crime in my *work* life as a criminologist, I've tried in this book to look for the meaning and impact of psychopathy in my *personal* life.

I also wrote this book to pass on the knowledge and hard-earned wisdom I've gained as someone who's dealt with all types of Dark Triad individuals. For example, I knew, as a criminologist, I might deal with murderers clinically and study them dispassionately at an arm's length as strangers from a different cultural milieu. Never would I have guessed that they'd ever come from the very fabric of my life. With luck, my story will spare you from being a victim of antisocial, even criminal, behavior by people who walk, work, and sometimes even live next door to us.

Before you start reading about the bad guys, I begin with a brief "story" about one of the good guys. It's fact-based like a few other "stories" in the book, which are also told from a third-person, all knowing, point of view. These stories are intended to be out of the usual chronological order of this book. For instance, the detective's story is from 1979, ten years *after* the start of this book's main story.

PART I – THE UNICORN KILLER

A Detective's Story

March 1979

It's not every day you serve a warrant on a so-called celebrity. Detective Michael Chitwood fumbles to attach a temporary red light atop his dashboard as he navigates busy traffic. Without sirens but with red lights flashing when needed, he and his seven-man team speed across Philadelphia in unmarked cars. There's subfreezing windy weather this morning and the threat of slippery black ice on the streets. But Chitwood's determined not to mess up and has meticulously prepared for this raid, cautioning the team to kill their flashing lights within two blocks of the suspect's home.

When a groggy-sounding tenant answers the intercom, Chitwood apologizes for the early-hour intrusion and informs him he has a search warrant.

"To search what?" the tenant mumbles.

"The balcony, porch, whatever it's called, at the rear of your apartment."

It takes some moments for the lock to buzz. The eight climb a flight of stairs to reach the apartment. The guy at the door is essentially nude, clad only in an open robe that he makes no effort to close, much to the team's disgust. Chitwood flashes back, opening his coat and revealing his police badge, and hands him a copy of the warrant. Glancing at the front of the thirty-five-page warrant, the man mutters something to the effect of "Yes, I once had a live-in girlfriend, but she ducked out for groceries and never returned."

Ignoring the tenant and most of his apartment, Chitwood speeds through a long hallway to a living room overrun with books and papers on every surface, including the floor. Pushing aside a maroon blanket hanging on one wall, Chitwood discovers a door, which he opens. He motions to two forensic techs, and they all enter a small porch enclosed by windows looking down on a yard. The three stare at a heavy-duty padlock on a closet door. As Chitwood and the techs don rubber gloves, another tech enters and photographs the padlock. *Flash!* Chitwood then asks the tenant, "Got a key to this lock?"

He says, head down and still in a mumble, "No idea where it is."

"Well, I'm going to have to break it." The guy shrugs, looking bored and disengaged from the proceedings.

Chitwood takes a crowbar from a tech and breaks the lock with two hearty strokes. The tech photographs the broken lock. Flash!

When Chitwood opens the door to the closet, he sees shelves filled with cardboard boxes. and a purse atop a green suitcase on the floor. Chitwood tips the suitcase toward himself and sees, hidden behind it, a black steamer trunk, the type people once took on cruise ships.

Chitwood removes items from the shelves and suitcase, having aides photograph and catalog clusters of items, such as clothes, home wares, and sketchbooks. The purse contains a driver's license, a social security card, and a worn library card, all belonging to someone named Helen Maddux.

The tenant, moving back and forth through the porch door, begins to lose a bit of his cool as he continues to observe what's unfolding. Chitwood becomes agitated too as an unpleasant odor wafts upwards when he pulls the trunk out of the closet. He undoes two side latches but then says, "No key to this either?" The tenant, who's changed into pants and a shirt, nods.

Chitwood breaks the lock at the center of the trunk. He takes off his suit jacket and pauses. When he finally lifts the trunk's lid, an awful stench causes some of his team to wince or choke, covering their mouths with their hands. A few reach for their handkerchiefs. The photographer can't because he keeps shooting—reluctantly, it seems, as his face has gone pale. He's been ordered to document every step of the search.

Chitwood looks down into the trunk and shoves aside a layer of polyfoam pieces, the type used to stuff cushions. Then he slides a stack of old newspapers to one side as well.

Whoosh! A human hand lunges at him!

"Jesus!" he yells, jumping back, eyes filled with fear. Everyone else but the tenant leans forward to look. After noticing the hand is now motionless and withered, Chitwood calms down. He proceeds to clear away material from the hand's shriveled forearm, clothed in a flannel shirt.

Chitwood motions for photos then moves back into the apartment to the kitchen sink, takes off his gloves and asks one of three officers watching the tenant to summon the coroner. While washing his hands, Chitwood turns to the tenant for a reaction.

Nothing.

Then Chitwood says, "Found a body. Looks like it's Helen's."

Shrugging his shoulders, the tenant, who is now a suspect, says, "You found what you found."

As an officer reaches for handcuffs on his belt, he makes eye contact with Chitwood. The detective shakes his head no, acknowledging the suspect's celebrity and passivity. Chitwood then reads the suspect his Miranda rights, and when he asks if he wishes to remain silent, the man nods yes.

A tech measures the trunk—over four feet long, thirty inches wide, thirty inches deep—and another readies a cataloging clipboard. They both move closer to the trunk and put on masks to better tolerate the smell, an odor best described as a combination of formaldehyde and decomposing flesh.

A tech resumes the process of digging deeper in the trunk while another writes down the items found: Bone fragments. Three air fresheners. Clumps of hair encrusted in blood. *Flash!*

Soon, the tech uncovers a skull smashed in several places. As he removes crumpled-up plastic bags used as filler, he finds the skull is connected to a half-decomposed, half-mummified body. It's in a fetal position.

Chitwood tells the tech to stop.

Shortly, the coroner, a deputy prosecutor, another homicide detective, and a private investigator hired by Helen's family enter the premises. A couple of them, bearing additional search warrants, start examining the rest of the apartment. More cameras flash.

The suspect remains quiet through all this, even when techs use power saws to cut sample floorboard pieces from the bottom of the closet. The tenant below had complained of a substance oozing from his ceiling.

Because the suspect is a local celebrity, no one worries about him escaping when he's finally escorted to a waiting vehicle outside.

CHAPTER I

Ira Interrogates.
Eve Enters the Garden.

March *1968*

From the start of 1968, violence and nonviolence battled for the soul of America overseas and at home. Overseas, unspeakable violence raged at the height of America's investment of lives, talent, and treasure in the war in Vietnam. But despite a tactical victory during the massive Tet Offensive, respected TV news anchor Walter Cronkite joined the still-nonviolent antiwar movement at home and called for a negotiated peace.

Responding to Cronkite's pessimism, President Lyndon Johnson allegedly said something like, "If I've lost him, I've lost middle America's support." And soon, on March 31, Johnson announced he wouldn't run for a second term as president, but would push for peace and try to reunite a country torn apart by an unpopular, faraway war. I watched the president's startling declaration on a TV at Chicago's O'Hare airport on a layover en route home. Just hours before, my mother had committed suicide. Her death had shocked and numbed me, so LBJ's "startling" news rolled over me like water off a duck's back.

****

With my fiancée Sharon Belton's help, I managed to pull myself together after my mom's death. But Johnson failed to pull the country together after his announcement. If anything, his decision created other rifts—as in the now-rudderless Democratic Party—which prevented him from reuniting the country. And certainly, reunification became even harder after a wave of assassination attempts across America, succeeding in the cases of MLK, Jr., Bobby Kennedy, and nearly so so with artist Andy Warhol.

Sharon and I endured all this upheaval and the continued raging of the war overseas. Still, we retained enough idealism to participate in a nonviolence role-playing exercise in Santa Cruz, California just after getting married in nearby Palo Alto. Dubbed the Peace Games and funded by friend, folksinger, and stalwart of the antiwar movement, Joan Baez, the two-day exercise was intended to develop new ways to employ nonviolence. It took place in late August just before the Democrats met to choose a substitute presidential candidate for Johnson amid riot-like battles between the police and demonstrators outside their convention in Chicago.

Philadelphia – University of Pennsylvania – August 1968

When Sharon and I arrive in Philly after the Games to resume grad school, my acquaintance Ira Einhorn, considered the Prince of Nonviolence by locals, soon hears of our involvement in the Games. And recalling I know Joan from my youth, Ira insists I tell him about the Games.

I join Ira at the table where he holds court at a pricey café, La Terrasse, snapping his fingers when waitresses ignore him. He calls himself the Unicorn—Einhorn means "one horn" in German—akin to the mythical, gentle creature, tamable only by a virgin. While Ira's got no horn atop his head, his unkempt long brown hair and beard, combined with a six-foot-plus frame carrying 220 pudgy pounds, make him as odd-looking as a unicorn. He's known for his mix of erudition, otherworldly nonviolence, and real-world, um, single horniness.

Ira lights a cigarette, which rarely masks his renowned body odor, a result of his contempt for conventional hygiene. But his odor puts off very few of the many women who wait in line to consort with him. And the fact that he devours women with abandon, as he does books, also doesn't bother them.

I explain to Ira that Roy Kepler, bookshop owner and Joan's money advisor, spent time explain to Ira that Roy Kepler, bookshop owner and Joan's money advisor, spent time preparing Sharon, me, and two dozen others for the outdoor Games. We then traveled one weekend to a Quaker retreat in the Santa Cruz mountains. The role-play started as six of our group, chosen to be armed soldiers¬, invaded twenty of us playing nonviolent resisters. We represented holdouts during an on-going invasion of the U.S. by Chinese Communists and People's Liberation Army.

Kepler scripted the beginning action of the role-play Games after visiting an institute in Canada committed to experimenting with nonviolence. Like most pacifists, Kepler had long admired the hundreds of thousands of WWII Europeans who'd nonviolently resisted the Nazis.

I pause to be sure Ira's okay with being a listener, not the talker, as he usually is.

"Your Games," he asks, "took place just after the Soviets invaded Czechoslovakia?"

"Yes. Pretty timely. A real Communist invasion...no pretending."

Ira slams the table, saying as the cups clatter in their saucers, "What a week! That, then the Chicago rioting." Ira's intense blue eyes go from enthusiasm to wildness for a second.

A few cafe patrons stare at us, but I continue, "We resisters had decided not to defend territory or buildings but to insist on American rights like freedom to speak and assemble at any time. Thus, we generally moved around freely, refusing to be corralled by soldiers."

"*Capture the Flag* for hippies?" Ira jokes.

"Kinda. I got captured right away however, and Sharon cried. But unlike Capture-the-Flag, no one could spring me from jail."

"Cried?"

"Sharon swore her tears were real, just like those shed during the pretend electric-shock role-plays at Yale."

"And Baez? What'd she do? Talented. Pretty." Ira's fervor to meet the star with a wondrous pure soprano seems almost palpable.

"Wasn't there. She knew her superstar presence would ruin things."

Ira's usually curious eyes go dull and I have a fleeting thought, *Maybe the rumor's true? He wants to bed a celeb?*

I continue, "Just before dark, Sharon read a news release that the Chinese had snatched me to force me to reveal where we resisters hid our weapons. Apparently, she feared I'd be tortured, and she fainted. After a fellow resister revived her, Sharon said, 'They'll hurt Karl, even though he did gift the soldiers his portable typewriter to facilitate their paperwork.'"

"Nonviolent gift-giving doesn't always work," Ira chortles.

"Female pleading, even flirting, didn't work either."

"Why?"

"'Cuz the Chinese soldiers wore mirrored sunglasses. The glasses prevented eye contact, emotional connection. Plus, the invaders pretended not to understand English... and us praising American freedoms had no effect on strictly-supervised troops."

"Never tasted 'freedom,' huh?"

"Yup. So, having struck out, resisters retreated to their bunkhouse to sleep. Tired and dejected too, I curled up on the floor of my jail cell, a repurposed bathroom. Guards kept my 'cell' locked and took turns checking on me through the night."

Ira's lips form into a wry half smile. "The Chinese just didn't trust you resisters. Clearly, 'what we got here is failure to communicate.'" He takes a drag on his cigarette.

I smile. "Come morning, the Chinese commander ordered all of us to sign a surrender-and-cooperate document, or pay a price. When no one did, he stomped away."

Ira grins and leans forward.

"Then the sound of machine-gun fire thundered forth from my prison cell."

Ira almost rises from his chair, shouting, "That prop weapon must've made a damn-convincing noise! Go on! Go on!"

"Several resisters shouted, versions of 'We've lost Brother Karl, but not the battle.' They then linked arms and started singing, but others rushed to sign the document."

"Oh, no."

"About then, my guards hustled me, very much alive, to the crowd of resisters. Stunned, the signers realized they'd been duped. Amid the confusion, the Commander ordered soldiers to really shoot me.

Sharon wailed as I crumpled to the ground. At that point, Kepler, who was refereeing the Games, called out, 'Exercise over!'"

"Wow!" Ira gushes. "You were killed as a nonviolent soldier, just like Gandhi!"

Then, glancing at his watch, Ira stands up, saying, "Forgot I have an appointment. Can you pick up the tab?"

I watch Ira run out the door and think, *Joan doesn't need another womanizer after her, especially a cheap one.*

****

Days after depicting my role-play death, I deal with the real death of one of my professors, whose plane crashed during a weekend trip to Dartmouth College. Walking to his memorial service, Sharon and I pass a number of undergrads partying in ivy-covered brick frat houses. Ivy is obligatory at Ivies such Penn. So is partying for a few Gatsby types.

We enter Dietrich Hall, where criminology and sociology programs share space with the Wharton School of Business, and try to find seats in a richly paneled room full up with people attending the service for Peter Nettl. Despite the somberness of the occasion, I'm proud to be with Sharon, a blue-eyed version of Audrey Hepburn. Some of my fellow grad students, like Mike Hogan, nod to her before me. They know Sharon's large eyes see the world as a fine artist, but her delicate mouth can keep up with them swear word for swear word, even drink for drink. Nettl barely got his seminar on "power" under way before his death. I took it because if I reject violence as a way to exert power, then I'd better understand the other types of power out there, like Ira's "charismatic" power. Ira's charisma motivated me enough to want to be friends with him, impress him with my Games experience, and even pay his food and drink tab like so many others had.

Faculty share stories of Nettl's brilliance, humanity, and use of "Oh so terribly noice," a holdover from his native Britain. They note his books, especially one about Rosa Luxemburg, a heroine to this day of East Germany's Marxist state. This makes me think of my brother, flirting with Marxism at Cal Berkeley.

But my reverie is broken by a professor talking about the tragedy of Nettl dying so young. Suddenly, I feel very sad. Then lightheaded. I wonder if my olive-complected face now matches Sharon's usually pale, porcelain face. *Why can't my fifty-two-year-old mom still talk to me, and Nettl still meet our seminar this week?*

After the service, I don't want to ignore my feelings of sadness and grief by socializing at a reception in front of my professors, especially Erving Goffman, who studies forced, inauthentic behavior. As Sharon and I slip out, I overhear two of my fellow grad-students buds talking.

"No Marvelous Marv today," says Jon Snodgrass, raised in Panama and an activist despite of, or because of, military service in Germany.

"Yup. Globetrotting Marvin Wolfgang misses yet another event," Carl Klockars sneers, already scarfing down a free munchie despite being against free lunches for needy school kids.

****

Before starting home, Sharon dashes into the Wistar Institute diagonal from Dietrich Hall, where she works when not studying at the Pennsylvania Academy of the Fine Arts, to pick up something. Minutes later, we arrive at our apartment, located in a block-long row of three-story brick houses, sharing sidewalls. Thankfully, our windows face attractive Mansard-roofed detached buildings on the other side of street.

Our West Philly row house, like all the others we're attached to, has a separate entryway raised above the sidewalk by a few steps. There's no variation in most of the red brick facades, and not all have readable addresses. So, visitors, like Hogan, often buzz the wrong tenants. Rather than counting a certain number of trees to find our entryway, Hogan now just takes a taxi whenever he visits, trusting cabdrivers' abilities to guess addresses. Taxis make sense to Hogan, a lifelong New York City resident, since he knows nothing about driving, owning, or repairing a car. Though he knows cabbies cost, he often asks them to wait for him. Sometimes he forgets they're waiting, stretches out a visit...then runs up a huge fare. He's a sociological theorist.

As I climb stairs to our third-floor place, I read a letter from my dad I'd grabbed out of our mailbox. Addressed to "Family and Friends," it's written like the holiday newsletter he and Mom used to send, but always in December. He writes that Housing and Urban Development has just received a mandate to fight housing discrimination, and this won't be easy. He continues, writing he's begun seeing Eve Malouf, who he'd recently met in the San Francisco apartment building he moved to from Palo Alto after Mom's death. He describes the coincidence that he and Eve have had similar lives, growing up in Washington State and working for the Feds.

"What the hell?" I shout as I enter our flat. "Read this, honey!"

After skimming the letter, she exclaims, "Ahhh. Just as you thought!"

Despite the high cost of phone calls, I dial Dad's number and dispense with niceties, stating, "Can't believe you'd lie, Dad."

"Whoa! What d'ya mean?"

"Your letter," I say, grabbing a can and can opener from our cupboard. "You twist the truth big time."

"I don't understand—"

"Just bumping into someone like Eve. It's absurd," I say after finally succeeding with a manual can opener.

"Shows Aunt Irene was right—"

"Irene's a Stenerson, Mom's side of the family. They've had to blame someone for your mom's suicide."

"C'mon, Dad! Eve's someone you've known from years of HUD oversight trips to the Seattle Housing Authority." I pick up a spoon after the cat we're babysitting nudges my ankles forcefully.

"Believe what you want, son. I just met Eve."

"I don't believe you—"

"Trust me. Know you've always suspected, but when we have time to talk, I'll—"

"Sure."

"Gotta go, Son. Was rushing out the door when you called. Sorry to cut this short."

I sigh, pause, then bend over and feed the cat.

****

I'm at the campus paper's offices, and the editor of the *Daily Pennsylvanian* has just accepted my political cartoon lampooning racist presidential candidate George Wallace. I'm on a roll. The editor's run five of my pen-and-ink cartoons this term. (When I need a brief break from studying, I often sketch and sometimes a decent social comment cartoon emerges.)

As I leave the editor's office, I spot Ira Einhorn chatting up a reporter across the newsroom. Ira's eyes find mine, and he yells to me, "I wanna hear about Baez. Now! Over coffee?"

"Take him!" the reporter shouts. "This freeloader will drink all our coffee. . .our lifeblood."

"Pagano's?" I shout. "Cheap, in case I end up paying again."

"Just get him outta here," the reporter pleads. "Had it with his endless self-promotion."

****

As we walk toward Pagano's, I say, "You're a moth to a flame, Ira. Can't get enough newspaper coverage."

"Naw! Just spreading the message of peace and love..."

"Like Jesus," I snuffle nasally, as I'm wont to do as a cleft-kid.

"Don't need the *Daily Pennsylvanian*. Got the *Distant Drummer*'s love."

"I've read your *Drummer* pieces. Lots about drugs, hippies versus radicals—"

"My *Drummer* persona! I try to live up to it, unicorn-like. 'Smile on your brother, everybody get together—'"

"'Try to love one another right now'...but you're disruptive too," I say as we wait to be seated. Ira objects, saying he calms situations. In fact, he says he just played peacemaker in a dispute between a biker gang and a draft-resistance commune. It boiled over when a Warlock assaulted a draft resister, thinking he'd put sand in his and his buddies' gas tanks. The resister denied it, but said the gang deserved it for attending a right-wing George Wallace rally. Tensions grew between the two Powelton Village groups.

As the informal mayor of Powelton, a neighborhood abutting Penn, Ira claims he schmoozed both sides a bit and organized an artsy happening to raise money to fix the damaged Harleys. The rift healed in no time, according to Ira.

As we slide into a booth and order coffee, Ira says, "Enough about peacekeeping. Dish about Joan."

"Well," I take a deep breath, "she immersed herself in her Nonviolence Institute to get over Bob Dylan. It worked. She just married a draft resister."

"Lucky guy!"

"Hold on; Feds just convicted him of draft evasion. Still free, but soon he'll be in a Texas prison."

"Tell me when they incarcerate him, and she's back on the market—"

"Look out," I caution. "Roy Kepler watches out for her."

"The Peace Games guy?"

"Yeah. He organized 'em with the help of Stanford's Free University."

"I started Penn's Free U."

"Joan kept our Free U alive after Stanford kicked it off campus. My people, the local Unitarians, came to the rescue too, providing classrooms."

Ever competitive, Ira says he organized marijuana Smoke-Ins and acid Be-Ins to save his Free U. And then I tell him a couple of Joan stories, including the time she kissed me.

"Je-sus, Karl! What kind of kiss?"

"More than a peck on the cheek ...but I didn't kiss back."

"Christ, man!"

"Sharon and I had just committed to each other."

"You idiot!"

"Her romance with Bob Dylan had just ended—"

"Didn't stop her husband—"

I explain that I felt, too, she'd overwhelm me with her complex, contradictory lifestyle, spartan at times—sitting on concrete floors at her institute, meditating alongside me—and indulgent at others, like clothes shopping at pricey stores and joyriding her Jaguar XK-E convertible around Carmel.

"How'd you meet?"

"School ...where she and her mentor, a Gandhi scholar, promoted nonviolence. Having been bullied for my cleft lip and palate, it seemed like a way to be assertive without risking a punch to my surgically fixed face."

"You then chose Quaker-inspired Penn to study how to implement nonviolence—"

"Especially in police work."

Swallowing the last of his coffee, Ira says, "Come to my place and see my nonviolence library."

"Just a flyby. Gotta get home."

****

Ira's rundown building, called the Rock Pile because its facade sloughs off rock that piles up in flower beds, attracts stoners and burnouts. Kids in perpetual disrepair crash in its huge basement, partly because Ira encourages it. I wonder, *Does he do this to atone for those who can't handle the drug culture he promotes?*

Ira's apartment has books everywhere: crammed in bookshelves, piled on tables, stacked on the floor creating pathways.

"Wanna get rid of 'em all," he murmurs.

"Don't!" I exclaim, recoiling. "Good books are hard to find. And costly too."

Ira grabs Sharp's 1967 *Civilian Defense* off a shelf, causing other books to fall to the floor.

My eyes light up. "Sharp facilitated the birth of the Games. The Von Clausewitz of nonviolent warfare."

Ira mumbles as he finds Fischer's *The Life of Mahatma Gandhi.*

I say, "His book's where I first learned about Satyagraha."

"Sanskrit for 'nonviolence!'"

"Not quite. Gandhi used it to refer to the 'power and forcefulness of truth.'"

Ira ignores my correction, saying, "I practice Satyagraha to save the planet. Hurting the environment is violence."

"No surprise; you're the Prince of—"

"When cops raided a party here last year, I used nonviolence as they searched everyone and the premises. I even challenged a belligerent cop to match me with push-ups."

I laugh and say, "Gandhi probably never thought of push-ups as nonviolence."

"Months later, cops pounded on my door again, in the morning. They couldn't find anything." Ira beams. "I'd hung my stash out a window, hiding it under the windowsill."

"Pretty savvy."

"They still took me, my overnight friend, and some pills to headquarters. During the interrogation, they baited us, calling me a faggot and her a whore."

"Faggots sleeping with whores? Hmm. What'd you say?"

"'I can hurt you guys 'cuz I'm a black belt, but don't want to.' All along, I'm smiling, loving, nonviolent."

"And?"

"The mean cop, who wanted to beat me up from the git-go, calmed down."

"Not sure about the black-belt bit," I say. "But," patting Ira on his massive back, "it was a real encounter, not a Games exercise."

"The cops released me, determined my pills were meds, as I'd claimed."

"Sweet."

"They can bust me, but they can't pin anything on me."

CHAPTER 2

Hecklers, Holly,
and the Hansons

Philadelphia, Pennsylvania – February 16, *1969*

Scoffers yelling through windows at us inside College Hall finally get to me. I lose my cool, shouting, "Stop it, for God's sake! Learn the facts. Then join us. You know we're right!"

I'm sitting in to protest Penn officials wanting to displace thousands of poor people living next to the campus. The same expansionism caused violence at Columbia University last year.

Einhorn rarely protests, but supports causes by speechifying and the odd theatrical stunt. He claims his fingerprints are all over this housing fight, since many of the residents Penn threatens to displace live near his place.

So I sit in, Ira jawbones, and my dad fights via HUD (Housing and Urban Development) for housing reform. Ira has loads more time to do battle than I because he doesn't bother working for a living. I've got to grade, lead discussion sessions, and perform other TA tasks besides conducting my own graduate work. My sit-in time is limited to alternate days.

Penn officials keep their cool, but campus cops grow restless as the days drag on. Whenever cops seem close to losing it, we chant "Not another Columbia," hoping events won't take a similar turn. Police in NYC cleared occupied Columbia buildings last April, injuring hundreds and arresting almost a thousand.

Knowing that emotions are as high as the stakes are, I put my sociological skills to work by surveying the fifty-one protestors who decide to sleep-in Saturday night. My results show most advocate nonviolence and expect the protest to remain calm. A small number feel violence will occur, and not so much due to the administration's campus cops, but to Philly's cops led by hardline Police Commissioner Frank Rizzo.

Believing in transparency and the power of self-fulfilling prophecies, I publicize the nonviolent disposition of dedicated protesters by sharing my findings with less-dedicated ones and Penn administrators via the *Daily Pennsylvanian*. Becoming aware of our commitment to nonviolence may've motivated administrators to continue showing restraint. Their willingness to change Penn's priorities and decision-making processes—plus the negotiating savvy of our leaders—allowed the protest to end peacefully on Sunday.

I am gratified that nonviolence and mutual concessions bridged the gap between Penn's activists and administrators. No buildings were destroyed, and we built a hell of a lot. We achieved many of our goals without Columbia's violence, which was actually followed by another round almost a month later, when NYC police injured over fifty students and arrested nearly two hundred.

****

During one of my trips outside Philly to promote conflict resolution programs among neighboring colleges like Swarthmore and Haverford, Sharon tags along to tour the gorgeous Bryn Mawr campus. On our train ride back to Philly, Sharon tells me of meeting a woman, Holly Maddux, who had uncanny similarities to herself. I remark that she even resembled Sharon physically, having seen Holly say goodbye to Sharon just as I entered the Student Center to rejoin Sharon. Holly is a blonde like Sharon, who is now peroxiding her hair, and Holly has delicate features like Sharon.

Sharon says that when she arrived at the Center, she noticed a woman sketching at a table by herself. Sharon asked her if she could look at the drawing, saying she attended Philly's Art Academy. Holly invited Sharon to sit with her and spoke enthusiastically about transferring soon to the Rhode Island School of Design in Providence.

Sharon, too, had changed colleges but hadn't taken a year off for nonacademic reasons or lived back at home as Holly had. Home for Holly was humid, sports-crazed Tyler in east Texas, where she'd been the salutatorian of her senior class and also a willowy cheerleader. I thought, *Holly and Sharon, while gifted enough to excel academically anywhere, have inner voices that keep returning them to artistic pursuits.*

As our train passes into Philly proper, Sharon continues her twins-separated-at-birth story. Both their dads were WWII vets, upset with the antiwar activism of most of their daughters' boyfriends, blaming their activism on sophisticated universities on both coasts. Both dads were happy with American capitalism, pleased with their Episcopalian roots, and very protective of their pretty daughters. Holly's dad grilled her many boyfriends over the years and Sharon's did the same, plus surprising us in Philly last year to see if we were living in sin. We were.

Sharon says, "We talked candidly, as perfect strangers often do, about both often feeling like outsiders – as artists, introverts, and transplants to the Northeast."

"True, for you," I say.

"And our lack of confidence about social and political stuff. We speculated it's 'cuz we both grew up with a loud, opinionated parent dominating a quiet, better-educated one."

"Also true, for you, but unsure if the cause is what you two speculated about."

Sharon concludes her story, saying, "Holly and I also talked about having to grow up fast in college due to being naïvely traditional as youngsters."

"You weren't the oldest Virgin Mary in your Christmas pageant for nuttin'," I joke.

"Never shoulda told you that," Sharon retorts. "I break rules these days."

"Well, the Art Academy expects you to break 'em."

****

That I might see my field notes by moonlight, I stand outside an unmarked patrol car and scribble "seventh time out with Gang Control Unit." I've been riding mostly with Willie Robinson from a subunit of the Philly Police Department's youth division.

Earlier on, he and I had sat in the Gang Control office talking about different ways of handling gangbangers. I'd asked Robinson if he'd give a second chance to a kid who'd stolen, burgled, or committed another penal code wobbler.

"Yeah, when faced with a wobbler between a misdemeanor or felony for a juvenile, I always charge the former." I congratulated him, saying, "You're helping reverse the research finding that cops often contribute to kids' lifelong resentment toward authority figures."

Suddenly, Robinson got a call, strapped on his gun belt, and we rushed to the scene of a gang fight.

I strain to hear what he's saying to a young kid he's dragged to the periphery of a huge fist-fight between rival gangs that's being carefully watched by a few other Gang officers. After Robinson gets the kid's version of how the fight started, he warns him, "Go home now, or I'll arrest you! No good'll come of an arrest record."

I smile, hearing him be firm but fair, a milder version of what the *Tough Love* book, just out, advocates for troubled youth. However, Robinson may've also acted humanely knowing the cavalry's coming. Sure enough, a swarm of marked squad cars swoops in and regular officers wade into the fracas with nightsticks drawn to stop the fighting.

There's little beyond police prodding tonight because no one saw the glint of a knife or shiv in the moonlight. Nor has anyone seen guns. If dispatch had reported such, Robinson would've slowed our unmarked car, making sure I, as a researcher, arrived after any fireworks.

Returning to me and the car, Robinson says, "Uniformed cops will arrest only a few youths tonight, and I'll interview 'em tomorrow, especially if anyone's been seriously injured in the melee. If kids blame someone who 'got away,' I'll use the PD's extensive file of names, addresses, and rap sheets to ID 'em and then arrest 'em."

As we drive back, I screw up my courage and ask, "Did you give my letter to your sergeant?"

"Yeah, and he sent it upstairs to the captain."

My heart skips. *Access to police data's never easy. But this effort's been a bear.*

"What'd the captain say?"

"He's not keen that you want to turn cops into social workers." Robinson smiles.

"So what'd he decide?"

"He's giving you access."

"Hallelujah!" I shout, slapping my knee.

"Said he couldn't deny a request from one of Wolfgang's boys. Said he remembers when Wolfgang's mentor, Thorsten Sellin, first put American Criminology on the map."

****

Later in the week, I spot Wolfgang half a block ahead of me on campus and hustle, knowing how hard it is to collar the Sociology Department chair and criminology superstar. Breathless when I finally draw even, I say, "Great news, Dr. Wolfgang. Got the final data I need to start my thesis."

"Nonviolent policing, right?"

"Pretty much. Comparing humanitarian and authoritarian policing."

"Let's phone your committee head and get your thesis launched."

Once we're in Wolfgang's office, he bellows into his phone, "Hey, Digby, Schonborn just got access to his final batch of data. He's now got data from family crisis cops in NYC and from gang cops here in Philly."

Wolfgang listens and repeats Professor Baltzell's words to me. "Also, data from National Guard 'n' 82nd Airborne riot troops. And from UN peacekeepers."

Wolfgang cradles the phone with his shoulder while repeating, "He's using the data to test hypotheses from his theory of nonviolent third-party intervention."

After lighting a cigarette, Wolfgang explains, "Both Karl and I have seen bobbies using nonviolence in England. American cops need to try that, though we got more guns here 'n they do in England."

Wolfgang listens again, then asks Baltzell, "You're speaking for your committee, Digby?...Oh?...They OK'd the thesis launch a while ago, pending this final data acquisition?...Great! Thanks, Digby."

Wolfgang smiles at me as he hangs up.

"T-Thank you so much!" I exclaim and stand up to leave.

"We all like your broad—local cops to UN peacekeepers— approach. And your multi-discipline approach; that's really necessary when researching violence."

****

I burst into our apartment, shouting that the faculty green-lighted my thesis. Sharon hugs me and says we should go out for drinks.

I nod and then say, "I married my longtime girl this year. Now I'm marrying nonviolence to police work."

"You're an idealist, all right."

"It's a genetic defect."

Sharon grabs a fancy envelope and hands it to me. "Sorry. This may ruin your high. Came in today's mail."

"Huh?" I say as I pull out a wedding invitation and read it. " Oh, Jesus! Dad's marrying Eve!"

"At the Hansons'."

I lunge for the phone to call my brother in Berkeley.

Scott answers on the first ring, saying, "Knew it was you. Can't believe it either. He's remarrying so soon."

"Who is she?"

"I just met her. She's okay. Like Dad, she lost a spouse recently. Probably needy too."

"Still, couldn't Dad have waited a bit?" I moan. "Especially from a public-relations standpoint?"

"Everyone will now say Aunt Irene, Mom's sister-in-law, was right, that Mom killed herself because Dad was having an affair."

Scott tells me a bit more about Eve, saying she worked in an office in Seattle and likes to sing. Her spouse crawled through buildings, wiring 'em up for demolition.

Scott then updates me about the Hansons, whom we knew as fellow Unitarian Church members. After Mom's suicide, Dad's friendship with Dr. Kent Hanson, a hotshot psychiatrist in San Francisco, rekindled. While Dad always commuted to S.F. for work, he moved there shortly after Mom's death in March.

At the end of the phone call, Sharon and I go out for drinks. We talk more about family drama than the okay to launch my thesis.

San Francisco, California – July 1969

Approaching the Hanson home in the exclusive San Francisco neighborhood of Forest Hills-St. Francis Wood has always thrilled me. Winding, leafy green streets—not the squared-off blocks of most cities—prevail on the sunny side of Twin Peaks. The two-story Hanson brown-shingled home impresses because it's perched high above the street with a small lawn sloping down to a five-foot retaining wall running along the sidewalk. Each story boasts a set of windows, composed of four door-sized windows subdivided by mullions, looking out onto the street.

As Sharon and I exit our rental car, we admire the other stately homes around us. We walk up a flight of concrete steps to a landing bordered by small, sculpted trees, and climb another flight to a neatly manicured lawn. After crossing a courtyard-like area created by the L-shaped footprint of the house, we arrive the front door. Sharon strikes the door knocker, and a woman in a caterer's uniform opens it, saying, "Welcome to the Hanson residence." She ushers us into a sunken living room where son Bill—tall, fair, with long hair—greets me as a friend. I introduce him to Sharon, and we chat amiably.

Out of the corner of my eye, across the large, classically decorated living room with crown molding and decorative trim, I see Dad standing next to a petite, curvaceous brunette whose hair is pulled up in a stylish do. I explain to Bill we haven't met Eve yet, so must break away. After hugging us both, Dad introduces us to Eve.

I extend my hand, quickly shaking hers, and murmur, "Pleased to meet you."

"Likewise," she says, awkwardly making eye contact. "Your dad's so proud of you—"

While Sharon shakes her hand, she asks, "Do you like living in San Francisco?"

"The fog's like Seattle's rain. Moving to Palo Alto soon. It'll be warmer. I'm half Lebanese, so I like it hot."

"Half Irish too," Dad interjects. "That combo means she's not afraid to confront me or fight me."

"Family must be important to you?" I ask.

"Love my sister's three girls to death...because I missed out on kids. Got just five relatives."

"I hear you sing," Sharon says.

"Want to sing in the Unitarian choir, if the church'll have me," she responds, laughing an odd laugh.

"Sure it'll have you," Kent Hanson says as he joins us. He's lean, wiry, of average height. "In fact, the church wants you right now. Reverend Shaefer sent me to bring you and Jack to the kitchen for paperwork."

As the three leave, Bill and his sister Gwen approach us. I introduce Sharon to Gwen, who's fair, medium height, and sports black-rimmed glasses. "This is my still-new bride," I say. "Our wedding happened last July."

"Congrats!" Gwen says. "Your brother said you all danced 'til the sun came up. Where is Scott-Boy anyway?"

"Running late, as usual." Sharon chuckles.

"Don't mind that," Gwen says, "but I do mind that he hates to dance."

I turn to Bill. "The S.F. church still holding weekend retreats for Bay Area Unitarian kids?"

"Yeah. Last one I attended focused on 'Unlocking American Prisons' and—"

Scott approaches our group. We all hug him. He's fair, curly-haired, slightly shorter than swarthy, straight-haired me. After pleasantries, Gwen tells Scott we were just talking about Unitarian youth retreats.

"Wow!" Scott reacts. "Did anyone go to the one on abolishing the death penalty?"

"Death intrigues me," Bill says. "Maybe that's why I'm into motorcycles ...That retreat would've been good for my conscientious objector's essay. Dad's after me to write it. Keep me from Vietnam."

"My dad too," Scott says. "He'll proofread it. Has Reverend Shaefer helped with your C.O. application?"

"Not really," Bill says, "nor has my dad." He looks down. "He's always too busy."

"Back to retreats," Gwen says. "We'd always sleep on the church pews. Mom thought sleepovers there were innocent. Little did she know."

"San Francisco's summer of love, the sexual revolution," Sharon says. "Something must've started in those pews."

During the lavish rehearsal dinner, I toast Dad and Eve, as do others. Probably only Dad detects I'm lukewarm about his impending nuptials, but I'm still mad at him ...and Eve.

After dinner, since none of us are needed for the wedding rehearsal, Sharon, Gayle and Gwen chat while Scott and I accompany Bill upstairs to his room to see his collection of model airplanes, mostly hanging from his ceiling. I'm surprised at the number of warplanes and fighter jets Bill has, given his parents' antiwar stance and wish for C.O. status for him. A half-built plane occupies his large desk. Not a book in sight. Ever the hardworking grad-student, I wonder, *Is Bill devoting enough time to the college courses he's repeating this summer?*

****

Sharon and I drive to Berkeley after the rehearsal dinner to stay with former Yale roommate Ned Hooper. He's offering us his spare bedroom for our entire stay during the wedding trip, as Dad claims his big apartment is too small for us.

The next day, we attend a party in San Francisco for Dad's work friends and late-arriving family, including my sister Gayle, who's a female version of brown-eyed, dark-haired me. She and her husband, Ben, moved to Philly about the time I did, for Ben's post-doc fellowship. Since they live in downtown Philly, across the Schuylkill River from Penn, Sharon and I don't see them often. It's fun catching up with Ben and my sis.

After the sun sets pink, purple, and orange behind the iconic Golden Gate, Sharon and I find we've made the rounds of all the people we know. So we approach a stranger to us, discover he's an East Coast HUD guy, and innocently ask, "Have you ever met Eve before?"

He responds, "Not 'til your dad introduced her to me tonight. But then I got to thinking and realized I've known her for several years. Her distinctive surname, Malouf, has been on Seattle HUD correspondence for years."

I look at Sharon, whose eyes have widened.

Is this the smoking gun?

CHAPTER 3
Biting Eve's Apple.
Cracking the Zodiac's Code

Driving to Dad's afternoon wedding, I decide not to share the smoking-gun news, even with sibs, wanting to avoid July Fourth emotional fireworks. Bill and Gwen Hanson greet Sharon and me at the door, and Sharon quips, "We gotta stop meeting like this." I ask their mom, Myrna, if she needs any help. She says caterers have things under control and we should just find seats amid the rows of white chairs in the living room.

It's the perfect setting for a wedding, as Sharon, ever the artist, points out. White trim for the four huge windows provides a nice accent for the off-white walls of the high-ceilinged room. Floor-length beige drapes add more elegance, as does the large fireplace with multilayered white molding surrounding it. Candles and greenery adorn the mantel.

Dad and Eve stand on the hearth looking at Reverend Shaefer in front of them and at relatives, friends, and co-workers filling the room. Sharon mimics society-page accounts by whispering about the couple's appearance to me, who could never describe my high school dates' clothes or hairdos to Mom after dances:

"Eve wears a lime-green, sleeveless, form-fitting silk dress. Her brown hair is up in an almost-beehive do, and she looks younger than her forty-four years. Jack wears a dark suit."

I whisper back, "Jack looks older than his fifty-three years...and you're radiant in your satiny deep-pink dress."

Sharon says softly, "Shut up" with a wry grin. "Brides are the radiant ones."

As the ceremony gets underway, Gwen—sitting next to me—starts crying.

"Everything okay?" I ask.

"They're just so great together."

"Really?"

"Yeah. I rarely see such happiness around here."

When Shaefer concludes the brief ceremony, we all stand and move to the sides of the living room. As Kent's best man toast drags on, Sharon mutters, "What gives? I'm here for the champagne!"

After drinks and socializing, Sharon and I serve ourselves from a sumptuous buffet. We then sit on the floor above, where it steps down to the sunken living room, next to longtime friends of Dad's, a HUD architect and his Costa Rican wife.

I tease, "You know Corbusier's 'towers in a park' housing is being blamed now for crime in low-income areas."

He smiles. "Don't blame me, I only design the bathrooms."

As we finish our meals, Dad and Eve approach us with their plates piled with food. They pause, looking down at us all.

The architect's wife looks up. "Why is it, even in Costa Rica, brides and grooms are always the last to eat?"

Myrna Hanson then shows up. "Anyone want coffee?"

Dad asks, "Does this mean there's no more champagne?"

"Heavens no, Jack! Coffee's for the lightweights now. Heavyweights should join me in the kitchen, where I'm just getting started. When we're outta champagne, I'll bring vino up from the wine cellar."

With that, Myrna and the architect and his wife head to the kitchen. Sharon and I stand up and move to a room off the living room.

Soon, Dad's sister Marian and her husband George approach us, all smiles.

"We're just so excited for Jack and Eve," gushes Aunt Marian. "You know they're honeymooning at our cabin in Washington?"

Uncle George follows up, saying, "Maybe they'll even buy a cabin near ours on Hood Canal."

As more people pour into the side room, we drift apart, though I overhear Marian talking to Kent Hanson and twice hear "Laura" and "schizophrenia" in the same sentence.

When Kent moves on, I confront Marian, "Are you looking for medical ammo to counter our theory of why Mom suicided?"

"How dare you eavesdrop! And why would you ask that?"

"Well, Dad's quick re-marriage pretty much supports the affair theory."

"Karl, the whole family knows your mom was depressed."

"Not the Stenerson side, especially Aunt Irene."

George joins us and says, "Overheard you two. Not here. Outside for any fireworks."

Ignoring George's eavesdropping, I say to Marian, "Depressed I'll grant you, but only short-term depressed ...because Dad cheated and wanted out of the marriage. No way was Mom long-term depressed, and certainly never schizophrenic."

Marian huffs, "I'm done with you, Karl." She grabs George's arm and pulls him away.

Later, I tell my siblings about the exchange. Gayle takes Marian's side, Scott mine. Then Scott reveals that Eve was on crutches but a month ago. "Wrecked her ankle on an irregular patch of sidewalk near Dad's apartment. Her insurance covered her expenses, but she sued San Francisco anyway."

"She win?" Gayle asks.

"She's been cagey about whether she won," Scott says. "She did drag Dad into everything from the start, having him help write letters to the city."

"So what?" Gayle says. "Dad used to write ill-tempered letters to corporations, to Congress–"

"But he never sued anyone," Scott retorts.

"Imagine the guilt Dad might've felt," I chime in, "every time he looked at S.F. City Hall out his HUD window, only a hundred yards away. He knows how little S.F. can afford to pay off litigious residents."

****

To clear my head, I go outside to the Hansons' small backyard. I think I'm alone until I see Bill sitting on a chair in khakis and a button-down shirt. To put him at ease, I strip off my jacket and loosen my tie before pulling up a chair. I tell him I'm a khaki kinda guy too, though I wear Nehru-like collarless shirts as often as button-downs. Bill responds that Gwen's boyfriend wins the hippie prize for often wearing a friar's frock with scores of buttons down the front.

"So how's it going?" I ask.

"I'm upset. Just met with my college dean. Wants me out. Lousy GPA."

"Bummer."

"'Specially 'round here," he says, waving his arm to encompass the neighborhood. "My dad stayed in school 'til he was forty-five!"

"The GI bill motivated his generation to attend college, get advanced degrees."

"I'm tired of hearing about our dads' generation, their work ethic."

"Can you pull out of your GPA nosedive?"

"Thing is, don't wanna. Just wanna earn enough to move out."

"Your dad probably likes having you home. Can spend time with you...finally."

"Rarely does. Anyway, he's always on me. Thinks college and C.O. status are the only things that'll keep me outta Vietnam."

Trying to lighten things, I quip, "The army will probably 4-F you for your long hair. They 4-F'd me for my clefts."

"Hell! Won't need any of his nonsense soon. Lottery's replacing the draft."

"Forgot about that. You could be dealt a 'Get out of Vietnam Free' card in December."

"Even if I lose, there're other outs," Bill says, as he gets up and enters the house.

Through a window, I see him climbing the stairs to his room.

Philadelphia – Summer-Fall 1969

Although ambivalent about staying in close touch, I phone Dad. He tells of a serial killer terrorizing the Bay Area, and he thinks, as a budding criminologist, I should know about him. Someone calling himself the Zodiac has written letters to local newspapers and taunted police departments. He claims to have killed two teenagers parked on a lovers' lane in Vallejo in December last year and to have shot another couple this July in the same area.

In the last attack, the male victim survived and said a man, likely the Zodiac, approached their parked car, shined a flashlight into the car to locate them, and then opened fire. He walked away but returned when he heard moaning, shooting them again, killing the female.

Dad says the *Chronicle*, *Examiner*, and *Times Herald* have each published the portion of a symbol code the Zodiac sent them.

"Why are they propagating anything related to this psychopath?" I ask.

"Psychopath?"

"Psychopaths are people unencumbered by guilt, anguish, or insecurity. Often have no friends, even jobs, as a result."

"Well," Dad says, "newspapers report it 'cuz the Zodiac said he'd keep killing if they didn't, and he promised to reveal his identity in the cryptogram. No one's cracked the code, so papers have asked for readers' help."

"So a killer and an extortionist. Surefire psychopath?"

"As a former journalist, I'm intrigued by all this...and especially the code. Wanna help me crack it?"

"No time now. I'm a TA, assisting a prof teach a class. Ford Foundation fellowship doesn't require me to be a TA, but I need to learn how to 'teach'."

"Okay, I'll get my Press Club friends to help."

****

When Dad and I talk a while later, he asks right off about family news. I tell him Sharon and I are delighted Scott's using our place as his home base during an extended East Coast visit. We're glad we've gotten to know Gayle's husband Ben better over dinners with Scott.

I explain too I'm loving my studies with Wolfgang and with Goffman, whose Stigma and Asylums showcased sociological social-psych. Most weekends, I protest the war in some way, though I did put politics on pause recently by grabbing a beer with an Italian criminologist before heading to a Yale-Penn football game. And I did have dinner with pro-war friend, Carl Klockars.

Dad then says, "While my Press Club buddies couldn't crack Zodiac's code, a couple in Salinas, California did. And Zodiac lied, didn't reveal his identity in the cryptogram."

"A predictable psychopath. A liar."

"But he did reveal his motive for killing: 'to garner slaves for when he's reborn in paradice [sic]'."

"Likely more BS."

Dad closes with the information that the Zodiac struck again in late September, tying up and then stabbing a college couple picnicking at Lake Berryessa in Napa County. The male survived, and he described the killer as wearing an executioner-style hood with a symbol resembling a target crosshairs or a Celtic cross. The killer scribbled the same symbol on the side of the male's car using a black felt-tipped pen.

After talking with Dad, I think, *The Zodiac is more cautious now, hiding his face. He doesn't want to get caught anymore because he likes playing mind games with journalists and cops.*

In mid-October, Dad calls with yet another update.

"Zodiac shot and killed a cabbie who was letting the Zodiac out in the Presidio Heights area of San Francisco. Three teenagers across the street from the murder scene called police."

Turns out the responding officer noticed a white man—in his thirties, at least 5'8"—walking away from the bloody scene but didn't take action because he thought the dispatcher said, "Look for a Black suspect." With the help of the teens' input, though, sketch artists perfected an earlier drawing, resulting in a widely disseminated image. Soon, the Zodiac wrote a sixth letter to authorities complaining that because these youngsters complicated his life, he'd start shooting at young people on school buses.

CHAPTER 4
Moratorium, Russian Roulette, and Earth Day

Philadelphia – October 1969

Loving that our new secondhand VW is so reliable, Sharon and I head to Bryn Mawr for a speech and candlelight vigil at a draft board. It's part of an antiwar protest calling for work stoppages and demonstrations the next day. Sharon easily spots Ira on the sidewalk in his trademark sandals, flannel shirt, bushy beard, and ponytail.

I slam on the brakes and yell, "Einhorn! Schonborn. Here!"

Ira stops, comes up to Sharon's open window, and asks, "Latest Baez news?"

"U.S. marshals just came to Joan's Struggle Mountain commune near Palo Alto," I say,

"Why?" Ira asks.

"To take Joan's husband to a federal prison in Texas," I say.

"She's pregnant. Their child's due in November," Sharon says.

"Blew my chance," Ira says. "Gonna write her off too, 'cuz unicorns need virgins."

"You're disgusting," Sharon says, "but come with us to Bryn Mawr. See MLK Jr.'s heir, Bayard Rustin."

"Can't. Sorry."

"Aww," I say. "Thought of you during a recent War Resisters confab."

"Now I would've liked that," Ira says. "Was at Woodstock then."

"Woodstock was the following weekend," Sharon counters. "So, make amends. Go to the March on Washington."

"Can't," Ira says. "I'll be hanging with my yippie buds Jerry Rubin and Abbie Hoffman. And after, with my hippie buds Allen Ginsberg and Richard Alpert—"

Sharon interrupts, "Alpert's 'Baba Ram Dass' now—"

"I know, but I'm not a marcher. I'm a catalyst, a planetary enzyme." As Ira turns to leave, he says, "Anyway, yippie theater's my preferred form of protest."

"But only if you play the leading role," Sharon says as he strides away. She's not worried if he overhears.

The next day, millions of us strike and march across the U.S., Canada, and England.

Washington, D.C. – November 15, 1969

A month later, the March against Death, as part of a follow-up to the strike, starts Thursday in D.C. and continues throughout the night. Over forty thousand people walk silently from Arlington National Cemetery to the U.S. Capitol. As they pass the White House, each marcher, bearing a placard with the name of a dead American soldier, shouts out a name. They then continue down Pennsylvania Avenue to the Capitol, where they place their placards in wood coffins. Hour after hour, for two days and a night, Death Marchers come—that's how many war dead there are.

As Sharon and I travel to D.C. on Saturday, we keep hoping that demonstrators will remain nonviolent. A conflict did flare up Friday night, at DuPont Circle. Police tear-gassed violent protestors.

Arriving in D.C., we join a monster rally in front of the White House. Illustrative of President Nixon's siege mentality, he's completely encircled his seat of power with buses, parked bumper to bumper. Police officers on-site guarantee the wall of buses remains impenetrable.

Antiwar congressmen speak. The folk trio Peter, Paul, and Mary sing. And at one point, folksinger Pete Seeger leads a half a million of us in "All we are saying..." the chorus of John Lennon's new song "Give Peace a Chance." Seeger, an inspiration to Joan, interjects often during our ten minutes of chorusing: "Are you listening, Nixon?" "Are you listening, Pentagon?"

Responding the next day, Nixon states, "As far as this kind of activity is concerned, we expect it; however, under no circumstances will I be affected whatever by it." With these words, he dismisses the largest antiwar protest in the history of America. *Nixon's the most psychopathic politician ever.*

Philadelphia – Winter 1969 to Spring 1970

Two weeks later, the Feds hold their lottery for men born 1944 through 1950 to determine who'll be called to fight next. This is partly to answer critics who say draft boards let privileged whites slip through cracks. On December 1, the earth's about to quake for those whose randomly selected birthdays make them immediate candidates for induction. Many believe recruitment's a death sentence, as most will be sent to Vietnam.

Sharon and I watch Lottery Night live from Washington, and it's pretty intense because it'll impact both our brothers. We can only imagine how intense it is for them, Bill Hanson, and the countless other young men sitting around TVs at home or in college dorms.

Here's how it worked. The Feds mixed up 366 blue plastic capsules containing slips of paper with birthdates, including one for leap year. Officials then drew capsules out of a huge glass container. The first birthdate drawn was September 14. It received the number "1," meaning men with that birthday will be drafted immediately.

We call our brothers after the drawing. Sharon's has a good number, and is safe. I then dial Scott, who shouts that he's got a great number, 359. I breathe a sigh of relief, then kid him, "No need for a college deferment now. You can drop outta college."

"Just talked to Bill," Scott says. "He's safe too, but my good friend Tom who applied for a C.O. isn't. If he gets C.O. status, he's got two years' alternative service. If he doesn't, it's Vietnam."

I reminisce about my own C.O. app. *If Tom's board hates giving out C.O.s for any reason, they'll deny him the C.O. like my board did, giving me a 4-F instead. My board even assigned me a social worker to help with common taunts for failing a physical, like "They'll draft women and children before drafting you!"*

****

The sun's rays melt the last of Philly's snow, and I run into Ira more often now on the street. He's rid himself of his huge book collection, and with it, any hope of becoming a professor discussing the wisdom the books contain. Instead of such a conventional life, he says he's creating his own path and own wisdom, which he'll pass on to businessmen as well as anarchists and counter-culturalists. He says he's also studying parapsychological ESP and mental telepathy, having met Andrija Puharich, a charismatic medical doctor, once with the CIA, who researches such fringe physics.

I relay further to Sharon that Ira's also into environmental politics ever since a Penn grad student knocked on his door. He asked Ira to help promote Senator Gaylord Nelson's April 22 Earth Day celebration in 1970. Ira wouldn't be an organizer per se, but he'd like him to get Powelton residents and his numerous business friends to support a week of Earth Day activities.

"As Ira tells it, he greeted the student in the nude and stayed naked during their hours-long meeting."

"Hmm."

"There are parts of Ira that're still a mystery to me, in spite of our friendship. Like, I doubt he's bisexual, but I'd say he constantly projects a provocative seductiveness."

"Christ!" Sharon says. "That's the perfect description of that Holly gal I met at Bryn Mawr. Couldn't put my finger on it then, but your phrase explains how she could attract so many men despite being standoffish."

"You hadn't mentioned that earlier. You did learn a lot about her in a short period of time."

"Women can do that, exchange lotsa info in a flash."

Ira's whirlwind of activity in the spring—promoting Earth Day, organizing a "Smoke In," and writing his "Unicorn Speaks" *Drummer* column—matches mine. I study for and take days-long doctoral-qualifying exams, continue my thesis research, and grade endless stacks of blue books and term papers.

****

A while later, after passing my PhD qualifying exams, I celebrate by spending time at some Earth Week events with Sharon. Economist, environmentalist, and conflict-resolution scholar Kenneth Boulding speaks on campus early in the week. The responsive crowd in immense Irvine Hall galvanizes me. I've relied on Boulding's writings about nonviolence over time and almost chose him and his university, Michigan, for grad school.

In his speech, Boulding discusses the economics of Spaceship Earth, by describing the world's past economy as open, one of unlimited resources. He then suggests that with the realization, thanks to Rachel Carson's *Silent Spring*, that the earth's resources are truly limited, the world now has a closed economy. Like a spaceship, it requires recycling of resources. This notion startles most of us. As Boulding's talk garners intensifying applause, I think, *Finally, an academic advocate of nonviolence gets a rock star's reception.*

After congratulating Boulding backstage, Sharon and I join our Penn pals at the Bull and Barrel, where we consume communal pitchers of beer, charred burgers for next to nothing, and peanuts whose shells are to be tossed on the floor.

****

A couple of days later, Sharon and I walk through Powelton to Fairmount Park for Earth Day itself, the culmination of the week's events. We'd missed consumer advocate Ralph Nader at an earlier gathering at Independence Hall where the Broadway cast of *Hair* sang "Let the Sun Shine In," keeping their clothes on because of news network cameras everywhere.

At the Park, we sway back and forth with 30,000 others while watching Redbone, a Native rock band, perform on a temporary stage. As folksingers Ian and Sylvia take the stage, I notice Ira behind them waving his arms as he argues with several people. The events during Earth Week required a delicate alliance with corporations who organizers thought were often part of the pollution problem. Organizers appreciated Ira's help scoring corporate donations as he tried to move from '60s hippie guru to '70s business consultant. However, they didn't want him grandstanding at events.

After the entertainment, organizers speak briefly and then allow Ira to the podium for a few words. He shouts into the mic, "I've been waiting for this day. The day when people realize the Earth is theirs and must take care of it. This is that day."

"Environmental stress is a form of earth pollution, just as stress is a form of body pollution. The crowd politely lets Ira continue.

"The Earth's pollution is toxic. The environment can't handle it. Likewise, the body's pollution is information that the body can't handle." Now, some crowd members aren't sure what Ira's saying.

Ira bulls on, "Both types of stress– climate change for the earth and cancer for the body–present great challenges for us."

Ira pauses to scan the huge crowd, and a key Penn organizer, Ed Furia, is furious. Catching Ira's eye, he points to his watch and then to a noted Harvard biologist standing by, waiting to speak.

Ira eventually ends his flight of fancy and introduces the biologist, who talks about toxic raw sewage in drinking water, all the while taking jabs at President Nixon. As he finishes his talk, Ira races back to the podium before organizers can restrain him.

"I'm at the center of a huge network of scientists, scholars, activists, and corporate leaders," Ira exults. "When something happens in environmental-edge disciplines, I hear about it quickly. I'm not only in the flow, but I'm also the conduit for the flow."

Ira continues holding forth and lapses into other riffs about consciousness, psychokinesis, and Uri Geller. The crowd gets increasingly restless and the organizers get apoplectic in the background.

Straining to be heard over Ira's booming voice from the loudspeakers, I tell Sharon, "Classic Ira-on-drugs. Wish I had his supreme self-confidence, but not his ineptness at reading social cues."

"Pushy and inappropriate as usual," Sharon says.

Finally, Ira finishes...and announces, "The true dignitary of the day is here—the Democrat senator from Maine, the Honorable Edmund Muskie."

With that, Ira lunges toward Muskie and kisses him on the lips.

Judging from a thousand gasps, the crowd can't believe what's happened. But unflappable Muskie carries on and delivers a rousing speech, saying that polluting industries often produce stuff we don't need. Muskie ends by asserting that, tragically, they also produce too much war-making stuff.

Ira grabs the mic yet again, welcoming friend and poet Allen Ginsburg to the podium. During his remarks, the renowned beatnik includes the signature phrase, "the best minds of my generation destroyed," from his poem *Howl*.. Ginsberg then concludes the world's first Earth Day celebration by leading thousands of us in chanting a meditative "om" over and over.

CHAPTER 5

A Slasher's Story

Slamming down the phone, he screamed, "I can't believe this! It totally sucks."

He stormed out of his place and drove to the Sport Chalet, talking out loud to himself.

"Goddamn it. This can't be happening." He paused while he tuned in a radio station. Then, "I don't deserve this."

****

Walking into the large store, he quickly found what he wanted beneath a see-through counter. He drummed his fingers on the glass, then stared at a clerk dealing with another customer.

Finally, he speaks up, "Uh, over here, please, when you can."

He then notices a second knife that interests him.

His patience almost exhausted, he almost bellowed, "Can't you hurry it up, Mister? Over here!"

When the clerk finally got to him, he noticed the customer's days-old stubble as he asked, "What can I do for you?"

"I wanna see that one, the tactical knife."

It was in his hands but a second before he said, "Nah, how about that one?" He examined the new knife carefully. "Tactical or combat?" he asked.

"Combat."

"Is it a Bowie?"

"Yes. You know your stuff," the clerk rejoins.

"Not really."

After sliding his thumb across the blade, he frowned and said, "Too long" and handed it back to the clerk. Inspecting the remaining choices, he then said, "What about that one, the folding knife?"

After sliding his thumb across the blade, he frowned and said, "Too long" and handed it back to the clerk. Inspecting the remaining choices, he then said, "What about that one, the folding knife?"

"It's really a hunting knife, meaning it's lockable," the clerk said as he handed it to him.

Feeling its blade, he smiled slightly. He folded up the knife, smiling again. He unfolded it and locked the blade.

"I like it. It's a Buck, right?"

"Right."

"I'll take it."

And while the clerk walked to the cashier to hand off the knife, he muttered to himself, "Am I in too deep now?"

The clerk ignored his mumbling and rushed off to another customer.

He quickly realized the irony that his "in too deep" worry paralleled his plan to thrust a knife deep into human flesh.

At the register, he stared confrontationally at the cashier after getting his receipt.

"Don't worry," the cashier said. "I'll put it in a paper bag. We always bag knives."

CHAPTER 6

Four Dead in Ohio.
Premonitions

Philadelphia – April *1970*

No time to enjoy the intense fragrance of cherry blossoms this spring. Sharon prepares an exhibit of her paintings, and I continue analyzing two thousand cases of peacekeepers intervening in violent incidents. Then, a week after Earth Day, President Nixon reveals he's invaded Cambodia. (He broke his promise that he wouldn't since the South Vietnamese fighters we trained appeared competent.) He also says he needs to draft 150,000 more Americans for the fight.

Sharon and I rally outside Penn's main library, part of almost five hundred campus protests across America. When we run into Ira, I say, "You've gotta fill in for us next antiwar crisis. We're swamped with studies and work. Not enough time to keep up with everything."

"Got no time either," he says. "Really busy. Just yesterday, a local paper asked me to explain the views of our generation. And then Bell Telephone asked me to forecast where the world's headed!"

****

Days later, at an anti-Nixon protest at Ohio's Kent State, the National Guard opens fire on protestors, killing four. In response, millions of students of all ages go on strike across the country. Penn votes to strike for a week. Dad and Eve, in D.C. on business, inform me that one hundred thousand people marched and then rallied at the White House.

I'm doubly mad about the Kent State tragedy. Mad politically that Nixon ignores the ever-growing antiwar sentiment in America. And mad professionally, that third-party National Guardsmen at Kent

State blew their chance to be role models for nonviolence. Channeling my anger, I train youth marshals to keep the peace at a march to Philly's Independence Hall.

Days after Kent State, a similar tragedy at Jackson State where two students were killed by 70 local police firing into crowds too.

I tell Jon Snodgrass, "If only the Scranton Commission's plea for fresh peacekeeping tactics had been implemented–"

"Then no Ohio or Mississippi tragedies. Even my Army buddies back in the day wouldn't have been so inept and trigger happy."

****

Finished with finals at Berkeley, Scott flies to Philly as Dad and Eve travel up from D.C. for a mini reunion here. Scott's with us, and the folks are at Gayle and Ben's near Temple University in North Philly. The gathering's bittersweet for Sharon and me, because Gayle announces Ben's just landed a tenured professor slot at the University of Illinois, and they'll be leaving Philly soon.

After the reunion, Sharon and I travel with Dad and Eve to Manhattan, and while the three of them tour the city during the day, I go to the United Nations and the NYPD to clarify certain aspects of their peacekeeping datasets. The next day, I sit down with a professor in Manhattan who's mentoring me about family violence interventions. A former street cop, he's tough and less idealistic than I about nudging cops to be more humanitarian, but we get along. Finally, I also do a rare-for-me NYPD *daytime* ride-along to better understand police work.

At the end of my work in Manhattan, Sharon and I say goodbye to the folks and return to Philly, where I begin the process of looking for a professorship for myself. Given my involvement in our grad-student uprising critical, among other things, of Chair Wolfgang's absences, which created an almost-rudderless department, I don't expect him to help me much. So I strategize with other faculty with whom I've worked.

****

Sharon and I push our tired VW to the limit: driving to conferences to job hunt, attending antiwar protests, and camping with our Penn pals and their families. On one trip to D.C. for a demonstration, we link up with Dad at his home away from home, the Graylyn Hotel. During a walk in Rock Creek Park, I see Dad wince and suddenly look for a trail bench. He sits down and reaches into a small container for a tiny yellow pill, placing it under his tongue.

"Anything wrong, Dad?" I ask with trepidation.

"Just nitroglycerine. For angina."

When I recall what I know about angina from med school, I straightaway sit next to him, thinking, *First Mom. Now Dad?*

"You worried?" I ask, as I put an arm around his broad shoulders.

"Naw, the pills stop the chest pain, and I go on my merry way."

"They're just a Band-Aid, Dad. You need to eat healthier, exercise more. But no walking or hiking by yourself."

"I'll let Eve know. Don't tell her, but I'm worth more dead than alive." We grin.

****

Sharon accompanies me on another thesis-related trip to Manhattan so we can visit New England afterwards. At one point after meeting with my mentor and riding along with the NYPD, I share my observations with Sharon as I've usually done after outings with all manner of crisis interventions. Sharon knows how privileged we are to be so-called "starving" students, and not "starving-for-real" indigents, in our big city. But I describe a drug den I've just seen and a squalid apartment shared by infants, teens, and their folks, unfit to be parents using any metric.

"Ride-alongs have always been an eye-opener," I say, "but I try not to judge. Squalor *does* cause some cops to stereotype the poor."

"You've seen stuff most academics, researchers, even journalists, haven't seen," Sharon says.

"Yes. Many liberals and conservatives who spout off about poverty don't know what they're talking about. Ironically, armed cops, authorized to use violence, have allowed me—an unarmed, nonviolent guy—to see the world as it is, often seedy and dangerous."

"Do you think seeing squalor and sordidness will shatter your idealism?"

"Hope not."

New England – August 1970

The next morning, Sharon and I head north to New Haven and Yale, and then to Mystic, also in Connecticut, to see our mutual high-school classmate John Hand. He and his fiancée, Janis, run a seasonal business there in the summer and take care of a large farmhouse in nearby Sterling the rest of the year. We enjoy getting to know Janis as we visit the Mystic Outdoor Art Festival and talk long into the night before we crash onto four sleeping cots in the back of their small shop. John floats the idea of us staying at the farmhouse next summer, gratis.

"Perfect for writing a thesis," he says. "And you'd be helping us out, since the owners like us to spend more time there in the summer than we can."

We nod "Yes" in unison, knowing the Philly rent savings would be huge.

Afterwards, we drive to Hyannis Port, Massachusetts, to check out the Kennedy Family compound and head further east to Provincetown at the tip of Cape Cod, where the crowds of tourists make Sharon feel uncomfortable and lightheaded. We retreat from the throngs and visit some friends in Boston and in a quaint New England town before heading home.

Atlantic Seaboard, Philadelphia – Fall 1970

I take breaks from working on my thesis to research faculty and courses offered at various universities to find an assistant professor position that's a good fit. In the process, I realize fact-based academia has similarities with its opposite, faith-based ministry, in that idealism flourishes. In any case, academia's not like business, where realism rules. Academia's a calling, like the ministry...with pay to match.

I keep thinking that I should start my career in the S.F. Bay Area to be near Dad, whose angina argues for maximizing our time together. Since the greater Bay Area has mostly public universities, one faculty advisor who's partial to private universities insists I cast a wider net. And so I arrange interviews at the annual Crim and Soc national meetings with faculty from schools that interest me. Luckily, both meetings are in greater D.C. this year, and so I drive south and stay with different friends. Other grad students who've "sold out" – that is, ditched their heartfelt interests for topics with easy, abundant funding – stay at nice hotels when attending such conferences.

So my couch-surfing constitutes "relative" deprivation, but I enjoy the privilege of being otherwise middle class...and white. By contrast, I see a great number of the Black Panther delegates attending the September Revolutionary People's Constitutional Convention surviving hand-to-mouth in Philly. Interestingly, despite Klockars' and others' fear that Panthers would brandish guns in public as they did at California's capitol three years ago, they didn't. The days-long confab to write a new constitution remained peaceful.

****

Even though my thesis and job search keep me busy, as do Sharon's Wistar job and art Academy classes, we host a number of Friday sherry parties at our apartment. Since the uprising, Wolfgang now promotes gatherings to foster better student-faculty relations. He attends, often regaling everyone with inside baseball info about criminology and our visiting profs Franco Ferracuti from Rome and Sir Leon Radzinowicz from Cambridge. With free-flowing sherry, it pays to watch how much one imbibes, since faculty members expedite job hunts.

Wisconsin – Winter 1970

Sharon and I spend the holidays with her family, the Beltons, who now live outside Minneapolis. The partially frozen lake fronting the Beltons' home reminds me of one where Lee Sims and I walked onto some thin ice in Connecticut during college, warm-weather fools that we were. We got our shoes, pantlegs, and spirits dampened after nearly falling through the ice.

After Christmas, Sharon and I celebrate New Year's Eve with fellow grad student, Hal Pepinsky, in nearby Minneapolis where he's visiting his new bride's parents. A recent Harvard Law grad who studies "law and society" issues at Penn, Pepinsky and his wife host us and a few other couples. Though Hal entertains us with guitar and song, he seems most interested tonight in learning as much about nonviolence from me as he can.

The next day, Sharon and I set out in the afternoon to return to Wisconsin. We delight in the bright sunshine as we cruise along a slightly elevated two-lane highway in the Beltons' front-wheel drive Oldsmobile. Suddenly, the car lurches to the right and flies through the air, landing with a thud in snow ten feet below the shoulder. Certain we've totaled the car, we manage to crawl through open windows, get up the embankment, and flag down a trucker. He uses his citizens band radio to call a tow truck. After the tow guy pulls the heavy Olds up onto the highway and starts filling out paperwork, I look at him.

Getting no reaction, I ask, "What now?"

"Just get in and turn the key."

"But it's totaled, right?"

"Nah. Good as new, A soft landing after a little black ice. Happens all the time."

Feeling guilty and skeptical about the Olds, I argue with Sharon all the way home. I want to tell her parents. She says she withholds, even lies to them, on a regular basis. When she gives in days later and I confess, the Beltons insist we get spinal X-rays. Overall, it's a scary start to the new year, but nothing compared to what's to come six months later.

CHAPTER 7

A Schmoozing Politician
and a Boozing Extremist

Philadelphia – *1970-1971*

Walking down Sansome Street, I'm startled to see Ira holding court at LaTerasse with a friend of my Dad who I'd met years before. I rush into the café and gingerly interrupt their conversation.

"Russell Byers, right?" I ask, extending my hand. "I'm Jack Schonborn's boy, Karl."

"Jack's son? I remember you," Byers says, beginning to stand.

"Stay seated. Just wanted to say hi and let you know Ira, here, is a good guy."

"So, your dad knows Byers," Ira says without looking up. He's fixated on the croissants on his plate.

"Yes, my dad directs a regional HUD office just as Mr. Byers does."

"Please join us?" Byers asks, not cognizant that Ira prefers working his table his way.

"Thanks," I say. "But got an appointment."

Ira snorts, "No matter, Byers. Karl won't get a word in edgewise once I finish eating."

Byers looks at me, winking, "Luckily I pay Ira by the hour, not by the word."

"You're spending taxpayer dollars here anyway, so I better scram," I say, turning to leave.

"I'm filling his head with Bucky Fuller's ideas," Ira says.

"Well," Byers quips, "Ira's a cheaper date than Bucky."

"Imagine," Ira says. "Fuller's geodesic domes might improve the safety of public housing compared to Corbusier's superblocks."

I turn back. "Forgot to give you an update on Joan, Ira. She and her baby flew to El Paso to pick up her hubby, who just got released from prison."

"Sorry to hear that. Never got 'round to—"

"Carry on, guys." I hold my breath, hoping Ira won't finish his sentence in front of Dad's friend.

As I walk from the café, I recall Ira boasting once of meeting Philly elites beyond just patrician politicians: execs like Byers... and the head of Bell Telephone Pennsylvania who manages thousands of workers who make sure twelve million Pennsylvanians are able to use their phones every day. I think, *Pretty impressive.*

That evening, I tell Sharon that Ira's transitioning from the '60s since he can't play the hippie card forever. If he helps clients envision the '70s by tapping into his futurism research, it's a win-win for everyone.

Sharon gives me a blank stare, so I elaborate, "Even if he's conning these people, at least he's entertaining 'em."

****

I still see my breath outdoors now, and with lingering cleft-palate issues, I snuffle more than usual when it's cold. As I take notes during my last Philly police department ride-alongs, I can't wait to fly west on the University of California's dime for some sun and the chance to talk to faculty committees interested in hiring me. When February finally arrives, I spend a week or more being grilled and regaled at several different campuses. At each place, I seek out students and others to get their perspectives. I also squeeze in a short visit with Dad.

Once back in Philly, I see less of my faculty and more of Penn's computer center because I'm deep into analyzing the data part of my study. When I get around to weaving these findings into my thesis, I find I'm still battling perfectionism, which popped up while writing papers in college. However, having gained a few insights into myself over time, I've devised tricks to keep the perfection demon at bay. Sharon also admits to being bedeviled by perfectionism, especially when painting. Perhaps that's one reason she's working more at Wistar and painting less at the Academy these days.

During my self-imposed daytime isolation for writing, I look forward to Sharon's return from the outside world. Over dinner, we discuss what's in the newspapers she brings home, and afterwards, I return to writing but am burned out by nine at night. To relax, Sharon and I often go to the Bull and Barrel to drink with Hogan, Snodgrass, and Klockars.

****

On March 9, Sharon reads a newspaper headline out loud. "'Guru Wants to be Philly Mayor.'"

"The Unicorn!" I shout.

She chuckles. "Hogan lives near Ira now. He'll have to take over his job as Powelton mayor if Ira wins."

"His main opponent will be Police Commissioner Rizzo."

"So, soft liner versus hardliner?"

"Well, they're both charismatic, though one wears a shirt flaunting a gun in his waistband and the other, a shirt showcasing gravy stains."

Sharon then reads aloud an exchange between reporters and Ira at a press conference.

"Q: What can you do for the city?

"A: Turn it on!

"Q: What're you doing now?

"A: I keep myself busy twenty-four hours a day as part of an international conspiracy to make the planet livable."

The media give Ira lots of coverage during his campaign, which features a unique mix of human-potential-New-Age truisms and pro-LSD, pro-Earth, and of course, pro-Ira catchphrases.

Ira's most-watched TV appearance occurs alongside other contenders and devolves into a circus-like sideshow. At one point, Ira combines sense with nonsense, saying he'd like to see Rizzo and Nixon down with some baby boomers and listen to them. . . after smoking a little pot together.

Shifting momentarily from being a political idealist to a realist, I tell everyone who wants a prediction: Ira will have some fun, get a lot of publicity, and then lose. "He doesn't really want to win the Democratic primary, because it *is* the mayoral election. So Rizzo will trounce him and go on to win the general election easily."

****

I'm jubilant when I finish the rough draft of my thesis. I give it to committee members and hope they like it and speak well of it when universities interested in hiring me ask about it. Everything's on the line.

While I wait for committee members' written and oral evaluations, I take on deferred tasks. John Hand and I finalize the details of his Connecticut farmhouse offer. It's an opportunity for Sharon and me to put saved rent money toward getting a larger car to move our stuff westward for my first grown-up job.

****

Turns out my thesis draft and my performance during various interviews were good enough to land me offers from some big public universities on the West Coast, plus the University of Chicago. My committee says they'll sign off on my thesis if I rewrite some of it to clarify things they've flagged. I start the process and eventually accept a public university's offer in part because my liberalism pushes me to serve students less privileged than those who can afford private schools.

As Sharon and I walk home from celebrating at a pub that night, she tells me the S.F. East Bay would be a dream come true. It's her old undergrad stomping ground. Her folks' too, though her mom dropped out of Berkeley to follow her dad to Stanford for an MBA. I tell Sharon of former roommate Ned's offer to put us up when we arrive in Berkeley.

****

I start off the month of May by taking my orals, a kind of no-holds-barred inquisition of PhD candidates by faculty members. After successfully defending my thesis and fielding questions covering my specialty areas, I face some unexpected zingers. A couple of faculty still can't understand why I've turned down Chicago, a private school, to teach at a public one in the west.

William Evan, Sociology of Law Professor and inveterate Easterner, says, "Some schools out west have bought excellence overnight or stolen Nobel laureates from the east by trumpeting West Coast weather. The universities are still relative Johnny-come-latelys."

I sputter in response, "Like you, Dr. Evan, all my post-secondary education's been at Eastern private schools, but I need to return to California, to my roots."

"Just be sure you're somewhere you could enjoy being stuck at forever," another faculty member says. "The days of moving freely among universities has ended…at least for white males."

"Truth be told," I say, "I want to be near my dad in the Bay Area. He's got angina. My mom's sudden death three years ago, during my Prelim Exams, taught me how fleeting life is."

Dr. Evan touches my arm, saying, "I understand. You're doing the right thing."

****

Hogan throws a farewell party in June with a mix of Penn and local types like Ira, who's subdued and slips out early as he's just conceded the primary to Rizzo.

During a toast, I gush, "I've sensed a heartfelt closeness among many of us here."

"Agreed!" Klockars says, then counters, "True camaraderie, despite our political differences."

"We love you and Sharon," Hogan adds. "Be sure to invite us to California to work on our tans before the Big One."

"Well, if we fail to, don't blame us. It'll be the San Andreas' fault."
Everyone groans.

Somehow, though, during the evening, somebody isn't feeling the same love: one of the women finds her purse has been stolen. *A bunch of oblivious criminologists-to-be? Criminologists do tend to be theory-oriented. Maybe "applied" guys, like criminalists or criminal justice types, might've hindered or prevented it.*

Sterling, Connecticut – Summer 1971

Sharon and I head for the farmhouse in Sterling, halfway up the state of Connecticut, next to the Rhode Island border. We travel US 395 and veer off for Sterling at tiny Plainfield. When we arrive at the farmhouse, I think, *It looks somewhat like Ed Gein's farmhouse in Plainfield, Wisconsin, a thousand miles away.* The white clapboard structure appears large from the outside, with a double-windowed dormer breaking through the front façade's steep roof, and a two-story addition at right angles to the farmhouse proper.

The front door has a small roof jutting out only a foot over it. (We will soon discover this means we have to get inside fast if we don't want to get drenched outdoors when sudden thunderstorms force us to run for shelter.) A slender spire built alongside the two-story chimney reminds me of a smaller L.A. Watts Tower. I surmise *It must be a lightning rod or antenna.*

John and Janis greet us with warmth, drinks, dinner, and a description of the owner, a stocky sheet metal worker who lives in Manhattan. They speculate that Gerald feels more at home here than there because he usually visits solo, away from his alcoholic wife, Birdie.

John says, "Gerald asks only that whoever stays here shuttle him to and from the Plainfield train station when he comes up for weekends."

"And feed Thrace, his semi-wild dog, two times a day," Janis says.

We get advice about operating a few of Gerald's eccentric household devices. John says, "They work about as well as the antenna: sporadically, if at all. Are you okay with often being cut off from the outside world?"

"We are," Sharon says, "As you know. I plan hone my painting and cooking skills while Karl edits his thesis."

The next morning, after encouraging our friends to have a remunerative summer as they leave for their Mystic shop, we unload our VW of our scant worldly possessions.

Despite the farmhouse's size, the useable inside space is limited to the large kitchen and living area with a staircase to John and Janis' bedroom where we will sleep. Gerald has locked the doors to the four rooms off the halls in the addition.

After settling in, we start exploring the extensive acreage of the property. Given Gerald and Birdie like having people occupy the farmhouse year 'round, they live in a small cottage twenty yards distant. Yet more drawn curtains pique our curiosity. When we go further down the gravel road, we encounter ten-foot-tall thickets of bright green brush everywhere. We poke our heads into various parts of the thickets that have reclaimed what was once farmland.

"Holy crap!" Sharon shouts after pushing aside some brush.

I'm there in an instant as her big eyes stare in disbelief at a huge army-green vehicle.

"Military cargo truck. Army surplus, I'd guess. Canvas rain cover's rotting."

"Gerald must be a survivalist!" she exclaims. "Thinks he'll flee Manhattan and take a stand here?"

"Times Square is descending into anarchy, but doubt this rust bucket'll get him to the hills."

As I speak, I notice Thrace, who has been furtively following us. I speculate, *Gerald may've taught this pit bull to stalk people to unnerve any trespassers.*

By the end of our exploration, we've also stumbled upon a small barn and various outbuildings we can see into. One's a shed filled with junk, and another's a workshop containing creepy, unfamiliar tools. But despite our unsettling finds, the property's greenery trumps our West Philly neighborhood aesthetically and oddly mitigates the summer humidity.

Sharon soon creates a studio in the living room and starts a series of paintings, slightly abstract, of different vegetables from Janis's garden. I've commandeered one of the two large rustic tables in the place and plugged my electric typewriter into the only working outlet in the living room.

To clarify the sections of the thesis that my committee has flagged, I edit or rewrite. This means I must often retype entire pages, keeping 'em free of new typos. (Technically, I can't use correction fluid, but I fudge sometimes.) I often feel I'm Captain Ahab, but tussling with a four-hundred-page monster rather than a whale.

One day, after hearing Sharon complain that Academy student and faculty critiques have forced her to rework too many paintings, I say, "I feel your frustration. I must serve many masters too. Besides my department faculty, there're administrative deans and staffers of all sorts who're sticklers regarding theses."

"At least you can phone someone for clarification of the rules, say, for creating an index. I can't. And I barely kept mental notes, let alone written ones, during critiques."

"I hear you," I say as I wrap her in a hug. "A painting forces one to be naked in public."

She hugs me back.

****

A few weeks pass, and Gerald calls to say he and Birdie are coming on the late Friday afternoon train July Fourth weekend. I'm curious to meet them, and Gerald in particular, since our neighbors on River Road have begun to confirm our sense he's something of a scofflaw.

Only Gerald emerges from the train, and he's a mountain of a man. Dressed in workman's coveralls, he greets me with "Birdie's sick" muttered from underneath a full mustache that hides any expression he may have. The smell of whiskey engulfs me once we're inside our small VW Beetle with the doors closed. But Gerald's drinking hasn't affected his speech or mood as we talk about the farm during our five-minute trip home.

Saturday morning, Gerald comes to the farmhouse to "check on things," as he says. After awkward pleasantries, he goes to the addition and tries each of the doorknobs of the locked rooms with me in tow. After inspecting the kitchen, he complains that we've misused the crockpot he modified with what I call a "Gerry rigged" timer. I promise to fix its frayed cord right away and hand him one of John's fine cigars that John gave me to try.

Gerald admires the gift, then growls, "No fireworks this weekend. Understood?"

"Don't worry," Sharon says, nudging him toward the front door. "No one's into fireworks...or cigars. Ugh!"

As Gerald reaches the door, he says, "I've got enough guns and ammo to light up the sky. Won't use 'em unless I gotta teach someone a lesson."

I look at Sharon, yearning for answers. Her body language says "Beats me," while her words say, "Crackpot" and "Crackpot" after he's out the door.

****

Early one Monday morning weeks later, the phone rings and a faculty secretary informs me Wolfgang's got to leave the country unexpectedly and will have to sign off on my thesis as department chair earlier than planned. I phone Wolfgang, and he says, "Once you get the revised copy to us, we'll photocopy the reworked pages and distribute them to your thesis committee members, who've promised they'll read 'em post haste."

So I double down, editing sections with a pencil late into each night while Sharon, bless her demon typing skills, takes on the retyping chore.

Just before I drive to Philly with my revised thesis, we calculate how much of a loan is necessary for a larger VW to move our stuff and

Sharon's canvases cross-country. After submitting my thesis, I sprint to Girard Bank to get a loan, but they turn me down flat, even though I've banked there for years.

"You've got no credit, no credit score, since you've not borrowed from us, only deposited," the loan advisor says.

Back at the farmhouse, I look into dealership loans, which're steep as I expected, before calling our fathers. Scarred by the Depression, both insist on strict repayment schedules, and Sharon's businessman dad insists on also charging us interest.

****

We buy a small VW station wagon from a local dealer, and it has a new car smell when we pick up Gerald for another weekend stay. However, Saturday night, he goes berserk in the midst of a lightning storm, which had already frightened us. He freaks us out so much that it's all we can do to pack everything in our new car as fast as possible and get out of Dodge. We head for a motel near Plainfield, afraid to tell a soul about how scary things got.

CHAPTER 8
A Serial Killer's Story

He almost ripped his clothes, rushing out his front door when his jacket caught on the door jamb's strike plate. The guy on the phone said lots of people wanted the gun. "First come, first served," he said.

As he drove under a threatening red-purple sky, he wondered, *Do I have the guts to use a gun? I'm not a violent person.* As he drove through neighborhood after neighborhood, buildings began to look increasingly dilapidated. Eventually, he reached an area punctuated with vacant lots and abandoned buildings.

He stopped at a boarded-up house, doubting he had the right address, and was amazed the front door buzzer worked. He raced up the stairs to the third floor, less so out of excitement over the gun than a wish to get out of this neighborhood as fast as possible.

A confident-sounding voice asked him his purpose through the door. The man who finally opened the door to Apartment Ten, after asking more questions, shook visibly—undercutting his authoritative voice. The closing of the door behind him meant he was now at the mercy of this druggie and whoever else lived in this squalid apartment.

He watched as the man's fingers struggled to expose the gun wrapped in a T-shirt. He judged it to be the .22 caliber gun that Mr. Shaky described over the phone, but he couldn't clearly remember the details of handguns he'd just seen in *Guns & Ammo*.

Before taking the weapon Shaky offered for inspection, he asked, "Sure this hasn't been used in a crime?"

"Absolutely. My prints are all over it now, and I'm linked to this address. Cops could find me in two seconds. If the gun 'had blood on it,' I'd sell it on a street corner."

"How much?"

"One hundred fifty."

"That's a lot. I've only got one hundred twenty-five on me."

"As I said, many people want this gun. It's got a soft recoil."

"You said you've also got a shotgun?"

"Yeah, it's a clunker, but it's pump action. Shot it just yesterday, hunting ducks."

"Can I see it?"

As Shaky went into another room with the .22, he said, "I can give you the shotgun for twenty-five less. You seem like a stand-up guy. Give me what you've got now for the shotgun, but promise you'll come back tonight with money for the pistol."

"Lemme see it. Maybe you've got a deal."

"Need it for hunting?" Shaky asked, laying the long gun on a grimy table.

"No, self-defense."

"Me too. Bought this baby and its twin for home defense. But my woman left. So I only need one now."

"It's got a fake-wood stock."

"It's like real wood, though. You can grip it good, even if your hand's clammy," Shaky said. "Just don't short-shuck it."

"Short-shuck?"

"Means you didn't work the slide fully after the first shot, so then your next round won't load in the chamber."

"I'll take it...and I'll be back for the handgun."

He handed over his cash. As he headed for the door, Shaky said, "Better go to a shooting range...practice so you know what you're doing."

CHAPTER 9

Terror at a Farmhouse
Berkeley and the Hansons

During an early morning call from our motel to our grad-school friends who were planning to visit us at the farmhouse the next day, we agree to meet instead in Providence, RI and caravan to a beach on Cape Cod. The four of us then crash at Professor Baltzell's empty summer home in nearby Wellfleet, a town of two thousand that grows fivefold every summer due to tourists. The next morning, Sharon and I beg off going to Provincetown since we've decided, given our earlier than planned exit, to try to make it to the American Sociological Association (ASA) meetings en route to Berkeley.

We enjoy the freedom of the open road for a couple of days before arriving in Urbana, Illinois at 3 a.m. to stay with Gayle and Ben. Over a late breakfast the next morning, with Ben already with his students at the university, we relate our experience with Gerald to Gayle.

****

It starts with us waiting for Gerald at the Plainfield railroad station Saturday afternoon. The minute we hear his voice, we know he's imbibed more than usual on the trip up. Once he's situated in the front passenger seat of our VW, he bellows, "John never told me you guys were rich. Fancy new car and all. He said you were starving artists, students, or sumthun."

Sharon replies, "We—"

"Shoulda charged you rent."

"We *are* poor," I say, hastily adding, "We scrimped on everything through grad school. My fellowship was intended to support just me, not Sharon too. Had to borrow for this car, mostly from Sharon's dad."

"What's he do?"

"Works for Doughboy Plastics," Sharon says.

"They make crap wading pools?" Gerald barks.

"Don't think they make 'em anymore," she responds.

"I called those damn bastards. They didn't care that my pool leaked."

We quickly change the topic and calm Gerald down by the time we arrive home. We orient him toward his cottage and are amazed he doesn't fall walking the short distance.

We close all the curtains, hoping he'll leave us alone.

Then a while later, a knock at the front door, barely audible given the downpour and thunder in the distance. Gerald rages, "Let me in. I'm wet."

When I unlock the door, I stand so that he can't advance more than a foot or two.

"I'm pissed. Couldn't get up here Friday. Lousy weather. And now another bad day."

"Know you're upset."

"I'm pissed for another reason."

"Why?" I ask, starting to tremble.

"You drove my truck!"

"No way. Anyhow, it looks too rusty to run and probably needs gas."

"You're lying, damnit!" he shouts. "Gave it five gallons of gas last time I was here."

"If we'd driven it, the huge tires would've mashed down the weeds. Check 'em."

"Can't. It's pouring!"

Sharon approaches us and says, "The tall bushes would've been crushed too."

Thunder booms nearby, then lightning illuminates the overcast sky and even the house, revealing Gerald's flared nostrils.

Suddenly, Gerald pulls a handgun from his coveralls.

"You spoiled ingrates! Turning my property into a playground where you and your rich friends play."

"We've just been writing and painting here," I say. "Only had a couple of visitors."

"I should've bred pit bulls again last year," he bellows. "Would've kept people like you in line...better 'n Thrace."

I object, "B-But—"

"No 'buts!' " he shouts and waves his gun at Sharon, saying, "You're the rich one."

Sharon's eyes are wide open now.

"Please, Gerald, leave her alone," I implore.

"Go back to your cottage," Sharon says. "Go now! The rain's letting up."

"You freeloading little shits sicken me." He turns, slams the door behind himself, and careens toward the cottage.

Gayle's eyes return to normal.

I check that the door is locked and do the same for the back door. I lock all the manual window locks behind the drawn curtains while Sharon grabs some food. We race upstairs and then climb a pull-down ladder to hide in the attic. After holding each other a moment to calm down, we tiptoe around in semi-darkness to find things to sit on.

For an hour, we only whisper. Then I sneak downstairs to test the phone. Finding it dead, I return to Sharon with books, flashlights, and more food.

Suddenly, around 9 p.m., more pounding on the front door, followed by rattling of each window as Gerald looks for an unlocked one.

He returns to the front door and threatens to send Thrace in somehow...to find us. Finally, after yelling obscenities at us, he screams, "Don't worry about the train tomorrow. I'll get myself a shit-ass taxi."

Silence for an hour.

Then a gunshot from the cottage.

We fear the worst but are too scared to investigate. Anyway, we can't phone for help.

It's still raining an hour later when I climb down the ladder-stairs to get blankets. I can't see whether lights are on or off at the cottage.

Sunday morning starts out stormy, awakening us from our unquiet slumber. No activity outside, so we figure Gerald's killed himself or is sleeping off a hangover. We creep downstairs to get breakfast food and are startled to hear a vehicle pull up. Peeking out, we see Gerald leaving his cottage for a taxi, and struggling with his half-closed suitcase in the rain.

****

Gayle can't believe the story. After asking us to elaborate on certain aspects, she says, "Guess you can't really trust strangers these days. Never know if they're psychopaths."

"Or if you do, have someone burly like Ira Einhorn on hand," I say.

"Oh god, totally forgot about him," Gayle says.

I then share that a barrel-chested guy like Ira might've handled Gerald better than I. Gandhi showed nonviolence coupled-with-might beats nonviolence coupled-with-cowardice.

"You're no coward," Sharon says. "I like your 'live-to-see-another-day' nonviolence just fine."

I crack a smile and say, "You know, Ira once said 'Powelton Village is a dumping ground for former psych patients—'"

"Like isolated farms are for the likes of Gerald," Sharon says.

"Ira went on to say he regretted letting so many of them crash at his apartment building."

Gayle intones, "Ira's as prejudiced against mental illness as the next guy."

I then share that I'm rethinking some of my knee-jerk idealism. Despite what we might soon hear from hippies on Berkeley's Telegraph Avenue, unconditional love isn't always enough to deal with the Geralds of the world.

Later in the day, when Sharon's napping, Gayle confides that she's been going through her own hell lately. She thinks her husband Ben's a manic depressive because he becomes loud and verbally abusive often, in contrast to his normally bland demeanor. After Gayle tearfully gives some examples, I tell her to phone me or Dad anytime...and for sure to call the police if Ben ever hits her.

****

Before the sun comes up, Sharon and I set out again, alternating drivers to Denver, where we stay a few days for the ASA meetings. We bunk with some Denver friends. And then it's mountain driving for us, across four states, before we get to the Bay Area...and the new home of old roommate, Ned, in Berkeley. After a good night's sleep, we start arranging our belongings at Ned's. He's led a privileged life but has never had a talented cook at his disposal. Sharon insists on paying rent in the form of personal chef services after our freeloading fiasco in Connecticut.

Berkeley, California – September 1971

Right off, Sharon and I visit Dad and Eve in San Francisco and have dinner with Ric Orsic, also new to the Sociology faculty, and his girlfriend Kathy. As I start outlines for the courses I've been assigned, I panic. What if my violence and conflict class gets large or my police and society seminar students need to catch up on some basics? I'll have to lecture. That means I'll need something to say at the first class session, the second, and so on throughout the term. *Duh! Prepping lectures is part of what I'm being paid for.*

Creating lectures from scratch week after week is all-consuming, forcing me to struggle to find enough time for Sharon and Ned. Luckily, Ned lets Sharon and me use the freestanding office he's just built behind his house. So while Sharon paints, I prep lectures. And I continue after she goes to the main house to cook, and then again after dinner until bedtime in the house.

Besides painting and cooking, Sharon chases after affordable digs in Berkeley. Since she's rarely first in line when a new apartment comes available, she realizes it'll take time to snag a good place. Because of this and the arrival of my first paycheck, we convince Ned we should also pay nominal rent for the time being.

****

My new faculty colleagues treat me with respect, and many invite Sharon and me to their homes for dinner at various times during the fall. They're delightful affairs, generally, but accomplished cook Sharon doesn't know what to make of the fact that, unless there's a secret memo, everyone serves us the same dish: beef stroganoff. Luckily, we love oodles of noodles.

Most of my colleagues are progressive liberals and a few, Marxist radicals espousing socialism. Some seem like closet conservatives, but almost none know much about crim justice reform and or what police studies entails. One Black colleague, moreover, objects to academics doing any kind of police research. Thinks police keep Blacks down.

****

I reward Sharon with a cat for finally snagging a two-floor townhouse with a patio for us, but am surprised that she greets this with a yawn and says, "Well, you can be its primary parent. I'm still not maternal at all."

When Scott hears we have finally found a decent rental, he suggests we celebrate at a coffee place in the Elmwood district near our new place.

After we seat ourselves, he says, "Congrats on a new chapter in your lives–"

"Requiring thrift stores because of sky-high rents," Sharon deadpans.

"Thanks for the congrats, Scott," I say. "We're late 'cuz I got off the phone with grad bud Klockars. He'd just fought with Bill Chambliss, a member of Klockars' new department at the University of Maryland."

Sharon adds, "Klockars' thesis probed the secret world of professional fences and pawnshops."

"Jeez," Scott replies, "I read lots of Chambliss in college...about how racist our crim justice system is. He probably accused conservative Klockars of lotsa things– like researching a lightweight thesis topic, or not labeling the pawnshop as 'the poor people's bank that rips 'em off.'"

"Well, Klockars studies cops now, like me—"

"Marxists such as Chambliss hate cops," Scott says. "See 'em as oppressors, and they're right."

"You sound like one of my Black colleagues," I say. "Cops *do* do a lot of good—intervening in family fights, handling gang violence, dealing with protests. Someone's gotta do that."

"Well," Scott says with agitation, "Chambliss claims police brutality and corruption, like planting evidence, offset all that good stuff!"

"Now, guys, take it easy," Sharon says.

Scott persists anyway, "Most of all, cops feed the prison industry's appetite. Without cops, the U.S. couldn't keep building prisons."

Sharon changes the topic by inviting Scott to join us mere activist radicals, not Marxist radicals, at the big San Francisco antiwar march next weekend. He can reconnect with our childhood chum, Lee Sims.

****

To celebrate another move—theirs from San Francisco back to Palo Alto—Dad and Eve invite us, Scott, and the Hansons, to dinner a few days before Thanksgiving. I grumble to Sharon about hour-long drives to and from Palo Alto, before the holiday, and again on Thanksgiving. She counters that I chose the Bay Area to be near my dad. I grin sheepishly and stop complaining.

Before dinner, I enjoy talking to Gwen Hanson and her boyfriend, who still wears a hippie-like friar's frock plus a peace-symbol medallion. (Sharon and I wear peace symbol pins mainly during protests.) Wearing pants and a turtleneck, Gwen says, "I'm in step with '70s fashion in America where women often dress less flamboyantly than men do."

When Bill Hanson joins us, his shoulder-length hair seems to be his only concession to counterculture fashion, which colors the Bay Area landscape much more than it did back East.

At dinner, I ask Bill, seated across from me, "Still on leave from college?"

"Yeah...and I never applied for C.O. status."

"Jeez. Took a risk."

Kent Hanson overhears and says, without his usual therapist-neutral tone, "Damn right. He took a big risk."

"No I didn't," Bill retorts. "I won the lottery."

"Won too," Scott yells from the other end of the table. "My lucky number meant the C.O. process, and writing my C.O .essay, were a waste."

"Wrong, Scott," Dr. Hanson says. "You thought things through. Researched issues, talked to people. You grew as a result."

"And I didn't?" Bill demands.

"You punted, son. Not very adult of you."

Gwen quickly interjects, "Scott, let's catch Cecil Williams at Glide Memorial Sunday. That foot-stomping, handclapping gospel's great."

"Great!" Scott says. "I live only a block away from Glide now."

Myrna throws her hands up. "So what's wrong with the Unitarian Church? Our music is wonderful."

"Now, Myrna," my dad says, putting his arm around her shoulders to restrain her flailing arms. "Our kids don't mean any offense . . ."

"Then, Jack, why do they keep kickin' us in the teeth?" Myrna snaps, liquor loosened. "Your father and I work hard, Gwen, to keep the Unitarian Church a happening place."

"C'mon, Myrna. Leave Gwen alone," Eve says.

Myrna gives up and drains her wine glass.

****

Days later, our Thanksgiving dinner with Dad, Eve, and Scott is tranquil by comparison. Soon after, I spend much time grading exams, reading term papers, and determining final grades before the holiday break. *Professing is a lot of work. Thank God for TAs.*

Sharon and I enjoy having her Wisconsin-based parents and brother for Christmas at our new place. Santa Claus brings Sharon painting supplies and me books, as well as lamps and end tables for our apartment. We then celebrate the New Year's Eve with new friends like the Orsics and old ones like Ned and another Yale roommate, Jerry Starkweather. "Stark" agreed to fly to the Bay Area after spending Christmas at home in Portland and before heading back to continue his first-year as a professor at University of Rhode Island.

Whether it's old loveable Stark or the alcohol we're drinking, we find ourselves alone with privacy and start to joke about our newfound power to be judge, jury, and executioner when grading final exams.

"So, I tell my students," Stark says, "'We're having an essay contest. I pick the questions, and—oh, so sweet—I alone determine the winners.'"

Getting into the swing, I say, "We decide which contest answers, I mean, entries, are rote and jargon-loaded, and which are original and wonderful."

"And if a contestant shows he never did the reading, I decorate his entry with my rubber stamp that says 'B.S.'"

"Then we get to be the firing squad." I chuckle.

"You be chicken-sheeeeyut, Schorny, 'cuz you want a squad, your TA graders, to help execute. I prefer being a solo executioner."

"Busted! But before the 'You still flunked' statement, I ask the student, I mean entrant, if he has read the fine print—not the Price-Waterhouse contest rules– but the damn questions."

"My grading metrics are fair, known, universal, and irreversible," Stark guffaws.

Weak with laughter, I roar, "'Next time, study harder, longer, smarter.'"

"Or see the Chair."

When I come to my senses, I say, "To be serious a sec, Stark. I'm a pushover."

"Me too, and I'm V-E-R-Y careful to kid around only with guys like you, Schorny."

Spent from our cathartic silliness, we rejoin the gang.

****

After the New Year, I get my first chance to teach criminology. I give lectures and short assignments about the crime wave engulfing America. FBI data show five million serious crimes in the last year, a seventeen-percent increase over the prior year and almost double the figure for 1960. While the wave's alarming, I argue it's due mostly to a disproportionate number of baby boomer teen and young adult males. The violent ones scare us, but they're usually immature under-eighteens, and deserve special treatment like second chances plus separate detention and court facilities.

It's enjoyable having fired-up students in class, though their energy's partly due to nonstop media covering developments in the 1969 Manson murders. Many of my students followed the trials of Manson and his family (especially Tex Watson). They ended in guilty verdicts and death sentences for Manson and four others in 1971. (However, the sentences got reduced to life in prison after California abolished the death penalty in 1972.) My students never tire of pondering how Manson could persuade his cult followers to kill for him...and yet never kill himself.

It's also enjoyable having partners in crime. Besides co-writing an article on the police down near Glendale with an urban geographer Don Holtgrieve, who serves as a reserve cop also, I get advice from criminologist Lewis Yablonsky, whose book on violent gangs influenced my thesis. Also, with Sharon, I befriend social historian Ted Roszak and his wife Betty, who live across the street from us.

Roszak edited *Peace News* in London before authoring *The Making of the Counterculture*, which made him an academic superstar a couple of years ago. A whip smart wordsmith, Roszak becomes a friend and mentor.

Point Reyes Seashore – Marin County

Sharon and I make several weekend trips to see Lee Sims at his place in Marshall where he works at the *Point Reyes Light*. Sometimes we take the Orsics because Ric's curious about the Synanon rehab program. Other times, the Roszaks. Or we take female friends we want Lee to meet. When the blind dates don't work, some of us end up drinking too much scotch, in the form of Marshall Milks in small canning jars at the rundown Marshall Tavern where Lee tends bar to make ends meet.

On one occasion, we even took Dad and Eve to see Lee so they could revel in the beauty of Point Reyes. As we drove there, Eve opened Dad's thick address book, a testament to how outgoing and friendly he'd been for years, and flipped through the "A" pages.

Eve asked Dad, "How about the Amirians?

"What d'ya mean?" Dad responded.

"I wanna rip out their address slip."

"You wanna what?"

"Get rid of them. You never visit or phone 'em."

"But I've just retired. Now I can stay in touch more."

"Okay. What about the Andersons? You don't talk about them much."

"I s'pose you're right."

With that, Eve ripped a 2" x 3" sheet out of the book and threw it on the car floor.

Sharon and I looked at each other. Dad didn't speak.

After some more A's hit the floor, Eve asked, "The Byers?"

"I really like Russell." Dad says. "I'll phone him soon."

"Okay, then, how 'bout …"

****

A week or so after returning to Berkeley from a recent visit to Point Reyes, I come home in the afternoon because of a canceled faculty meeting. I'm surprised to find Sharon drinking and ask if something terrible has happened. "No," she says, "but I often drink when you're gone, particularly ride-along evenings which seem unnecessary."

"Cops do critical work evenings. That's when families fight, criminals strike. There's gotta be another reason you drink?"

"Because I can, I guess. I've got time to kill."

"But –"

"To be honest," she whispers, avoiding my eyes, "I drink too because I can't seem to paint or stick to a painting schedule."

"Maybe the structure of another grad program would help?"

"I couldn't...again. You spent your fellowship money on my Academy courses."

"Was worth it."

After a long pause, she says, "I *would* be willing to work towards an MFA here. Only catch, Cal admits very few students."

"Go for it! And don't worry, we'll find the money."

Sharon soon spends time applying to Berkeley's MFA program: putting together a portfolio, getting recommendation letters, and being interviewed. She then must wait months for a decision, and so I try to indulge our mutual interest in art. We visit local art museums, gallery openings in San Francisco, and several artists' studios in the area.

****

To counter my exposure to so much *urban* policing, I do research ride alongs with Officer James Medina in *suburban* San Leandro, south of Oakland. During the ride, Medina comments on an unusual attack that just occurred in San Francisco. The assailant had concealed a knife in a paper bag in order to get close to his victim in the men's room of the city's main bus station. Located at Folsom and Beale streets, the station's south of Market Street, which is a wide artery dividing downtown San Francisco. North of Market—office buildings, department stores, high-rise hotels, and tourists jostling to ride cable cars up steep hills. South—cheap hotels, well-worn bars, and beat up two-story industrial buildings A dreary skid-row feel pervades.

Medina describes the attack, saying, "Because the attacker struck fast in a restroom with few people around to observe, no one got a clear view of the assailant. The victim only heard the crinkle of a paper bag before he collapsed."

"So weird," I say. "Wonder if it was the Zodiac."

"If it's him, he's getting ballsy, killing indoors."

"He killed inside a taxi, but maybe that's outdoors. Presidio Heights in San Francisco."

"Stay in S.F. Zodiac! Don't come to my beat."

"Damn straight! No messing with sleepy San Leandro."

Typical gallows humor that cops, and now I, have.

PART II – THE PAPER BAG KILLER

CHAPTER 10
The Stalking of a Serial Killer

Diplomacy finally ends American involvement in Vietnam. It's nice not to have to march or demonstrate so often. But it's not nice that the war killed so many troops and so much trust. To be fair, the assassinations of JFK, RFK, MLK Jr., and others also killed off trust. And the willingness to serve the public good.

****

Despite my interest in resolving conflict between nations and improving race relations in communities, my main focus now is police peacekeeping between individuals during family fights. I ride along with family crisis interveners in the Operation Outreach program I've helped implement in Hayward, next to San Leandro. Sharon finds my police Outreach stories more interesting than the usual ride-along ones featuring heroin and meth addicts.

Outreach officers defuse tense, often violent, situations through the use of de-escalation skills that crisis-intervention experts teach them. I see a role that nonlethal weapons can play in these situations. To inform myself about nonlethal weapons, I contact MB Associates, who manufacture them, and Senator Ted Kennedy, who's interested in them. I learn, though, after months of investigation that getting cops to use nonlethal weapons will require a parallel effort to end Americans' love affair with their guns. Those are both issues I fight for when I can.

In the course of all this, I learn more and more about the notion of cop culture. I've had to battle the notion in my effort to convince police departments that crisis intervention, really social work, is as important as traditional police work. Culture is like background music. It's familiar, comforting, and not really in our consciousness. In the case of cop culture, researchers have found it entails occupational codes that often override individual ethics.

Cop culture affects the working personality of police officers that I and others claim is often authoritarian, suspicious, safety conscious, and concerned with loyalty and honor. To illustrate just the safety component, many superiors tell officers before each shift "Be safe. You wanna go home to your families." Officers are conditioned to think policing's ultra-risky, when coal-mining and fishing-at-sea, to cite just two jobs, are riskier. Cops learn to support one another no matter what, even if it means a code of silence about another cop's wrongdoing. Cop culture, and related occupational codes, pose challenges to my effort to get American cops to adopt the English bobbies' approach to policing.

San Francisco – February 19, 1973

The Hansons invite us to dinner on Monday of Washington's birthday weekend, giving Sharon and me a break from our winter routines. We bring Gwen, studying at Berkeley now and without a car, along with us across the Bay Bridge to see her folks and Bill. Dad and Eve meet us at the Hansons' home, as does Scott, who, renouncing his recently earned BA, has joined his beloved proletariat as a carpenter's apprentice in San Francisco

During cocktails in the Hansons' living room, Dad notices Sharon staring at two large Rorschach-like paintings and says, "They weren't hanging at our wedding."

"They're dour, melancholy, but probably deep," Sharon replies.

"A patient did them," Dr. Hanson says as he joins us.

"Jeez, I didn't mean to—"

"Don't worry about offending anyone, Sharon," Dr. Hanson says. "If art makes you feel a certain way, that's all right,"

Myrna walks over and breaks in with, "Some people call them gruesome."

"My airbrush paintings seem shallow by contrast," Sharon says.

After a delicious dinner, Bill, Scott, and I end up in the backyard. When Bill notices me looking at the garden, he says, "Mom's let it go. She should garden more and drink less."

"Ah ha!" Scott says. "That's why she hires me to weed it now and then."

"So, Bill, how's the College of San Mateo?" I ask. "Heard you transferred."

"Beats San Francisco City College for sure."

"Bit of a commute, though?" Scott asks.

"Don't mind it. See that?" Bill gestures toward a van in their driveway. "I make good money delivering stuff. Pretty soon, my girl and I will move south of S.F...to San Mateo."

"Coincidentally," Scott says, "my girl and I just moved in together. Her husband went AWOL from the military. Left for Canada, and says he'll never return to this 'imperialistic' country."

"Congrats to both of you!" I remark. "You've both got the girl–"

"And can ride off into the sunset," Bill snorts. "If I do, it'll be on a motorcycle."

East Bay – February 20, 1973

The next day, just as Sharon tells me she's going to bake the cake for Ric and Kath's upcoming wedding, we catch over the radio:

"Police seek a young man in an attack on a businessman on Powell Street today near the Macy's at Union Square. The victim, who survived, says the attacker ran toward him with something in a paper bag. It was a knife. They struggled, and the assailant fled up the street. Police won't discuss the case, but people fear the Zodiac Killer has struck again. The city feels terrorized."

Sharon turns off the radio, saying, "The gall of criminals today! Maybe we should've stayed in Sterling."

"How quickly you forget. We left because we felt terrorized!"

"But that was at night. This last attacker is gutsy to strike in broad daylight."

****

A few months later, San Leandro PD Officer Medina updates me on the Macy's attack while I'm doing another research ride-along in his squad car. "Remember that businessman who got stabbed outside Macy's in the city?"

"Yeah."

"They arrested a guy and had to let him go."

"Why?"

"The businessman didn't show up for a key hearing. Believed his deals in Phoenix more important than testifying in court."

"Ouch! DAs hate that."

"Cops even more."

"Happens all the time with family fights. The way laws are, DAs gotta turn violent men loose when women don't press charges or testify against 'em."

"Hate it!" Medina says. "I interrupt my shift, even my off-duty life, to go to court, only to have cases dismissed."

"Well, I hope the Macy's suspect, God forbid, isn't the Zodiac."

"And starts messing around the East Bay."

Berkeley – Fall 1973

"Hey, Karl, look," Sharon shouts, staring at a women's magazine in her lap. "It's Scott. Can't believe it! In *Cosmopolitan!*"

I scurry to see a full-page photo of Scott. Nude. He's sitting with his knees against his chest, arms around his calves, his privates hidden. I phone him, and he says his friend Star O'Breen got the idea of nude posters after actor Burt Reynolds' foldout issue sold out in April 1972. Star wanted posters of non-threatening guys, believing gals should be able to admire male bodies, and not just sexualized celebrity ones. So she created a company and chose Scott and four others she thought gentle and approachable. "So now you're selling your body?" I joke. "Is that okay for a Marxist?"

"Star's turning the tables on *Playboy* finally," he says, ignoring my remark.

"You worried about getting rich?"

"The orders poured in for a while after the huge *Cosmo* ad featuring my poster. No one got rich, however."

****

Soon, Sharon and I have something else to smile about. Berkeley's MFA program, based in the Anthro and Art building across from Barrows Hall which houses Sociology, admits her with several credits transferred from Philly's art Academy.

Sharon immediately moves materials out of her makeshift studio in the dining area of our Deakin Street apartment to a studio in the brutalist-concrete Bauer-Wurster Hall, home to the City Planning Department. She finds art faculty and fellow students get her creative juices flowing again, in part from frequent critiques of her work. She and I attend art parties and openings at the university's new art museum and the Worth Ryder gallery on campus. Sharon drinks less.

****

My creative juices start flowing too, as I apply my classroom Q&A skills to a weekly TV show, *World Without Borders*, some local UN Associations have invited me to host. They'd liked a film I'd done on UN peacekeeping troops in Cyprus in addition to my speeches at San Jose's Model UN assembly and at an Oakland City Council meeting to support a UN peacekeeping resolution. As a result, I've been interviewing UN peacekeeping generals and admirals plus high-level UN diplomats. Deputy Secretary-General Andrew Cordier even shared insider info like the time he once gathered top American and Soviet officials to the basement of his home to brainstorm ways to reduce Cold War tensions.

****

Dad and Eve stay with us in Berkeley now whenever possible. I'm pleased, but wonder *Does Dad feel obligated because they moved away after I moved to Berkeley in part to be near him in S.F.?* They're here in mid-October to attend Gwen Hanson's wedding, which Sharon and I can't make. After the nuptials, Dad reports they had a good time, but says, "I'll need some time to get used to a wedding featuring an out-of-wedlock child in the service." I think, *Dad's not the one to talk about the appropriate timing of a wedding.*

"Had a nice talk with Bill," Eve says. "He's doing just fine."

"Move to San Mateo yet?" I ask.

"Been too distracted lately, he told us," Eve says.

"*Scott's* the one who's moving," Dad says, "Going to Lake Tahoe to build ski condos...for the rich."

"At a place called Northstar," Eve says. "He's so brave, moving to cold, snowy Tahoe."

****

At a café with Scott, I lament, "When you move, I'll have no Marxist to fight with anymore."

"You've got Marxists in your department," he says.

"But I can't tell them they're full of crap—"

"Remind me why you hate Marxist radicals," Scott says. You are an Activist radical."

"First off, all you do is talk about is workers rebelling."

"But we need a revolution. That's why I'm ditching nonviolence, leaving you and Baez behind."

"You're ditching 'cuz the lottery spared you the need to be a nonviolent C.O., to avoid Vietnam?"

"No!" Scott rumbles. "College profs got me doubting nonviolence long before the lottery."

"Second, even Marx didn't think workers, or a minority underclass, were up to rebelling. And if they were, they weren't up to ruling a society. Just think of the communists in Burma, successful in their 1950-1960s uprisings and rebellions, who couldn't govern and soon relinquished power."

"Okay, okay. If no change by revolution...then by evolution."

A lull, then I ask, "Do you still buy Marx's claim that criminals are the real revolutionaries?"

"All I know is, Chambliss says the justice system protects the rich and powerful...'cuz they decide who the criminals are."

"Well, there's something we can agree on."

After discussing other topics and some family issues, we hug goodbye. I tell him he'll have a great social life in Tahoe. Not because of his Marxism but because of his nude poster.

San Francisco – post-October 17, 1973

While waiting at the airport to board their plane to Seattle, Dad and Eve talk to us about today's media reports that the Paper Bag Killer has struck yet again.

"As a former journalist," Dad says, "I'm concerned that the media fuels the fear sown by him and the Zodiac."

"San Francisco's on edge for sure," Eve affirms. "And this guy kills during the day!"

"People also freak out," Sharon says, "'cuz anyone's lunch bag might conceal a weapon."

I then share what Ishmael (Izzy) Chen, a San Francisco law-enforcement official and friend, told me. "Izzy knows the lead detective on the case, Frank Falzon, who responded with his partner to yesterday's Paper Bag attack in the sketchy South-of-Market industrial district."

"Hope he's up to this scary case," Sharon says, kneeling in front of the three of us in seats.

"Izzy says that even though Falzon's a college grad, a police rarity, he's not intimidated by rough precincts since he's tall, muscular, and has insisted on assignments in dicey areas like San Francisco's Tenderloin over his eleven years as a cop. Also, thirty-three-year-old's work in Vice means he can handle the South-of-Market prostitutes along with the swarms of sensation-seeking journalists that Vice cases often bring."

Dad says, "HUD's painfully aware of those sketchy areas." Eve's eyes dart from me to the big clock to an airport official at a podium in the waiting area where non-travelers are allowed.

Sharon says, "Get to the murder, Karl, before they've gotta leave."

"According to Izzy," I say, "Falzon and his partner weren't able to glean much from the murder scene at 345 Third Street. All they found was a rolled-up copy of the daily *Racing Form*. So, the victim never got to Bay Meadows for the day's horse races. Oh yeah, they found, a four-inch-diameter blood stain seeping into the chalk outline that responding officers drew. That was it. Nothing else. The lack of shell casing suggested the killer used a revolver. Such guns rarely leave shell jackets behind, and–"

"Flight 744 to Seattle, now boarding," blares over the loudspeakers.

Dad says, "Darn!" He and Eve hug us and insist we pass on future inside info from Izzy.

****

A few days later, Izzy spills again, and I phone the folks with Sharon listening in.

"Falzon and his partner found eyewitnesses who said the killer, gripping a lunch bag in his hand, ran up behind his victim. He fired three shots at close range through the bottom of the bag, whose obliterated pieces blew away in the wind. The killer then ran down the street and cut into a parking lot. In the sparsely populated area, few had seen the killer. A couple of residents knew the victim, a stocky, older man, by sight, but not by name."

"Hmm," Dad murmurs.

"Canvassing the area further, Falzon and his buddy found a resident who heard shots and looked out his third-floor window. He said he saw a blond-haired man run into a vast lot filled with cars, which partially hid his movements. The nervous resident reported the young man came to a stop, gun still in hand, at the far end of the lot. He tore off the yellow shirt he was wearing, tossing it on the ground."

"Pretty smart cookie," Eve says.

"He put on a green short-sleeved one and cut back through the lot to Third Street. Running halfway up the next block to a van parked at the curb, he got in, started it, and tore into an arterial street for a clean getaway.

"The reluctant witness said he couldn't make out any numbers on the van's license plate, nor could he elaborate any more on the suspect's appearance. So the detectives left.

"The detective duo then found a parking attendant who also saw the murderer and corroborated the description the first witnesses gave. Falzon pressed the attendant who, eventually, gave important other details about the suspect."

"Witnesses are key," Dad says. "Learned that as a cub reporter."

"Back at Homicide, Falzon and his partner compiled a tentative description of the Paper Bag Killer: a white male, eighteen to twenty-four in age, with a youngish face, a light complexion, and shoulder-length straight hair. Around 5' 9", 130 pounds, wearing faded jeans and a T-shirt. The tie-dyed yellow shirt, which they retrieved from the parking lot, though common in San Francisco, had a distinctive chain design in block-letter style on the front."

"Forget circulating a facial composite," Sharon says. "Get the media to show that T-shirt,"

After we all murmur agreement, I continue with Izzy's story: "Soon the detectives knew the victim's identity: Lorenzo Carniglia, aged seventy, a retired painting contractor. He was shot in the head, neck, and shoulder. One of the slugs that penetrated his body got trapped in his clothing, and the crime lab analyzed it. It came from a .22-caliber gun."

After relaying Izzy's info to the folks, I say, "A final key fact: the killer drove a white windowless van!"

The folks don't react. And after some small talk, we hang up. But Sharon stares at me for a moment, then whispers, "You'd better not drive our van for a while!"

****

A couple of weeks later, Izzy updates me further "To discover the all-important motive for the crime, Falzon investigated the victim, Carniglia, to see if he was connected to the Paper Bag Killer in any way.

I explain to Sharon, "'There were different leads we started looking into about Carniglia,' Falzon told Izzy. The victim was a hard-working man and left a rather nice estate to his family. After immigrating to the U.S., he began a house painting business, which soon became secondary to his effort to buy and rent real estate. However, most of Carniglia's properties sat in low-income or mixed neighborhoods like Hunters Point to the south of San Francisco. So he had to struggle to keep afloat despite his two incomes."

"Izzy elaborates, 'Falzon and his partner talked to a few of Carniglia's tenants, who were angry with how Carniglia treated them as he went about collecting rents and repairing his properties. One tenant even muttered *he had it coming*, when he heard about his death. Others were bitter about Carniglia and even hated him. But Falzon, a good judge of character, concluded none of these tenants would've hired a killer to get even.'"

"The best detectives have 'intuition'," Sharon says, an avid reader of mystery books.

I continue, "Carniglia liked betting on horses. Detectives wondered if he was killed over a gambling debt, but that hunch went nowhere. They learned Carniglia had separated from his wife, but the two had remained on cordial terms. Despite his age, he romanced many women after his separation, including partnered ones. Thus, detectives looked into whether any partners had found out and wanted to harm Carniglia. The officers chased down many leads without success, concluding Carniglia hadn't stepped on any toes."

"Carniglia's one interesting victim."

I squeeze Sharon as I continue, "You were a step ahead of the detectives, 'cuz they finally decided to publicize the distinctive yellow T-shirt. (Incidentally, the crime lab said it contained no spots or stains that might lead to the killer.) The *S.F. Chronicle* and several local TV news programs featured a photo of the shirt with its distinctive design. They included a description of the killer. After publicity like this, typically, someone calls the police, cranks and wannabe heroes at the very least. Not a single phone call came in."

"Jesus, must've been a downer for 'em."

"Falzon and his partner gave up at this point, Izzy says. They had other cases to deal with. They'd spent two weeks tracking thousands of leads, made countless phone calls, and conducted untold face-to-face interviews and cross-checks of records. After more than a decade of sleuthing all kinds of cases, Falzon felt more stymied by *this* case than any other."

****

My criminology students worry the greater Bay Area's becoming the murder capital of the US. So I discuss serial killer stats and the fact that this relatively new kind of criminal violence has caught researchers by surprise. The literature remains sparse beyond some nonscientific accounts of Jack the Ripper and a few other serial killers.

One student says, "I can't get enough of serial killers, especially ones who target and hunt students like me."

"Me too," says someone, and then a couple more.

One shouts out, "Like in Santa Cruz."

Students and I discuss the current media frenzy over the Coed Butcher in Santa Cruz and the Paper Bag Killer. Then we discuss psychological reasons for our fascination with serial killings.

Finally, I get them to discuss the earlier notion of why it's hard to study serial killings scientifically: too few occurrences.

****

Sharon slowly but steadily evolves a painting style she's happy with. Painters like Charles Sheeler and Richard Diebenkorn influence her, and especially Joan Brown, who's one of the instructors in her program. Sharon's technique involves creating simple shapes on surfaces with masking tape and then spray painting them with an air compressor. When she removes the tape, the result is a bold, hard-edged image. She creates layer after layer of images to end up with striking, though cold, scenes of industrial buildings among other things.

****

These days, I spend time writing *Dealing with Violence*, a book which expresses my idealistic notion that police and other peacekeepers can learn to intervene in hot crises nonviolently and humanely. I try to marshal passion as well as facts to argue my case, unlike the highly quantitative studies published in the *Journal of Conflict and Conflict Resolution*.

My publisher wants my *Dealing* manuscript yesterday, but I've still got to polish it, and criminologist Yablonsky is behind schedule in writing the foreword. Dad suggests that he look over the manuscript in the meantime. After all, he wrote for a living– as a reporter, magazine writer, scriptwriter, and government speechwriter. He's fifty-seven, retired early due to angina, and has time on his hands. I welcome his help.

****

One day, I phone Klockars to compare notes on research we're both doing into the moral and ethical dilemmas police face, especially regarding the use of force. Soon, we both admit we couldn't put down former cop Joseph Wambaugh's novel, *The Onion Field*, about the risks of police work and the toll it takes on officers.

As we wrap up the call, I ask, "You've heard the story that I was stuck without a phone to call the police when a survivalist with a gun threatened Sharon and me?"

"Yeah, quite a story."

"Well, just between us, I may have to give up being a progressive and settle for just being a liberal now."

"Hah. Just wait 'til you've been mugged. You'll be more conservative than I...because I'm mellowing as you're hardening."

We both laugh.

San Francisco – December 20-22, 1973

Just before Christmas, I'm startled to hear the Paper Bag Killer has struck yet again, and only three blocks away from his last murder. I race to the kitchen radio to hear:

"Witnesses on a crowded street near the Life Line Mission at Fifth and Folsom streets say a young man, wearing a blue-hooded jacket and a knit cap pulled down to his ears, killed a man in broad daylight. The attacker swiftly approached the older man, concealing something in a large supermarket paper bag. The victim looked up as the assailant came at him and stopped just feet away. In seconds, a deafening boom from a shotgun caused passersby to turn and look with open mouths. They saw the victim's face turn bloody. The victim, along with the paper bag, fell to the sidewalk. A moment later, the attacker, presumably the Paper Bag Killer, turned and walked quickly toward a gas station on the corner. In an alley behind the station, he got into a white van whose motor was running. He sped down the alleyway."

"Jesus!" I exclaim as I run upstairs to Sharon in our townhouse place. "The Paper Bag Killer's back," I pant.

"Jesus *H.* Christ!"

****

My first chance after the holidays, I phone Izzy to see what Falzon's found out now, given that he's got another murder scene and victim. Izzy's words paint quite a picture, which I relay to Sharon:

"Falzon's investigation revealed f9n9 that the latest victim also turned out to be an immigrant like Carniglia. From Armenia by way of Russia, Ara Kuznezow had immigrated first to NYC and then San Francisco. He appeared to have had few friends and no relatives in the city. An architect by training, he'd been out of work for some time. Only fifty-four, he'd settled into a life of welfare, rented rooms, and free food at the South-of-Market Mission—about to open for business the morning he died. He'd been pacing to compensate for the December wind nipping at his threadbare trousers. Despite pacing, one of his legs had become stiff from the cold, causing him to limp.

"As a result, Falzon finally gleaned some insight into the killer—he attacks heavyset men who're older or seem older because they're bald or seem to limp. Falzon also established that his victims didn't know one another—not surprising, though, as they came from different socioeconomic levels."

Sharon says, "Both immigrants. Wonder if that's key?"

"Vague and conflicting information from witnesses to the Kuznezow shotgun murder led to only one new fact about the killer: he had a slight mustache. When fingerprints on the large, somewhat glossy grocery bag—one of perhaps ten thousand issued by Safeway every day in San Francisco—didn't match any on file, Falzon turned to his last hope, the white van ID'd as a Ford Econoline.

"Falzon concluded the locations of three of the four attacks suggested the killer was a deliveryman based in the South-of-Market area. With help from two other officers, Falzon and his partner knocked on the door of every business in the several-square-mile area, asking proprietors if they owned vans. If they did, the officers asked for descriptions of any drivers. Because hair and mustaches can be altered, they interviewed only drivers who were young and slender."

Sharon opines, "This detective work is a long, hard slog, unlike the ones in my cozy mysteries ."

"You bet, not flashy work. Anyway, fully aware it might tip off a suspect, the four officers decided to publicize that they were canvassing the targeted area. It paid off, but not until they had interviewed more than one hundred drivers and checked out three to four hundred vans. The payoff came in the form of a stunning phone call just before they'd completed their canvassing."

CHAPTER 11
The Making of a Serial Killer

San Francisco – January 26, *1974*

Our phone rings on one of the first relaxing Saturdays since the busyness of a new academic term. It's Dad. He asks if I've caught any of the day's news.

"No. Sharon's been out, so no background radio."

"Good, because I-I-I've got shocking news. I've confirmed it with a *Chronicle* reporter I know. And then I talked to a key–"

"Can't shake your news roots, eh? Double checking everything?"

"Yup, but this story's tearing me apart."

"So what's the news?"

"The Paper Bag Killer's been caught!"

"Great!"

"My sources tell me detectives drove across San Francisco yesterday to Twin Peaks. They went up Magellan Avenue…"

"God, you love dragging out a story–"

"Style's more *New Yorker* 'n *New York Times*…Anyway, the detectives, hands on their gun holsters, knocked on a stately front door on Lopez."

"The Hansons live on Lopez!"

Dad bulls ahead, "Kent answered the door. Found out they wanted Bill."

"Whaaaat?" I yell. "Bill? Our Bill?"

"Yes!" Dad says. "I yelled too when I heard it."

"How do they know Bill's the one?"

"An informant…and they found guns, evidence in Bill's room. He confessed downtown after they showed him eyewitness and ballistics reports."

"A would-be C.O. with guns!"

"A terrible tragedy, Son-"

"How're Kent and Myrna?"

"After getting over his shock, Kent called me. Needed to talk, and for once, I was the shrink, not him. He's worried about Myrna. She doesn't handle stress well."

"And Gwen? She's got a full plate: a child to care for-"

"Glad you mentioned her. I'll see if Scott can call her."

****

When Sharon returns and hears the news, she screams, "Holy shit! Mild-mannered Bill?"

"What're the odds," I ask, "out of a hundred and twenty million Americans, I know a serial killer? And there may only be ten out there at any given time."

"Wait'll your students hear who their crim prof knows..."

"Poor Kent. I'm sure the headlines will scream 'Paper Bag Killer: Noted Psychiatrist's Son.'"

San Francisco – Winter 1974

I phone Izzy to see how Falzon cracked the case. I'm mum about knowing Bill because I feel shame for some reason. Izzy tells me Falzon got a call at his desk about the time the van search was ending. The person on the other end, perhaps playing a prank, hinted about knowing the Paper Bag Killer. When he said he knew cops were looking for a windowless Econoline Ford, Falzon's ears perked up since only a few people knew that level of detail.

"You know someone who drives one?" he asked Falzon.

"Y-Y-Yeah. And he told me something."

"What?"

"Can't tell you over the phone. Too dangerous."

"Okay. Can you come to the police department?"

"No way. And ya gotta promise me anonymity."

Sensing the caller a juvenile, entitled to anonymity anyway, Falzon agreed to his request for an immediate face to face. They negotiated a safe place to meet, but then the caller insisted the detectives be in plainclothes. After agreeing, Falzon got his boss, Lt. Charles Ellis, to accompany him and his partner.

The three then raced out of their office.

The man *was* young. Fidgeting, he said, "T-This friend's name is Bill Hanson. Once when I was in his bedroom, he showed me a handgun and a pump-action shotgun." The youth paused.

"Go on," said Lt. Ellis.

"Bill said to me, 'I wanna kill men who rape girls. I need your help.'"

"What else d'ya know about Bill?" Falzon asked, always wanting details about suspects before encountering them.

"I know a lot about him, like he works at Redco. Always thought him a good guy, on the level."

****

Falzon and his partner immediately visited the owner of Redco Delivery Service on Tehama Street, at the outer edge of the South-of-Market area where they hadn't canvassed yet. Bill's boss deemed him a steady, dependable worker who'd never caused problems. Still, Falzon decided they should take their nervous informant's story seriously.

The duo then checked to see if the police department had arrest or fingerprint records for Bill. They discovered to their dismay that they'd not been informed that Bill had been the guy who cops had arrested for the Macy's attack but released because his victim didn't show up for a key hearing. Adding to their annoyance about their police department's internal workings, the duo found too that the police department messed up the laborious search to find a match for prints from the slick part of the killer's grocery-store bag. Falzon had ordered a recheck, and Bill's prints matched those on the bag.

Armed with warrants, Falzon and his partner felt they knew enough about Bill and his upper-middle-class neighborhood to arrest him on a Saturday afternoon without backup officers.

After Dr. Hanson opened his door and heard the charges against Bill, he stood frozen in disbelief. He then listened to the duo summarize the evidence, and finally led them upstairs, where they encountered Bill lying on his bed. Bill didn't resist being handcuffed.

Detectives found a seemingly never-used handgun under Bill's pillow...and a loaded shotgun in his closet. They shuddered, realizing the arrest could've become deadly. They also found clothes and items linking Bill to the four Paper Bag crimes.

After being Mirandized, Bill remained silent en route to police headquarters downtown. But, as the detectives itemized the evidence against him, Bill broke down and confessed. When asked about the .22 used to kill Carniglia, he said he threw it off the Bay Bridge into the water.

"What a story, Izzy!" I say. After promising him yet another bottle of liquor, I hang up the phone and sigh deeply. I stand a while, dumbfounded. When I tell Sharon, she's stunned too, agreeing we must be careful revealing what we know to others, especially my dad, regarding the secrets all the Hansons kept from us about Bill's earlier Macy's arrest and aborted trial.

****

A grand jury immediately returns indictments against Bill for murdering Kuznezow and Carniglia. He's ordered to appear in court in ten days. Kent and Myrna hire attorney Patrick Hallinan, the radical son of a controversial, socialist lawyer.

****

During a phone call with me, Dad lets slip the fact that the Hansons want Bill to plead insanity.

"Jeez," I react. "Given the facts, it's insane to use the insanity plea."

"Kent's a psychiatrist. He should know," Dad says.

"BS! Psychiatrists, like all medical doctors, shouldn't diagnose family members. It's an ethical issue. Anyway, we've known Bill for years. He's not insane. Not psychotic. Doesn't hear voices."

"Kent thinks he's mentally ill."

"He sees mental illness everywhere...in Mom, in Scott."

"That's not something I'd broadcast, son. Still, ya gotta be insane to kill people."

"Sure, all murderers are insane at the moment they kill. It's called diminished capacity. But it's a legal loophole."

"Then what's Bill's problem?"

"If I had to guess, some kind of trauma, like child abuse."

"Kent and Myrna would never—"

"You know how they treated Bill decades ago?"

Dad doesn't answer.

"Abuse needn't be yelling, hitting. Could be psychological, like mixed messages, withdrawal of affection, insistence on perfection—"

"C'mon, Karl."

"A grad-school buddy surveyed all studies examining child abuse and criminality. He concluded most found high correlations between them."

"So how were the Hansons abusive?" Dad demands.

"Well, Kent first: While a resident with huge patient loads and on-call responsibilities, he likely neglected Bill. And continued neglecting him, as a prof moving up the academic ladder with increasing teaching loads added to the mix. Fast forward twenty-four years, maybe Bill transferred his anger toward him to other, older men—"

"Whoa!" Dad exclaims.

"And Myrna. She may've neglected Bill too, as her drinking progressed?"

"Just speculation, Karl. And what d'ya know about psych stuff... especially compared to Kent?"

"And what do you know, Dad?"

"I visited your mom at the Stanford mental ward for two weeks," he says.

"Doesn't count. An upper-middle-class woman with a nervous breakdown. Mental exhaustion, really."

"I still don't buy your take on her," Dad says with an edge.

"Not to pull rank, but remember, I visited mental wards as a college psych major, took thirty-plus hours of psychiatry courses in med school, and now work with counselors in neighborhoods that're essentially outpatient psych wards."

Perhaps chastened, Dad says, "Guess all that higher education paid off."

****

According to newspaper accounts of Bill's initial hearing, Judge Frank Hart speeds through preliminaries, then asks attorneys to address bail. Prosecutor James Lassart starts off, arguing Bill's far too dangerous to be out on bail given the randomness of his attacks and the consequent terror his killings have triggered. Patrick Hallinan responds, saying Bill's too naïve for jail and instead needs bail with house arrest as a condition. He needs special psychiatric care he can only get outside of jail. Hallinan also says Bill isn't a threat because he's done with violence. That's why he arranged to get caught by tipping off a friend. That's why he submitted to arrest and then confessed.

The judge rules Bill's too dangerous for bail. He then asks Hallinan what his client pleads.

"Insanity, Your Honor."

"And why...in a nutshell?" the judge asks.

The news accounts get specific at this point. "Defense Counsel Hallinan says Hanson claims some older man, perhaps with a limp, raped his girlfriend. From what Hanson divined, this man was raping women in San Francisco, especially south of Market. Since Hanson made many deliveries in this area, he claims he saw other victims of this man on the streets. Hanson could tell which of them (despite some wearing heavy eye makeup to attract 'Johns') had been victimized by the moisture—really tears, in his mind—in their eyes."

Judge Hart rolls his eyes.

"Significantly," Hallinan continues, "Hanson then, like Don Quixote, sought revenge against this man. His mental illness caused his sick imagination to create a fantasy world in which he got even. He was so naïve in his fantasy world, he didn't know what he was doing was wrong."

The judge then asks, "And the state's perspective?"

DA Lassart asserts that as detectives pieced together parts of the puzzle, all evidence pointed not only to Hanson, but also to the fact that he was sane, in control of his faculties. For example, when victims of Hanson's initial attacks didn't die, he adjusted his approach by escalating from a knife to a handgun...to a shotgun.

Lassart declares, "And, almost by definition, concealing weapons screams sanity. You know what you're doing is wrong and so you use paper bags-"

"Objection," Hallinan cries. The judge nods in affirmation.

Lassart continues, "Hanson knew the women out on the streets were prostitutes plying their trade, not an innocent like his girlfriend. And if he wanted to get caught, he should've surrendered. But like any sane person, he didn't want to get caught, so he kept a loaded gun under his pillow as he slept."

"I've heard enough!" Judge Hart says, annoyance in his voice. "We'll have a sanity-competency hearing soon."

****

Since my crim students have brought up the topic of serial killers often, and since Bill meets the FBI's definition of such, I'm tempted to share my personal tie to Bill with them. However, I tell Sharon that something holds me back and that sometimes I think we should only talk to family, not even friends, about Bill. I tell her I'm also embarrassed that neither criminology, nor my subfield psychology, can explain, let alone predict, serial killings.

"I wonder," I say, "if the social sciences are in the dark as much as religion has been for eons in trying to understand and manage evil?"

She replies, "Sounds like you have doubts about your profession, your calling? I've had 'em in spades about art."

"Not sure, but with so much psychology under my belt and Kent's, you'd think one of us would've detected something amiss with Bill."

Without batting an eye, she says, "Age-old problem: appearances can be deceiving. Boring!"

****

Frustrated, I phone Scott and find he's frustrated too, but for other reasons. He hates that snow limits his social life as well as his work life, preventing him from earning more money during Tahoe's building boom. He admits radical Marxists shouldn't feel this way.

After updating him about Bill, I grumble about the Hansons' decision to pay an expensive-but-ironically-socialist lawyer to exploit insanity loopholes in the law.

"Hired guns, whatever their politics, won't ever fight for justice" Scott says.

I agree and then tell him if Bill's judged insane, it's off to a country-club hospital with only secure locks while the many destitute murderers I've encountered in my work get prison—and sometimes even death—for mere manslaughter.

"As Marx says, the poor get screwed as the rich get richer."

"All through school, I believed in justice in America, but now in the real world, where it's not an abstraction, I'm not so sure. But the heck with that. Why d'ya think Bill killed?"

"Simple. Anger issues. Like some C.O.s and wannabe C.O.s, he's placid on the outside, able to talk nonviolence, but seething on the inside."

"C'mon, Scott. Though Joan jokes that pacifists love to argue and fight, you really—"

"Bill's anger and rage stem from hating his dad, who spent so much of Bill's youth listening to patients and other people's kids rather 'n his own."

"Agree. But why didn't Bill attack clones of his father, slender men with ample hair rather than stocky, bald men?"

"Maybe he just attacked older men. Kent's hearing aids make him seem old."

"Kent needs his hearing aids," I jest. "He listens for a living."

"Bill probably hates Myrna too. Wanted to humiliate her. She's not easy to be around. Hired me to look after her nasturtiums. If there's such a thing as an alcoholic perfectionist, she's it."

"Just around nasturtiums?" I ask.

"No. Many things. But what she probably cares most about is her rep among garden clubbers." He chuckles. "Gotta hang up and shovel snow."

"Okay, okay. But call Gwen and give her some support if you can."

****

Scott and Sharon get me thinking about reputations and appearances. *Maybe I'm embarrassed too that Bill's in my social circles and my rep among colleagues may take a hit. Among upper-middle-class academics, murderers seem so lower class.*

Oddly, Myrna's rep among garden-clubbers, Kent's among psychiatrists, and both theirs among Unitarians takes minimal hits for a few reasons. One big one: the ongoing saga of the Berkeley kidnapping of Patty Hearst a week or so after Bill's arrest dominates the media. It prevents negative publicity about the Hansons as parents because the public can't get enough of the Hearsts. The wealthy media family is the subject of a sensationalized story for once, and not just the financial beneficiaries of one.

Another big reason: local media also give major attention to the Zebra killings, which started three days after Bill murdered Carniglia and continued for five months into 1974. Because of ten or so Zebra racial attacks—many fatal—since Bill's last murder, San Francisco's mayor initiates a citywide policy of stopping all Black men who fit the description of the Zebra Killers. ("Zebra" refers to the police-radio channel, not Black-on-white attacks.) And not surprisingly, Gwen and Scott's favorite minister, Cecil Williams, calls the mayor's policy racist, asking, in effect, Why didn't cops stop all young, slender white males on the street before Bill was caught? Or older white guys, right now, since the Zodiac's still active?

****

The insanity plea still bugs me, so I devote time to it and Bill's case in crim class, without revealing my connection. I start by warning students that, as of six years ago, a major U.S. ruling stated that legal insanity is different from medical insanity, which is a persistent mental disorder or derangement. I then explain that the definition of legal insanity has been increasingly liberalized over recent decades.

Next, I write "Model Penal Code" on the overhead projector's celluloid and explain how the judge is supposed to assess Hanson: You're legally insane if you don't know that what you're doing is wrong or if you cannot resist the impulse to do it. So the assessment test has both cognitive and willpower components. I opine that the two criteria are the result of a clumsy attempt to lessen the rigidity of previous insanity tests.

A student speaks up, "Yeah, there've been half a dozen tests over time."

I respond, "And now judges and juries have few criteria beyond the two to steer them other than their own sense of fairness." I pause. "And they tend to honor the most persuasive psychiatric testimony, even if it inaccurately claims psychoses when there're only neuroses, schizoid splits when there're only fantasies."

A different student states, "I heard the character who fakes insanity in Kesey's *Cuckoo's Nest* is based on real bad guys who study psych books and fool shrinks."

"You're right," I respond. "Nothing worse than a gullible shrink."

I finally bring up labeling theory. I use the Hanson case to get across the idea, saying, "What attorney Hallinan wants from an insanity verdict are self-labels and public-labels that're more easily alterable after incarceration."

Another student asks, "Hanson will thus be able to change a mentally ill label in his own and society's eyes more easily than that if he were labeled a murderer or serial killer, right?"

"Right," I say. "Plus, much easier prison time."

****

Later that day, after discussing crisis intervention with a professor in the Psych Department, I notice another professor, Janet Noces, literally shoving a colleague out of her office.

"You okay, Janet?" I ask.

"She's fine," Professor Jed Drell says, hurrying away.

Professor Noces forces a smile, then asks, "What brings you to Psych?"

"Was talking about crisis cops with a department colleague of yours-"

"You're always welcome here, unlike that obnoxious Jed."

I grin, then say, "Tell me about that *Science* study of shrinks you once mentioned."

"Yeah, a Stanford psychologist replicated what Goffman did in the '60s."

"Did he check himself into St. Elizabeth's hospital in D.C. too?"

"Kinda. He, David Rosenhan, checked eight research assistants into twelve psych hospitals across the U.S. He had 'em fake mental illness. Called 'em pseudo-patients."

"Lemme guess, after a while, the pseudo-patients reverted to acting normal."

"Yup. Hospital shrinks and staff continued treating 'em as insane, prescribing thousands of antidepressants and antipsychotics before the study ended three years later."

"So Rosenhan's confirmed what Goffman reported in *Asylums:* psychiatrists can't distinguish the sane from the insane."

"Yup," Noces says.

****

After several hectic days on campus, I pick up Dad and Eve at the Oakland airport with a plan to drop them at a BART station for a chance to ride the brand-new transit system to San Francisco.

"Wish you could stay with us," I say.

"You guys're too busy," Eve says.

"Naw, you're really here to support the Hansons at the hearing."

"Just a coincidence," Dad says. "We've got people to see, things to do."

"You're a better reporter than apologist for a killer."

"Okay, you caught me, but what if I take notes at the hearing and share?"

"Deal, but only if it's straight reporting. No PR or spin favoring Bill."

"You're just upset at how the case is going," Eve says.

I recoil, and the car swerves. I think, a sign of my disgust?

"Hallinan's not cheap," I say. "Bill's got first-rate lawyers, unlike most killers, who get overworked public defenders."

"Well, Hallinan's no miracle worker," Eve says. "He failed to win bail for Bill."

I recoil again, accidentally hitting the horn while I exclaim, "He's an admitted killer!"

CHAPTER 12

Courts, the Insanity Plea, and the Synanon Psychopath

San Francisco – May *16, 1974*

Bill's sanity hearing has come up quickly for a case of this magnitude. According to our agreement, Dad reports on it to me since he's one of the few outsiders allowed in, courtesy of the Hansons. Dad starts his phone report, noting that besides survivors of victims, attorneys, a court reporter, and bailiffs standing next to Bill shackled to a chair, there's a new judge. Morton Convin replaces Frank Hart. I think, *Did Hallinan shop for a more lenient judge?*

The judge opens the hearing, saying the death penalty's off the table, but hard time in a tough prison isn't if Bill's found sane. Pausing, Judge Convin then says, "We're here today to determine if William Paul Hanson was insane at the time of the murders. That is, did he lack substantial capacity either to appreciate the criminality of his conduct or conform it to the requirements of the law."

Convin nods to the prosecutor to begin. DA Lassart asserts what's known: Trying to rectify wrongs done to young women in the city, Hanson constantly scanned the streets immediately north and south of Market Street while he drove for Redco. Totally premeditated and with malice, the requirements for first-degree murder, he slammed on the brakes whenever he saw a man resembling the description he'd heard of his girlfriend's rapist.3

"All this shows discretion, deliberation," DA Lassart claims, "not impulses he couldn't resist or control." The district attorney pauses. "Hanson would then leap from his van, catch up to his target—even if he had to enter a bus station men's room—and attack with a weapon he'd concealed in a paper bag."

After a moment, Lassart says, "Criminal, vengeful, horrific, yes! Irrational, illogical, without appreciation of the wrongfulness of murder, no!"

Lassart next calls the owner of Redco to the stand to repeat the character assessment he gave Detective Falzon. The owner testifies that, far from a crazy person, Hanson was a steady, dependable worker who never caused any difficulties.

Judge Convin then signals the defense to present.

"Your Honor," Hallinan says, "the defendant's imagination created a quixotic world for him where he had to avenge rapes committed by a man across San Francisco. As an avenging angel for those wronged, Hanson wore no disguises—"

"Objection!" Lassart cries. "Hanson employed many disguises. Growing a mustache. Wearing a hoodie or a knit cap pulled down to obscure his identity. Even changing from a yellow T-shirt to a blue one after one murder."

"Objection sustained," the judge says.

"Continuing, if I may, Your Honor," Hallinan says. "Due to a certifiable mental illness, the defendant cannot conform to the requirements of law. To prove that, I call now two psychiatrists who've evaluated him."

After being sworn to tell the truth, the psychiatrists explain how they arrived at, independently, their assessments that Hanson was insane during his crimes. They use the words fantasy and fanciful, as well as a good deal of psychiatric jargon.

DA Lassart has a chance to cross-examine the two. He gets them to admit to having had connections at one point in their careers to Dr. Hanson or his psychiatric hospital, UCSF's Langley Porter.

Dad emphasizes to me that, during this part of the cross, Kent looked down at his hands and others in the chambers shifted in their seats. Bill, though, continued to exhibit the quiet and subdued demeanor jailers have noted during most of his three months in custody.

Lassart then calls a psychiatrist for the prosecution to testify about various defense claims. After being sworn in, Lassart asks him, "Did Hanson ever refer to himself as an avenger?"

"Yes, often," the psychiatrist responds. "In fact, he came across so vigilante-like, I thought he'd watched *The Fugitive* TV series."

"Had he?" the judge interjects.

"Says he hasn't," the shrink answers, "but I'd expect him to lie because he feigned mental illness throughout my interviews. Technically, I find him a malingerer. He hasn't hallucinated, heard voices, or exhibited characteristics of an insane person."

The judge asks, "If he were a vigilante, what characteristics would he have?"

"He'd be rational, focused, sane."

"Objection, Your Honor!" Hallinan shouts. "Dr. Spielstein must cite studies of vigilantes to demonstrate this. Anyway, Detective Falzon's assessment of Hanson as a psycho is more relevant."

Lassart counters immediately, "Falzon undercut his so-called psycho assessment when he later said, 'You just don't expect a psycho to kill again in the same fashion.'" Lassart continues, "Hanson must've been sane, since he kept attacking in the same rational way, not in irrationally different ways. He had an M.O.!"

Judge Convin raises his hand. "Detective Falzon's comments are all hearsay, and there's no time to subpoena him. So...moving along, is there evidence Hanson even had a girlfriend in 1972 or 1973? Some stories in the press report Hanson was avenging the rape of a sister, not a girlfriend."

Silence ensues, until the prosecution psychiatrist says, "Given the counterculture lifestyle of Hanson's peers, it's unclear what constitutes a girlfriend among them. In Hanson's milieu, group dating has replaced individual dating. Sexual exclusivity's out."

"So," the judge responds, "Hanson's motive is still unclear at this point?"

Lassart says, "Correct. Anything's possible. Hanson may've hated immigrants—two of his dead were—"

The judge suddenly stands, saying, "I appreciate everyone's input today. I must now read the psychiatric reports with care. I'll be looking for, as I noted earlier, key arguments regarding sanity: Hanson's substantial capacity to know right from wrong and his ability to resist impulses to break the law."

When Dad finishes his detailed and surprisingly neutral report, I thank him and tell him I'm impressed with his ability to remember dialogue. However, I do say I'm not impressed with the cherry-picking of shrinks and the influence-peddling on behalf of Bill that Izzy Chen reported. When Dad asks about the latter, I tell him that Kent allegedly sought out Falzon and his partner after Bill's arrest. Kent shook their hands, thanking them profusely for the way they treated Bill.

****

Dad reports that, within record time again, another court session gets underway in the Hanson case. I think, *It's designed to get the case finished and out of the news.* Judge Convin's likely to announce the court's verdict, and declare a sentence. Dad says, judging by body language, there's palpable tension between the Hanson family and survivors of the victims in the Hall of Justice marble hallway, where every word is amplified. When a bailiff unlocks the doors of the courtroom, people rush in, anxious to be able to talk again without being overheard. Once everyone's seated, a hush falls over Department 23 of the San Francisco Superior Court. All stand, including Bill, as the judge enters.

After what seems an eternity of paper shuffling, Judge Convin says, "Regarding case number 73-100684, the court has found the defendant, William Paul Hanson, insane. And so, in accordance with the provisions of Title 6 and 7, Pleadings and Proceedings, the defendant is found not guilty by reason of insanity, section 1056 of California's penal code."

The words "not guilty" cause Bill to perk up and then look over at his family. Kent smiles, and Myrna and Gwen sob.

The judge continues, "Mr. Hanson is thereby sentenced forthwith to Atascadero State Hospital for treatment appropriate the criminally insane.6 This court is now adjourned."

After Convin strikes his gavel, the victims' surviving families hurry out of the courtroom, heads down. As bailiffs walk Bill across the courtroom, the Hansons and their supporters murmur or mouth comforting words to him.

****

Soon after this report from Dad, I relay Convin's decision to Sharon and Scott, who're disappointed. I also phone Gayle as promised.

"I do appreciate your calls, Karl," she says. "It's been tough — my divorce, subsequent move, and now trying to get a PhD in my ex's department."

"That's why I'm here for you...So, here's what went down with Bill."

I explain that, essentially, the fix was in. Kent's reputation and ability to game the system saved the day for Bill. The Court — really just one person, Judge Convin — ruled Bill insane and sent him to a mental hospital.

"Won't the hospital be full of bizarre people, sadistic guards —"

"No. Atascadero isn't at all like the decrepit hospital in Bridgewater, Massachusetts."

I'd told Gayle awhile back about Frederick Wiseman's exposé of a hospital for the criminally insane in the film *Titicut Follies*. He uncovered callous treatment by guards, social workers, and psychiatrists there. In grad school, Professor Wolfgang had sneaked a copy of the often banned documentary for us to see.

"Atascadero is newly built...near the coastal town of Morro Bay, halfway between San Francisco and L.A."

"It'll be a bit of a drive for Kent and Myrna," Gayle states.

"Yeah, but that area near San Luis Obispo is beautiful. They'll wanna hike there."

"They've been through a lot..." Gayle says.

"In no time, Bill will be free, one way or another. Drug guru Timothy Leary just escaped from CMC, a nearby minimal security prison."

"At least you still have a sense of humor, Karl. Know you're bummed."

"Seriously, though, Bill shouldn't be free for a while. We need a law that once hospitalized insane get better, they're transferred to prisons to serve out a full sentence for their crimes.

Berkeley – After the Verdict, 1974

Sharon and I arrive with Dad and Eve at Spenger's restaurant. As we're standing in a line down a corridor after getting drinks, which're always large to make the long wait for tables palatable, we let fly our feelings about Bill. Berkeley traffic noise prevented any discussion driving crosstown.

"Justice prevailed," Eve says gleefully.

"Not if justice means fairness," I say. "Rich get coddled. Poor get cudgeled."

"Bill is insane," Dad says.

"No way," I object. "If Convin had had an insanity checklist that some judges use, then¬–"

Eve demands, "What's Bill if he's not insane?"

"A sane serial killer," I answer.

"Serial killer? No way!" Dad exclaims.

"FBI defines 'em as killers of two or more...at different times or locations."

"Okay, okay," Dad says. "Just hate lumping our Bill with the Zodiac and Zebra Killers."

"Luckily, Bill got caught," I say. "Serial murder's a skill. Some murderers get better as they go and develop a taste for it."

"C'mon, Karl," Eve says.

"Let's just agree that, as time passed, Bill became more lethal. Better at lying, covering his tracks."

Eve frowns, then takes a long sip of her drink.

"I'm just getting to know the Hansons," Sharon says, "So I have no dog in this fight, but I'd guess Bill senses what people want, then gives it to them. A kind of lying-on-demand."

"Wow!" Dad says. "How'd you come up—"

"Not sure," Sharon says. "Maybe being addicted to crime novels."

"Kent pushed Bill for C.O. status," I say. "Bill was chameleon-like in his ability to go along, blend in, seem normal."

"Yeah, he does look normal," Eve concedes.

"It's a myth that serial killers look monstrous and live alone," I continue. "They've got jobs, families. They hide in plain sight."

"So, your diagnosis, Karl?" Dad insists.

"Psychopathic, organized revenge killer."

"Okay, I know psychopathic, though I disagree," Dad says. "Explain the rest."

"Bill's methodical, careful about his attacks—as opposed to disorganized, sloppy."

"The revenge part, I don't get," Eve says. "We've all sought revenge at some point."

"Revenge killers have deeper, more insistent anger than you or I."

Then Dad asks me how psychopathic killers develop. After pausing to drink and gather my thoughts, I explain that their psychopathy firms up by age fifteen, and their killing by their early twenties, like Bill. Their first victims often look or act like family members. Hence Bill's older male victims. Stats show they murder one to three victims a year if they're organized, not caught.

"So how'd Bill get so angry?" Dad asks.

"You guys'll hate me for this." I pull Dad and Eve out of the wait line, whispering, "Kent's aloofness and Myrna's alcoholism."

Dad coughs, spraying scotch on my shirt. Eve almost drops her drink, saving it amid a riot of ice clinking in her glass.

Other people in the line look at us. Some shake their heads.

I continue, "Rich parents can neglect their kids, scar 'em emotionally, just as easily as poor parents."

"Kent was emotionally unavailable," Sharon says, "and Myrna unpredictable, unreliable."

"Enough!" Dad says, raising his voice and his hand. "Remember, guys, you're talking about our good friends."

Again, people stare at us, mouths open.

Eve says, "You're asking us to swallow a lot."

"Speaking of swallowing," I say, "we're at the hostess' desk and we can now eat instead of fight."

Summer 1974

Late in the summer, Nixon resigns. Among the many reasons, Bob Woodward, an investigative journalist and college classmate of mine, collaborated with another *Washington Post* reporter to expose Nixon's role in the Watergate burglary case.

Berkeley anarchists and Marxists celebrate Nixon's resignation in a manner more common of late: destructively. These days, they tear up the town, and often the campus, whether they're mad or glad about something.

Point Reyes, California – September 1974

Ric Orsic and I enjoy a secret perk of academic life, and our wives in art and social work enjoy it too: the ability to travel off-peak to avoid traffic jams. So, after a busy summer, we all stop in Olema one Friday morning, en route to Lee's before Labor Day weekend. During the drive, I'd thought about some encounter-group feedback I'd just received about being more open and in touch with my feelings. I decide the time has come to take a risk.

Sharon and Kathy hike north and Ric and I south, hoping to glimpse the breathtaking West Marin coast. Right off, I say to Ric, "I'm embarrassed to say this, but I've known the Paper Bag Killer for some time."

"What?" he exclaims. "Man! Kathy would love to hear this."

"Go ahead and tell her; just make sure she knows it's confidential."

I tell Ric about my family's friendship with the Hansons and my personal and professional shame over not seeing any signs. Ric says he's embarrassed too, that he and social psych can't predict behavior better. He then asks questions; I try to answer them.

At one point, I explain how the FBI created a behavioral analysis unit a while back—to study serial killers like the Boston Strangler—and that Bill's an example of their organized killer. Then I tell Ric what I explained over dinner to the folks at Spenger's. Being organized, Bill was in control of his actions. He parked a distance from his victims, kept his engine running, attacked them, then ran in a zigzag manner to his van to escape. By contrast, an insane disorganized killer, responding, say, to paranoid-schizoid voices in his head, might kill even if a policeman were standing next to him, at his elbow in the classic M'Naughten insanity test.

"Glad they caught Bill before he got addicted to killing," Ric says, "like that guy who often fakes a broken arm to lure women at the University of Washington. Removable cast!"

"Bill fits other FBI findings for serial killers: displacing aggression, targeting the vulnerable, and racking up mileage trolling for victims. Oh, and having developed no conscience due to childhood trauma."

"Can't believe the bastard got a get-out-of-jail-free card," Ric says.

"Joel Fort says all of Bill's attacks were first-degree crimes."

"Oh, yeah, we both know Fort."

I remind Ric that Fort was the only psychiatrist who found the Coed Butcher, Ed Kemper, sane last year, even though others found him psychotic because of his cannibalism. Unlike wealthy Bill, indigent Ed got eight life sentences for his serial killings in Santa Cruz. Ric says Dr. Fort's not the kind of shrink or lawyer who loves cases like Bill's. No appeal possible, so they can shoot, refute, and then scoot with their hefty fees. We laugh.

Finished hiking, the four of us continue north to Lee at the Marshall Tavern, where he's bartending now besides working at the *Point*

Reyes Light. As we hit Marshall, we drop Ric and Kath off at Synanon, whose leader Ric suspects has twisted the program into a cult. Chuck Dederich requires that, among other things, women in Synanon shave their heads, and if married, break up with their partners and find new ones.

Meanwhile, Sharon and I buy groceries for our time with Lee. When we pick up Ric and Kathy, they say a few people they talked to, with Dederich gone on business, groused about his efforts to control them and growing violence and financial chicanery at Synanon. Ric is intrigued, since brainwashing is an academic interest of his.

Over drinks at the Tavern, Ric tells us—and Lee, who's all ears too—that he's learned that Dederich faced lawsuits and financial challenges in the '60s in Santa Monica, where he started Synanon. After high-profile celebs and politicians saved him and Synanon from ruin, Dederich found himself flush with cash. So he bought sixty acres of land overlooking Tomales Bay in 1964 and thousands more acres in the early '70s in order to relocate Synanon there. Fast-forwarding, Lee says locals can't believe the light-to-nonexistent sentences Dederich received in current lawsuits, and we all conclude that contacts and high-priced legal help make the difference.

Out with Lee in a small boat on narrow Tomales Bay the next day, all five of us agree how relieved we are that the San Francisco Police Department just arrested four Zebra suspects, After civil rights advocates ended the mayor's stop-and-question policy vis-a-vis Black males, Zebra killings had started again in April, until an informant, Julian Harris, responded to a sketch and a $30,000 reward with information. Harris said a group of male Black Muslims who called themselves the Death Angels constituted a sect of sorts. He claimed the Death Angels committed fifteen murders and attempted eight others, mostly against whites. However, some authorities speculated they killed as many as seventy, many being white unidentified vagrants, runaways, or prostitutes.

Sharon says, "From the looks of the suspects and the nature of their crimes, I bet judges won't be coddling them due to their less privileged status as they have Hanson and Dederich."

"All us underprivileged are in the same boat in that regard," Kath says, triggering laughter.

"Rowboat, you mean," Lee says, eliciting even more laughter that rocks the boat. Then he yells, "Hey, calm down! Really! We die if we go overboard. Tomales Bay sucks, literally. Treacherous currents here."

Berkeley – Fall 1974

Not long after our getaway and good times with Lee, former grad-school buddy Hogan, still at Penn, visits. In our catch-up conversation, Hogan leads off, noting that the Unicorn has had some hits and misses lately. Sharon's hyper curious look tells Hogan he'd better elaborate.

"Ira's created a network of thinkers to whom he mails photocopies of articles on Bell Telephone's dime, and he's getting lots of attention promoting that Israeli spoon-bender to American audiences."

"That paranormal guy, Uri Geller," I say.

"Ira actually snatched a hit from a miss." Hogan says. "After almost falling apart, Ira's Rock Pile building got renovated, and gentrified rents forced him to a small place nearby on Race Street. This gal moved in with him a week after they met. Rare for Ira to get serious, and even rarer to cohabit."

"Any genuine misses?" Sharon asks.

"His book with numbers for a title didn't sell," Hogan says, sporting a smirk-contaminated smile.

"Not surprised," I say. "When Doubleday insisted Ira title the book before we left Philly, he decided on its Library of Congress ISBN number out of spite."

"Had more problems than the odd title," Hogan says. "Many reviewers considered the book sophomoric drivel. And the endless pages of graphics made it like a comic book."

We all laugh.

Hogan continues, "I've heard Ira's trying to write another book ... about UFOs and paranormal stuff—"

"And weaponizing physicist Tesla's ideas for jamming communications?" I say.

"Yeah," Hogan replies. "ELF transmissions might cloud people's minds in propaganda warfare—"

"You guys've got Ira's shtick down," Sharon chuckles.

****

On a lazy December morning, I help Sharon plan a working holiday, during which she'll show her portfolio to art galleries in Seattle while we spend Christmas with the Schonborns, and to galleries in Los Angeles while we're with the Beltons, flying in from Minneapolis. Then we start the giant Sunday newspaper, chilling after Sharon's and Ric's joint birthday party the night before.

"Holy crap!" I shout as I read the headline of a short news bulletin inserted at the last minute on page one: "Professor's wife fighting for life after knife attack."

"W-What?" Sharon demands.

"A colleague I know, across campus in Psych, found his wife at home—bloody, near death."

"Jesus Christ," Sharon says, grabbing the paper and reading aloud, "Dr. Jed Drell told police that when he'd returned home from an early morning jog today, he was shocked to see his wife bleeding and unconscious and his home ransacked. Medics raced her to a hospital, where doctors discovered she'd been stabbed thirteen times in the chest and back...and strangled"

PART III – THE "PSYCHO"-OLOGIST

CHAPTER 13
Deceitful, Predatory Professor Drell

Oakland – Sunday, December 8, 1974

According to radio reports, surgeons at Highland Hospital struggled to keep Jed Drell's wife, Angela, alive. Out of surgery now, the thirty-one-year-old mother of two girls remains unconscious and in critical condition from her stab wounds and strangling. Meanwhile, in the foothills across town, detectives are at her home on Trinidad Drive, where responding officers found her lying on the floor in a hall. Jed, the colleague I saw Professor Noces push out of her office, tells police that while he was out jogging, a burglar must've stumbled upon Angela, then tried to kill her. Jed thinks he might've escaped by way of nearby Joaquin Miller Road. When officers follow the route Jed suggests, they find his wallet and Angela's purse, without money and credit cards, discarded a few miles away

Later Sunday afternoon, an Oakland sergeant, Jim Hahn, with whom I'm riding-along, reveals the latest, which he knows because PDs, if nothing else, communicate 24/7 internally. Hahn tells me detectives felt Jed's story too pat, including the too-easy discovery of discarded items. So they took Jed downtown for further questioning. They pressed hard about the state of his marriage and the coincidence that he'd taken their toddler daughters the day before the attack to spend a few days with his sister.

While able to verbally spar with the best of 'em, Jed soon realized he'd need to replace Story A with Story B. Hence, he told detectives he didn't think they'd believe he'd be out jogging so early in the morning.

The lead detective, leaning forward to encourage intimacy and trust, said, "And so?"

"I'm something of an insomniac," Jed said. "I'd tossed and turned for an hour or more that morning, so I went out for a drive around 4 a.m. I'm kinda like a baby that can only be soothed by a car ride. When I came back a while later, I found Angela bleeding and called an ambulance."

"Did you try to stop the bleeding?"

"No. Never learned first aid."

Just then, the lead detective got a coded call on his radio and stepped into another room for privacy. His partner looked through a desk for a robbery report form.

Moments later, the detective returned and said, "I'm sorry, Doctor. You're under arrest."

"B-B-But, Officer…"

As he cuffed him, the detective said, "My partner will read you your Miranda rights."

"W-Why?"

"Your wife just regained consciousness. Said there was no intruder. Said you tried to kill her. You better hope she pulls through, pal."

Sergeant Hahn pauses to let me absorb the news. He cautions that forensics will reveal the truth. It's a very remote possibility that an intruder attacked Angela and she decided to blame Jed for some reason when she came to.

I respond that she'd have to be incredibly angry, yet quick-witted, to be able to capitalize on a tragic event when she awoke. I then tell Hahn the OPD's got this one right. They know that it's not just everyday people who try to kill their spouses; it can be privileged, brilliant psychologists.

Because I've known Hahn for years, I take a risk and reveal that Jed's the second homicidal individual of late I've personally known. I tell him I thought I moved in different social circles than that. *So much for all those people out there committing violence. They include my kind now.*

****

After my ride-along, I detour en route home, taking the Joaquin Miller exit off the highway to see Jed's house, which hangs off the side of the Oakland Hills. I'm amazed that a faculty member hired just a year before me could afford to rent or buy a house with a commanding view of the Bay. I knew Jed had had prior modest-paying post-doctorate fellowships, so Angela would've had to have had a very good paying job then...and now.

Jed's house, typical of many hill-hugging homes in the area, presents itself to the world as a two-vehicle garage connected to Trinidad Drive with a car-length long bridge. A mailbox sits where the paved bridge joins the street, as does a set of stairs descending a story to the entrance of the house itself. Such houses typically cascade down a steep slope two or three stories, with plenty of rooms to raise two kids and still get away from a spouse after a quarrel.

The Bay sides of houses like Jed's feature large windows and often sliding glass doors out to decks. On a clear day, Jed would have a panoramic view from the San Mateo Bridge to the south to the Bay Bridge in the north, barring fog and overgrown trees. Except for trees to trim, there's rarely a yard to maintain. And natural wood exteriors, except on the west weather side where the sun and sunsets are, don't require much more than wood stain every ten years.

So life should've been sweet in the Oakland Hills for Jed. At thirty-three, he had plenty of square footage for his family and plenty of time for jogging, studying, and writing in his psych subfields of psychopharmacology and mammalian sexual behavior. A supersmart, hyperactive guy, he appeared farther along life's path than I, though his fast track might've been his undoing.

At some point, life began to deteriorate for Jed. Perhaps it started with the time demands of caring for his youngsters and the expenses of childrearing and a pricey mortgage. And deteriorate it did. I picture Angela, whom I've never met, in a fight for her life, her chest bloody and hands cut from fending off Jed's knife. She keeps screaming even after Jed plunges the knife into her back, but finally, she's silenced as he strangles her. No one hears her screams in part because the steep slope of the Trinidad hill means no houses exist across the street or near the lower part of the Drells' house.

Likely, Jed premeditated his attack by arranging for his kids to be away and striking early Sunday morning while neighbors slept soundly. The attack would look like a burglary gone awry, the perfect crime in Jed's mind. He'd downsize, hire his sister—or better yet, an attractive nanny—to restore the control and freedom he'd lost as a family man.

****

At Jed's arraignment December 13, Judge Sidney Silverman hears Jed plead not guilty to attempted murder and then sets bail at a reasonable $50,000. But then Silverman elicits gasps when he allows Jed to keep staying at a jail closer to his home than the ominous county jail, called Santa Rita. I ponder, *Did the judge think Jed's family could visit him more easily? If so, not smart, since Angela told reporters after fingering Jed that she planned to start divorce proceedings at once.*

Angela miraculously leaves the hospital just eleven days after being left curled up in a pool of blood. *She must've felt pressure to recover quickly because someone had to watch her toddlers.*

****

When I learn of Jed's special treatment, I rush over to Psych to hear faculty reactions and see if his department will sanction him. I get no comment from everyone I buttonhole, except Janet Noces. Her first words to me are "Ugh! The judge's decisions totally stink, but no worse 'n the university's. They're letting Jed skate!"

Noces says Jed had cultivated powerful males in Psych over time. They strongly opposed her call for sanctions despite her being on the department's disciplinary committee. Her feminist friends, who should've been outraged, remained silent. Because of this, deans and top administrators up the line decided to merely suspend Jed without pay.

"Officials should've fired him," I bark. "At minimum, stripped him of his tenure or forced him to reapply for his position."

Noces laments, "Not sure what I can do now, given that males bulldozed over me."

"You must be doubly ticked since you just added ethics as one of your subfields." I recall, *Janet was hired before me and got flack for doing field research that violated subjects' privacy. She reacted by developing processes to prevent harmful, unintended side effects in research.*

I later tell Ric of the failure of Psych faculty to sanction Jed. Ric throws up his hands. "I've lost all respect for them. Ain't gonna collaborate with those jerks anymore!"

"I thought psychologists cared about humans," I say, "even ones who use rat-mazes. They, of all people, know about shaping behavior with punishments...and rewards."

****

Sharon and I fly to Seattle to be with Dad and Eve for Christmas. After a few days of schlepping her portfolio to galleries in pouring rain, Sharon's happy we fly south to her brother's place at sunny Manhattan Beach to be with her parents. When I ask Sharon if I should tell her folks about Bill and now Jed, she cautions me that knowing such violent characters, I'll lose my identity in their eyes as a nonviolent warrior.

I lament, saying, "I'm already questioning part of my identity as a progressive liberal regarding crim justice reform."

"Oh, tell 'em that. Their Republican souls will love it."

Sharon shows her portfolio to art galleries on La Cienega Boulevard, encouraged by the lyrics of "Bright, Bright, Sunshiny Days" on her brother's car radio. But when no one wants to represent her work, she's crestfallen. I try to buoy her up by the old adage: "It's like parking spaces; you only need one."

"Okay, when we get home, I'll restart prospecting galleries in San Francisco No more Zebras or Paper Baggers," she says, uttering a strained laugh. She responds to my smile with another strained laugh. "Not sure I'm cut out for constant rejection. With experience at *Sunset* magazine, I could work at the *Daily Californian*."

"Nah. You'll get a gallery," I say, hugging her. "But I hear ya. I hate rejection, too, particularly form-letter ones for grants, books, articles."

Oakland – January 1975

At a special hearing, Judge Silverman refuses to lower Jed's bail, despite arguments by his lawyer, Lincoln Mintz. The judge does agree to Mintz's request that Jed continue staying locally rather than at the tough county jail twenty-six miles away. He says he'll consider a plea bargain after Mintz suggests Jed's willing to reverse his not guilty plea.

When Ric hears this, he storms into my campus office, fuming, "Jed's a total dick. A lying, flip-flopping son of a bitch. Gives us social scientists a bad name."

"Agreed! Can't believe Silverman's coddling him, keeping him from other evil guys. At least he didn't lower his bail."

"Jed may be smart, but students say he can't teach. His sorry ass shoulda been fired just for inept teaching."

"For moral turpitude too. I understand, but don't condone, people who snap and attack others during a heated, argument. But he stabbed her in cold blood, then left her to die."

Despite Ric wanting to keep psych jerks out of his life, I still need them as collaborators, knowing that police and violence research needs psychology as well as sociology perspectives. So I check in with Psych again and find a couple of faculty besides Noces now willing to violate the chair's code of silence. One says Jed's brown-nosing of administrators over the years paid off, and another believes deans forgave him because he'd been an acting dean just before his violence.

Oakland – February 14, 1975

Because newspaper editorials criticize Judge Silverman's handling of Drell's case so far, he opens his private chambers4 to the press on Valentine's to see how he gathers info to rule on the petition Jed filed for a plea bargain. Such controversial pleas allow a defendant to plead guilty to a lesser charge and get a lesser punishment, saving all sides the time and expense of a trial.

Silverman signals the prosecution to begin. DA George Nicholson opens with "Initially, the State planned to charge first-degree murder, punishable by death. But the victim lived."

Silverman responds, "We're aware of the facts, Counsel. So…?"

"The State charges assault with 'the intent to kill, plus perjury to mislead.' The difference between a murderer and an—"

"Objection, Your Honor," Attorney Mintz shouts. "Dr. Drell isn't a murderer."

"Sustained."

The district attorney continues, "The difference between murder and aggravated assault is a dead versus a live victim…and this depends on whether EMTs get there in time or docs are good enough to save a victim."

Mintz interrupts, "Precisely the point of our petition—Dr. Drell actually called 911 for help—"

"Wrong!" the district attorney says. "He only called to complete his alibi. Thought she'd likely die any second."

Mintz ignores the district attorney's words and says, "Your Honor, you've got our other arguments in our plea petition. I'll add this: given Dr. Drell's brilliance and academic achievement, he should be allowed to resume his work at the university as soon as possible."

The district attorney ignores Mintz' words in return. "To be clear, aggravated-assaulters generally want what murderers want—their victim dead. And, by the way, Mr. Drell's no medical doctor. Moreover, he doesn't deserve to be called 'Doctor' for a second reason: in his work as a psycho-pharmacologist, he regularly degrades doctors, calls 'em ignoramuses."

"Your point about doctors?" Judge Silverman asks.

"Mintz is stealing medical doctor status for Drell. If anything, Drell should enhance doctors' status, rather than steal their status. They saved his wife's life and, in so doing, saved his, since California voters have just reaffirmed their wish for the death penalty for murderers."

"Enough of your digressions, Counsel," Silverman admonishes. "Back to the case."

Nicholson continues, "Most importantly, Mr. Drell has intimidated his wife to the point that she's now afraid to testify against him. For this reason alone, Judge, the State asks you to deny the defendant's plea petition for leniency."

Judge Silverman then asks, "What does the State recommend?"

Nicholson answers, "That Drell learn a lesson. He needs five years of real time with real felons in state prison, not easy time with misdemeanants in cushy local lockups."

Silverman then recognizes Probation Officer Gwen Hopper, who says, "Our department agrees that prison time's essential for Drell. But first, the Court needs to do a ninety-day psychiatric evaluation of him."

"Why?" Silverman asks.

"Drell claims he's severely depressed, and that's why he attacked his wife."

"Last word goes to the defense."

Mintz says, "My client has served almost four months for an assault that grew out of a simple domestic quarrel. Give Dr. Drell probation so he can serve the community once again."

Judge Silverman says, "Thank you all. My decision will be forthcoming."

CHAPTER 14

Predator Plays the Court. Zebra Terrorize the Streets

Oakland, California – Hall of Justice – March 27, 1975

Having been given a rare opportunity to observe a private plea-bargaining session, I wonder if Silverman's going to be fair. As all the parties take their seats, Drell, who waived his privacy rights during this process, works a crossword puzzle as he waits. *Probably a cryptic puzzle*, I think, *as he's often boasted he only does the hard ones.*

Silverman gets right to his decision, saying, "The court has decided to accept the plea bargain petition wherein Mr. Drell promises to plead guilty to felonious assault rather than attempted murder. Do you so plead now?"

"I do, Your Honor," Drell says without standing or even putting down his crossword pencil.

"The Court herewith denies Ms. Hopper's suggested new five-year state prison incarceration. Instead the Court imposes five-year's probation and a six-month jail term at Santa Rita. Mr. Drell must also refrain from seeing his wife."

I gasp in disbelief, along with Prosecutor Nicholson and Probation Officer Hopper,

Drell's broad smile lasts just a few seconds, though. Silverman says, "But Mr. Drell must undergo psychiatric treatment and pay for it himself."

Attorney Mintz jumps up. "But, Your Honor, my client can't pay for therapy. He's poor. No university paychecks lately."

"If you petition and prove impoverishment, I'll modify my order," Silverman says.

Rising from her seat, Ms. Hopper asks to speak, and Silverman consents. She says, "Respectfully, I must report that the defendant doesn't believe in psychiatric treatment and feels it would be hypocritical to undergo it."

Silverman's blazing eyes drill into Hopper, Mintz, and Nicholson. He barks, "You all should've sorted this out before court. Get on it."

****

On the way home from court, I stop to see Janet. As she ushers me into her office, I blurt out the judge's sentence. She utters expletives, pounding her desk. I tell her that having witnessed *real* domestic quarrels during almost every ride-along, I believe Jed's using quarreling as a cover-up. Janet agrees, saying, "Jed once confided in me that he wanted sexual freedom but couldn't go through the trauma of divorce."

"Planned. Premeditated's always worse! … Pretend a minute that Jed *didn't* plan to kill Angela, that he acted out of anger. The justice system, in the guise of Silverman, would've been even more lenient. The judge would've also literally 'whitewashed' Jed's sentence because he's a white male. I know lots of Blacks who commit unplanned family violence, in a burst of momentary anger, and get serious state-prison time."

"So Silverman's racist as well as sexist?"

"Six months for a white male, when it could've been so much longer. I looked up the sentence that California mandates for most aggravated assaults, number 217 in the Penal Code. It's fourteen years!"

"Differential justice is un-American besides unethical."

"I figure Silverman treated white, supersmart Jed just like he would a star athlete or entertainer. You and your fellow Psych faculty are the only people who can really sanction Jed at this point."

Janet pats my arm. "I'll keep up the pressure. I'm as upset as you."

"Without further sanctions, Jed can someday tell people he was guilty of assault, which is technically any verbal threat to harm. And even if he adds, 'and battery,' he can follow up with 'you know, like shoving someone.' People will think 'No big deal.'"

Berkeley – Winter 1975

At the book launch for my *Dealing with Violence* in a non-descript campus lecture hall, I converse with friends and colleagues, particularly criminologist Yablonsky, who wrote the foreword, and friend Roszak. I do miss seeing Gayle, Scott, and my wordsmith dad, who's with Eve visiting friends in Malaysia. I especially miss that my family won't see the new me, sporting contact lenses and a more aesthetic cap for the undersized front tooth where my cleft meets my gums.

In my remarks to the crowd, some who know my politics detect a lessening of my commitment to progressive-liberal reforms. During the long lead time between writing and publication, I've dialed back some of the idealism I express in the book. Bill's and Jed's cases, and countless hours observing police in action, have made me more of a moderate regarding police reforms. Thus, I can't believe I'm hearing myself saying to the crowd, "Maybe America needs to disarm its citizens as it disarms its cops."

Further evidence of my becoming unmoored ideologically comes the next day. During the first radio interview on my book tour, KFOG host Charlie Stamper says in his deep voice, "I'd let down my listeners if I didn't ask you what you'd do if crime visited your family—idealist that you are?"

"Unfortunately, I just yell at guys in the Philly and New York subways who try to look up my wife's dress while she climbs those see-through iron-grid stairs. My wife and other women hate that."

"Yes, public civility's declining. Gotta have you back about this 'Broken Windows' theory that's getting some notice. But what about *violent* crime? Say a rapist attacks your wife?"

"No one knows exactly how they'd respond. I'd be angry as hell but wouldn't become a vigilante. I'd want the rapist to get significant prison time, especially if he's a privileged white guy."

"You're more forgiving as regards the underprivileged?"

"Yes."

After other interviews, I feel further unmoored, sensing more of my crim justice idealism slipping away. This is more than the usual postpartum fatigue after a book's published. It's a sadness, a world weariness about an imperfect world.

****

I walk near the Psych building early one morning. A man darting by startles me so much, I drop the book and papers I'm carrying. He slows to turn and look.

"Whoa!" I say while stooping to recover my stuff. "Hi, Jed."

"Hi, Karl. W-W-Working on Sunday? You must be a busy guy too," he shouts as he scurries into the building's breezeway. Before I know it, he's inside the building. I think, *Doesn't Jed work at an off-campus location? Bet he's violating work-furlough rules.*

Sure enough, reporters at local newspapers soon write about Drell's violations of Judge Silverman's orders. One paper's editorial board decries the fact the perpetrator of a brutal stabbing attack could be so grossly unsupervised in his work release. Due to the furor, Silverman tightens up his terms for Drell's release arrangement.

****

I read some time later that Jed has applied for a six-figure grant to study the post-release needs of county-jail inmates where he's serving time. He's created a research group, hoping government officials will choose his proposal over the other eleven submitted.

Almost crumpling the newspaper in my hands, I squawk to Sharon that Jed's trying to make a buck off his time in jail. "Can't believe the chutzpah of that guy."

"Born and raised in the Bronx, a fast-talking scrapper! I rest my case."

"These days, he's nice on the outside. But angry on the inside? Rumor has it that he used to lose his temper in classes, yelling at students."

"Maybe that's why he became an assistant dean?" Sharon says.

"Possibly. Students complain that he advocates legalizing most drugs."

"I've always wondered, why wouldn't a psychopharmacologist like him use an obscure drug to kill Angela?"

"Is crime fiction having an effect on you, Sharon? Drell's probably in line with research that shows people who 'hate' their intimates and loved ones prefer hands-on violence: stabbing, strangling."

"Then I don't have to bother buying a gun?" she says, chuckling.

Northern California – Summer and Fall – 1975

Out of nowhere, Lee Sims announces he's just moved to Auburn, a small Gold Rush town along the main highway to Lake Tahoe. Sharon and I had grown dependent on getaways to see grandly welcoming Lee in Tomales Bay. Moreover, Ric had become friends with Lee while helping the owners of the *Light* continue investigating Synanon.

There is a silver lining to Lee's move: we all get to try rafting on the American River, which runs relatively close to Lee and his girlfriend's place. And when they offer to act as guides for the Orsics and us in a raft that seats six, we all trust them implicitly. Though I think with a smile, *Lee tried to kill me once before, on a ski run.*

All's well and good the first day on our rubber craft as we get some rays and enjoy the beauty of the river. On the second day, whitewater rapids surprise us. Though we raftmates have bounced off many rocks and feel invincible with our helmets and safety training, we feel increasing dread as the river gets wilder. Soon, the raging rapids overwhelm our collective skill set, and we overturn, having to swim to shore in cold water.

Lee waits until we end our trip to mention that even though people die rafting, many more die going out on tranquil Tomales Bay in Point Reyes. In fact, he claims he nearly drowned there recently when the little-appreciated sneaker waves capsized him. A chill sweeps over me knowing the times I've been out on the water with Lee. Little do I know that more death chills lie ahead.

****

Sharon and I become super busy as fall unfolds along with our creativity. I like to think both Sharon's paintings and my writings have evolved into appealing hard-edged realism pieces. I submit two of my articles to journals: one about conflict resolution teams and the other about TV violence co-authored with a Psych professor. Sharon and I also start attending peer-to-peer groups in Berkeley—hers for assertiveness training, mine for personal-growth therapy.

Our schedules go into overdrive as pre-holiday activities kick in with the Orsics and Roszaks. We celebrate Christmas with Sharon's family at her brother's in Los Angeles and return to Berkeley for New Year's with mine, including Gayle from the Midwest.

Winter 1976

Once I prep a new seminar on conflict resolution, I return to the publish-or-perish game. I write *To Keep the Peace* about cutting-edge crisis-intervention programs. In the book, I analyze how police manage school violence, hostage situations, and landlord-tenant disputes. Plus, I examine the challenges police face dealing with victims, witnesses, and the mentally ill. Since the Feds fund pilot programs exploring these kinds of challenges, I recommend they use psychologists and social workers to train police who're called to intervene in crises after professionals like them go home from their nine-to-five jobs. I argue it's okay to blur the lines between police work and social work, though I'm understanding better why older police chiefs oppose it.

****

Old-school policework gets plenty of press during the extensive media coverage of the trial of four Death Angel suspects in the Zebra Killings. The San Francisco Police Department's Zebra team presents compelling testimony at one point regarding a .32 pistol found near the scene of the last killing. Zebra officers show how the gun was used in many of the murders and then trace the chain of ownership of the gun to a worker at Black Self-Help Moving and Storage, where most of the accused work.

After the cops' gun testimony, the defense's only hope is to discredit former Death Angel Anthony Harris, who turned state's evidence. But Harris reveals so many details over twelve days of testimony that his cred remains unimpeachable. After 108 days, this longest criminal trial ever in San Francisco ends with convictions and life sentences for the Death Angels, for killing fourteen and assaulting eight.

****

I growl after reading in the campus newspaper that both the Psych chairman and a university vice president assert that Drell will be allowed to teach the upcoming summer session. I confront Janet Noces at the door of her office, saying, "Guess you and your pals whiffed."

"I'm sorrier than you."

"And what does the vice president mean, saying he'll review Drell's performance, his whole situation before deciding about permanent reinstatement?"

"Well, because Jed's been one of them—an administrator, though for just one term—our chairman and the vice president have been ultra-cautious. We call them Doctors Song and Dance."

"Whatever you call 'em, they're compounding the injustice, adding their own blunders to those of Judge Silverman."

"Truth be told," her lower lip trembles, "the so-called disciplinary committee is packed with Jed's friends, union guys who intimidate everyone." She almost whispers, "Just between us, the union has threatened to file a grievance alleging job discrimination against Jed if he's let go. Gonna make it a *cause célèbre*."

"I doubt Song and Dance will stand up to the union."

"I'm mobilizing a coupla more feminists to fight, but everyone's shutting us out."

"Will they listen to the likes of me, a conflict-resolution expert?"
She gives me a Mona-Lisa smile. I decide not to intervene.

****

Sharon finds a former warehouse in the Berkeley flatlands that has a studio she can rent, and during one of Dad's visits, he helps us build a worktable and several shelves in her small space. We enjoy getting to know other artists at the Warehouse, as it's called. But we don't like that Yulia, the Marxist head of the enterprise, charges Sharon more rent than other artists "because Karl has a real job." Sharon keeps quiet about the secretarial work she does at the Chemistry Department on campus because Yulia would charge even more.

We also don't like that, soon after joining the Warehouse, a stranger rapes, hogties, and murders a young woman at a similar artists' co-op across from the San Francisco Art Institute. Sharon gets nervous about going to the Warehouse after dark, and we wonder about our plan to move there when a larger space with a kitchen and bathroom become vacant. Live-in artists have improved half the forty spaces so they no longer have to cook with hotplates or use the huge communal bathroom where ten can wash up at a time at a huge circular sink. The sink's fun for everyone, but women don't like the fact that urinals vastly outnumber stalls.

****

After Sharon sells her painting of Italian-Borsalino hats to a friend, we celebrate at McNally's Irish Pub. Upon our return to our apartment, Sharon answers our ringing phone.

"C'mere. It's your sister. She's crying."

CHAPTER 15

Death at my Doorstep. Dragon Lady

Spring *1976*

"Dad just died!" Gayle moans. "Eve called me."

"Holy Christ! It can't be. Not after Mom—"

"Heart attack. Collapsed this morning in front of their Hood Canal cabin. Eve gave him CPR, which she'd learned 'cuz of his angina."

"I can't believe it. He just turned sixty."

By now, Sharon's got an arm around me, straining to hear what Gayle's saying.

"Somehow, an ambulance found their cabin, but cars wouldn't yield to it fast enough along a two-lane road to Port Townsend's hospital nineteen miles away."

"Nothing closer?" I ask.

"Not sure. But with luck, Dad may've seen Whidbey Island on the way where we Schonborns camped during family reunions on Puget Sound."

Choking back tears, I ask, "W-Where's his body now?"

"Eve said he's at Kosec Funeral, where they're embalming him."

"Christ! Gotta stop that. Need an autopsy to know if he's had *silent* strokes or ischemia, other stuff, barely sixty."

"Ever the medical student," Gayle says. "But I agree."

"Look, I'll call Eve about the autopsy...and Dad's doctor if necessary."

"Good. I'll call Scott and others. Then gotta book us flights. Love you, Karl."

"Love you too. Bye," I mumble, dissolving into tears.

I get through to Eve, and after consoling her, convince her that even if the embalming's started, a partial autopsy's better than nothing.

I collapse into our sofa and think back to mid-January when I waved bye to Dad after a really good visit. *Thank God for that and many other visits. Good decision to take professorship near him and not in Chicago or even L.A.*

Seattle, Washington – May 1976

My sibs and I stay at Eve's house in Kirkland, across a long floating bridge from Seattle in an area soon to be key in the history of both Microsoft and Costco. Our visit with Dad's doctor turns tense when he reveals the autopsy shows Dad's coronary arteries were 80 percent obstructed. We can't get the doctor to admit he should've ordered bypass surgery for Dad.

We help Eve plan a memorial service for Dad at the local Unitarian church. After the reception, we drive south to a cemetery near Tacoma to inter Dad's ashes beside his parents. It makes me extra sad, though, that Dad chose not to inter Mom's ashes there eight years earlier. Instead, he kept them in a small box until he put them with a tree we planted in her honor at the Palo Alto Unitarian Church.

San Francisco Bay Area – May, 1976

Back in Berkeley, I catch up with professorial duties and help plan another service for Dad in Palo Alto, where Eve has returned. She kicked out the tenants to whom she and Dad had rented the family home before moving to Kirkland. Scott and I continue to struggle with grief, but we manage to host a few of Dad's many friends and relatives who stream into the Bay Area for the memorial service.

This second service satisfied me more than the first because we sibs wrote and gave the main eulogy to the hundreds who attended. Reverend Danford Lion's words, plus spontaneous comments by attendees, saddened me because of their poignancy. But they delighted me because Dad's wit attracted friends with the same gift. And attendees also uplifted me. I learned, for instance, that Dad sang in an *a capella* group at the University of Washington, that he was good friends with Joseph Eichler who built the Frank-Lloyd-Wright-style California houses we lived in, and that he'd recently rushed a child stricken with yellow fever to a hospital in Malaysia while visiting there.

****

We sibs have lives to lead and so don't get into the probating of Dad's will. (When Mom died, no probate necessary. With California's community property laws, Dad simply inherited Mom's half of their estate.) We trusted Eve when she said we sibs and she shared Dad's estate and that she'd already met with Dad's lawyer to facilitate the probate. Little did we know she'd fast-tracked a shocking court procedure.

****

After summer fades, Sharon startles me one morning by reading a headline out loud. "Convicted professor Jed Drell to resume full duties.

"What?"

Sharon reads on, "Top university officials reviewed reports and summer session evaluations of Dr. Jed Drell to assess his professorial fitness. They concluded there's no basis for preventing his permanent return to the Psychology Department."

Sharon gives me the paper, and I read the rest of the story, groaning, swearing, and clenching my fists. Then I phone Janet.

"Thought you'd call," she says. "I'm as pissed as you."

"You couldn't persuade the higher-ups?"

Janet explains everyone in the administration's concerned about PR and lawsuits. I feel sucker-punched. She says, "We couldn't budge academic union bigshots either. But that's not what shames me."

"Huh?"

"I chickened out, Karl. Didn't use all my ammo."

"Spill."

"From the day I met Jed, he's come onto me, though he's married."

"Jesus!" I drop the receiver on the kitchen counter, startling Sharon. I grab it, then say, "I thought Jed more nerd than womanizer."

"He persisted, Karl, so I slapped him every time he touched me. He got the message that I wasn't interested."

"So he stopped?"

"Not really. But I heard he hits on students too."

"He's a predator! Did you complain to your chair or senior faculty?"

"Yes. But they're sexist pigs, except for one female who's always on leave and another whom Jed won over early since she wants to become an administrator."

"And that's why you couldn't get the department to punish him for trying to kill his wife?"

"Yes. But there's another reason....I've kept it from you—"

"Fire away."

"Most of you in Sociology probably never knew this," she whispers, "but Jed and Angela attended a Psych party at my house the night before the attack! So some people suspect me—"

"Of being Jed's lover?"

"Correct." She pauses and then adds more to her revelations. After hearing her out, I hang up and stare at the floor, shoulders slumped.

Sharon re-enters the kitchen, waits a second, then harrumphs, "So how'd the killer furlough-cheat prevail this time?"

"Just before senior faculty threw Noces off the disciplinary committee, they let slip the rest of the truth."

"What?"

I explain that Drell twisted the arms of some friends from the Bronx who'd also ended up at our university. These guys helped establish a very assertive faculty union, which replaced our moderate one by a close vote. So these Bronx-driven union guys told university bigwigs and VPs that they'd sue if they fired Jed. The bullies claimed their union's disciplinary committee voted to lift Jed's suspension and reinstate him.5 They didn't consult rank-and-file union members like Ric and me. Of course, deans and VPs caved because they didn't want any further negative publicity for the university.

Sharon storms out of the kitchen, and I ruminate, *Wish I could tell Sharon it gets worse, but first gotta confirm the sex-predator allegations.*

****

"I can't figure out why Jed wanted Angela dead," Ric says as we jog around Lake Merritt, a small oasis that attracts joggers a few blocks east of downtown Oakland.

"I've heard a coupla theories, but first, I need to reality check something. Janet Noces claims Jed's hit on her repeatedly over the years."

Ric reacts by almost colliding with an oncoming runner. After recovering, he says, "Sorry. It's so laughable, I almost lost it."

"You don't believe her?"

"Funny thing, but I do. Why would she lie?"

"You heard anything else about Jed?"

"No. Though rumors always swirl about us faculty. Where we live, our marital status–"

"Janet says he hits on students too."

"Jed's more of an asshole than I thought," Ric says. "So, what're the theories?"

I relate Janet's theory that Jed wished he'd married up, wished Angela was more than just a secretary. Maybe a professional like Janet, or if not, at least more sophisticated about sex or okay with an open marriage.

I explain another theory, a Psych prof's, that Jed's "got a screw loose." Prof thinks Jed misses the forest for the trees. Though brilliant, he hadn't thought out being a widower with small kids. Realizing he'd need help, he deluded himself that he could find a new partner who wouldn't mind raising his kids *and* wouldn't guilt trip him for extramarital sex.

Ric reacts, "Jed's definitely twisted. But back to Janet. Why didn't she complain to senior faculty?"

"She did. Got nowhere. Thinks they're all sexist."

"Unlike senior profs in Sociology?" Ric snickers.

"Speaking of which, Ric, one knocked on our apartment door recently, knowing I'd be at a conference. Holding a bag of groceries, he told Sharon he'd cook dinner for them both. She slammed the door in his face."

"That bastard!" he yells. Who?"

"Can't tell ya. He's got too much power—"

"Shit, Karl."

"Watch out, Ric, another jogger!" I shout. "Incoming fire everywhere you turn!"

****

At the insistence of friends, Scott and I visit Dad's lawyer, who describes how Dad's "life estate" works. For we three siblings, it means Eve can live in the Palo Alto house until she dies, but we kids, not Eve, own it. This provision doesn't apply to Dad's less valuable properties in Washington. As we're leaving the lawyer's office, he whispers, "Conflict's built into a life estate. Consider getting your own lawyer. Soon." I think, *Amazing confession from the guy who drew up this will for Dad while his new wife looked on. Still, Eve's planning to stay in our childhood house a long time, she's assured us.*

Wrong! Stinkin' thinkin.' Eve informs us siblings the next day, in writing, that she's put the house up for sale because she needs cash … and doesn't like California anymore. I phone Scott, who's as angry as I am. And I phone Gayle, saying, "Sounds fishy, especially the cash part, since Eve said she'd just received Dad's life insurance payout."

"I know it smells," Gayle says, "but Eve's our mother now. She wouldn't harm us."

"But our house is a gold mine! I can manage renting it. Scott can keep it repaired. Prices are skyrocketing now in Silicon Valley. When the boom's over, we can sell it if Eve insists."

"Try to talk her out of selling, Karl, but she helped me out of my marriage. I trust her."

I plead with Eve to let us rent out the house, but she won't budge. I then talk to a financial planner and a lawyer friend who both say Eve's selling our life estate *is* dangerous. That's because once the real asset becomes liquid, Eve might invest it poorly and our inheritance would vanish.

I call Eve again, and explain all this and how we all can profit from holding, not selling.

"Don't try to block the sale," she snaps. "I'm the executor of the estate!"

"You can't be cash poor. You just got Dad's life insurance...and soon you're getting his pension, investments, and other real estate."

"Not your business what I've got...or what I do with it! Goodbye!"

I call Scott, who says he's learned Eve's charmed two of Dad's three sisters, but the kids of the third, two of our cousins, call her "Dragon Lady." When I explain to Scott that charm's often a trait of sociopaths, he responds by saying we should hire an attorney to fight for our inheritance. After calling Gayle again and finding she's still in Eve's camp, I share everything with Sharon, who counsels, "Sounds inevitable: you and your bro versus Eve and your sis...in court."

We hire a probate attorney in Oakland, and for a considerable fee, he promises to slow the house sale and force Eve to be transparent by monitoring each step she takes. He discovers, though, Eve's moved faster than we thought: she's sold Dad's vehicles and the Hood Canal cabin where he collapsed before dying. Worst of all, he's discovered she's found a judge who's helped to accelerate the normally slow probate process by setting an imminent court date. Our attorney says she learned a lot of tricks not only executing her first husband's estate, but also her father's before that.

CHAPTER 16

Legal Shenanigans

San Francisco East Bay – 1977

Scott and I lose big time in court! Despite our lawyer's cogent arguments, we're up against a judge who believes in giving young Silicon Valley a boost by churning its real estate. He sells our house during the hearing to a buyer Eve's lined up.

We leave the courthouse angry, avoiding eye contact with Eve and Gayle. We're upset about the loss of our childhood home and the fact that we must hire a second attorney to watch what Eve does in Washington with our share of the money from the sale.

We're downright livid when we later learn the identity of the buyer Eve brought to court to persuade the judge. He's a real estate agent, and friend of Gayle's, who Eve and Gayle tipped off that our house was for sale in probate. Since the realtor also speculates and flips, he knew he could buy our house under-market, without a bidding war because probate sales are only publicized in tiny notices in the legal sections of newspapers.

****

Sharon switches her office secretary job from the Chem Department to the City Planning one, located in the same building where she had her personal MFA studio. She still finds time to paint a large mural on the sixth floor of nearby Evans Hall.

"I'm so proud of you," I tell her after watching math majors get off the elevator and break into smiles upon seeing her huge shape-scape of cones and truncated cylinders against a blue sky. I tell her some students told me the mural humanizes the place.

"Ironic," Sharon says, "There aren't any humans in that piece. I rarely put 'em in my work."

****

Soon, Yulia at the Warehouse tells us that an artist is relinquishing his livable space in a few months. We debate the pros and cons of moving there permanently, and then visit the gigantic space. The kitchen meets Sharon's requirements, and the recently built bathroom and plywood shower, though quaint, seem serviceable. We decide then and there to buy the space, knowing that improved spaces rarely pop up.

A few weeks later, though, Sharon expresses some buyer's remorse. She resolves her remorse by realizing that living at the Warehouse will simplify her life. Currently, she works on campus, paints at her small Warehouse space, and returns to our apartment to sleep after doing her half of the cooking and cleanup.

****

My simpler life involves teaching and researching on campus and writing at home. Presently, I'm promoting the use of disturbing-the-peace provisions in the penal code for temporary restraining orders in family violence cases. They're easier to implement than any other statute. I also promote using other eyes and ears besides those of the police to identify existing or potential family violence victims. School teachers can report student injuries they observe. Beauticians, barbers, likewise. And so too, bartenders and taxi drivers. There's pushback from some in these occupations, though, who claim there's an implicit promise of confidentiality, which makes them resist requests to narc on their clients.

During the holidays in Southern California with Sharon's family and relatives, I visit the Glendale Police Department to sow the seeds for future research there. Strange, this mixing in a little work with seasonal joy reduces the sadness I feel being estranged from Gayle and five hundred miles from Scott and good friends during the holidays.

****

Back in Berkeley, Scott and I make a New Year's resolution to save money and not use lawyers for informal questions for Eve. We write her and ask: if she dies tomorrow, will her only heirs, her sister and two nieces, inherit what our parents worked so hard for over three decades of marriage? Or, if Eve remarries, might her new husband get our inheritance? Additionally, we ask if she ever plans to chuck the Schonborn photo albums and heirlooms she still possesses. I remember her tossing names from Dad's address book.

Eve never responds, so we're forced to pay our Oakland and Seattle lawyers to ask some of the same questions as part of ongoing formal inquiries. Months pass, and our side's peeved that many inquiries remain unanswered. Finally, in November, Eve's side responds and, among other things, her lawyers reveal Eve's already inherited three times what she's led us to believe.

****

Since Sharon and my days in our Deakin Street apartment are numbered, we throw small and large parties for our neighbors and friends, most of whom love to argue into the night about politics. They all agree on two things, though: our parties rock and Sharon's a fabulous cook. What most don't know, however, is that while Sharon loves the kitchen kudos she gets, she's more and more exhausted rather than energized by people in general.

About this time, Sharon and I watch an unsettling TV movie, *The War Between the Tates*, about a professor and his wife and the impact of the '60s and '70s on their relationship. We talk about the movie for days, realizing we too have been stressed, as a married couple, through the tumult of Vietnam, civil rights, student unrest, and sexual liberation. And, in our early thirties, we don't have a conventional life with a house and kids like so many people our age.

Since moving to the Warehouse will continue our unconventional lifestyle, I ask Sharon if she's okay with our decision. She says, "Yes."

Relatedly I ask myself, as well as agemates in a peer counseling group, about whether I'm okay with: living communally in the Warehouse, my shifting stance on certain crim justice issues, and the stress of relatives taking sides over Mom's suicide and Eve's legal maneuvers. I also begin individual counseling to work through grief over my parents' deaths and to address the fact that Dad's heart attack reawakened youthful concerns about my own heart.

Among other things, I learn from counseling that losses, like losing political idealism —and particularly uncommon losses, like the premature deaths of parents—are necessary. They're required for growth, but there's no set formula, despite Kubler-Ross' wisdom, for working through such losses.

CHAPTER 17
Holly Screams

Fire Island, New York – Early September – *1977*

Holly Maddux, former high school cheerleader turned rebellious-hippie, determined the time for a fresh start had come. The thirty-year-old had finally gathered the courage to end the volatile relationship she'd had with Ira Einhorn since 1972. They'd been in Europe to escape Philly's humid summer. However, she'd left midsummer to return to the States, making clear to Ira her intention to forge a new life. He'd protested and promised to end his put-downs and infidelities, but to no avail.

Though Ira phoned Holly often as he continued touring European countries, she stuck to her guns, as she did when he returned to the U.S. a month early to coax her back. In August, Ira became increasingly desperate, and understandably so, after a falling out with another key person in his life, paranormal scholar Andrija Puharich.

Ira kept badgering Holly through the Labor Day weekend to probe whether she was in a new relationship and instill guilt over her rejecting him. She continued to say she was happy living on a thin barrier island off Long Island. When he browbeat her into finally confessing that there was another man in her life, Ira demanded she come to Philly to talk.

Despite knowing he was livid, she relented and visited him on September 6 with the understanding they'd only talk. Instead, Ira likely forced himself on her sexually, promising to start a family if she stayed. Upset and unconvinced, she returned to New York on the 7th as she'd planned, but not before Ira extracted from her that she and her new man, Saul Lapidus, planned to spend twelve days together on a boat trip.

A storm raging within, Ira called Holly several times Friday, September 9 freaking out and insisting she return to Philly to get her possessions. After threatening suicide, he also said he'd throw her things into the street if she didn't fetch them. Holly couldn't reach Philly friends she thought might be able to calm Ira, so she reluctantly decided to do it herself and traveled to Philly again.

She managed to soothe Ira, and the couple even went to see Star Wars, whose futuristic, techie quality intrigued Ira. Once the couple got back to 3411 Race Street, it's anyone guess as to how things progressed. There was a report of a fight in Ira's apartment around this time, which included the sounds of loud banging on the floor and a terrified scream.

CHAPTER 18

A Unicorn's Story: Cleaning and Scheming

Philadelphia – September 9, 1977

Almost jumping up and down like a guy dying to take a leak, he knew he had to act normal as he entered the huge store, with endless aisles of merchandise.

Spying a hapless clerk, he asked, "D'ya have a heavy-duty cleaning product that doesn't smell like bleach?"

"What's on the shelf's all we got," the clerk said.

"So which shelf?" he demanded.

Staring at his clothes with some disgust, the clerk said snidely, "Somewhere on Aisle 17, in Hardware." She strode away.

"Bitch," he muttered.

Hearing this, the clerk stopped, turned, and glared, then exclaimed, "Customers!"

In Ira's rush, he overshot Aisle 17 and frantically backtracked, thinking, *Guess I'll need one of those...what d'ya call 'em...scrub brushes.*

He pondered his choices—all contained bleach—and then reached for a gallon of lemon-scented Clorox. When he realized how heavy it was, he raced back to the front of the store to trade his carry-basket for a cart, cursing under his breath.

After putting three gallons of bleach and a large scrub brush into his cart, he paused and scanned more shelves. He then grabbed a dozen air-freshener aerosols and began looking for cloth towels.

As he sped down the adjacent aisle, he grumbled, "Shit, can't find towels! No time for another store." He tore around the corner into the next aisle, still looking for towels. He was about to search for another clerk when he remembered he'd need trash bags, so he tried to find his way back to the cleaning aisle, mumbling, "Homeware, Houseware, Hardware—whatever the crap they call it."

He grabbed a box of plastic trash bags and started searching again for towels, realizing he'd have to settle for paper ones. When he finally found them, he loaded his cart over its brim with rolls and grabbed a pair of rubber gloves displayed nearby.

As he wheeled his cart to a checkout stand, he exclaimed, "Wasted too much time. Probably forgot something. Shoulda made a shopping list." Then realizing he was speaking too loud, he mumbled, "Goddamn, cops woulda loved finding a list like that."

During the checkout process, he skimmed a tabloid, holding it high to hide his face from the cashier. He paid with twenties.

****

Back at his place, he scrubbed floorboards everywhere, getting into every little crack. His maniacal cleaning and rinsing—not to mention the bagging of human detritus—exhausted him. But every time he glanced at the body in his bathtub, he got another burst of adrenaline-fed energy to complete his many tasks.

****

During the quiet after his storm of shopping and cleaning on Sunday, he phoned antique shops and finally found one that would deliver a steamer trunk to his place, but only if he paid extra for a Sunday delivery by two teenagers.

With the trunk on site, he then called two suburban women he knew, asking them to drive into the city and he'd regale them about the biology of fall colors along the Schuylkill River.3 He'd taught them last spring, at his apartment, some of the psychic arts like telepathy, psychokinesis, and astral (soul) projection for achieving an out-of-body experience, ironic now with his getting-rid-of-a-body challenge.

Traveling alongside the river as a passenger in their 1976 Plymouth Volare, Ira told them he had to dispose of some top-secret documents that could get him in big trouble. Would they help him transport a trunk he'd filled with them and dump it in the river? They hesitated when hearing it contained reports about Russian KGB mind-control experiments. So they asked him to lead them to the exact spot they'd access the river. When they stopped to look at the drop point, they asked Ira to measure various dimensions of their car, which, alas, revealed it couldn't accommodate the trunk. Dejected but edgy, he asked them to return him to Penn's Archeo-Anthro Museum instead of his apartment.

The women seemed relieved driving to the campus, but not Ira. Still antsy saying his goodbyes, he rushed to the museum's gift store to buy a Plan B essential. He knew that, because of the museum's impressive Egyptology collection, it carried all manner of books, including ones on the ancient art of mummification.

CHAPTER 19
Destroying Art and a Relationship

Berkeley – Late Summer

At the start of a three-day weekend, Sharon and I take advantage of the extra time to move to the Warehouse. In the middle of putting wrapped dishes in boxes, I make eye contact with Sharon and fold her box flaps down to keep her from packing for a moment. "Do you think we've been living parallel lives lately—all our mutual busy-ness?"

"Well, you'd annoy me if you weren't busy. Anyway, the Warehouse will make my life easier...and artists there will keep me creative."

"What about pro-creative? You know, having babies?"

"No time for that now."

"But time's a-tickin' for us...or do you still hate kids?"

"I do, but mostly, I hate squally, runny-nosed kids."

"There'll be lots of those in the Warehouse hallways."

"I'll turn up the radio. But I can't do that if they're ours."

****

Once we settle into our space, Sharon complains the bathroom and kitchen seem coarser than she'd remembered them to be. I hire Scott to help me add refinements to them as well as soundproof a small, enclosed space I've created for my office under our loft. We commiserate with one another how the once too-fast probate battle has slowed to a glacial pace. We decide "Justice delayed is justice denied."

Photographer Richard Misrack, whose space abuts ours, hosts a welcoming party for us. I enjoy chatting with an old friend, Bill Owens, who documented the newly expanding suburb of Livermore while a newspaper photographer there. Owens agrees the Warehouse lifestyle entails about as different a way of life as is imaginable from that in suburbia. We also agree the Bay Area has sprawled in every direction from the compact assortment of near-the-Bay communities we both knew growing up here.

With room to spare in our gymnasium-sized space, Sharon starts work on a humongous canvas to be hung on a San Francisco billboard for a month by a foundation, which selects the artists for an annual show. Midway through her project, Sharon's happy to accompany me to Chicago, where I present a paper and meet with a book editor, who offers me a contract. Sharon's folks, who've moved from Wisconsin to a Chicago suburb, put us up. While we're away, Scott builds a handrail for the stairs leading to our sleeping loft and installs a secondhand counter-flow heater to warm our immense space.

Sharon and I feel the pinch of lawyers' bills, Scott's wages, and art supplies that feed the appetite of her paint-hungry air compressor and airbrush. But it's exciting to watch Sharon's billboard develop—a collage of urban blight and billboards blocking residents' views of the Golden Gate Bridge. It's also exciting finally to watch a crane lift her canvas, rolled up like a carpet, for workers to lash to a North Beach billboard. Along with other billboard artists, we attend openings of some of the twenty exhibits hung around San Francisco. We conclude a fun November with Scott, the Orsics, and other friends at a Thanksgiving potluck at a very long worktable Scott and I build in our space.

Weeks later, Sharon and I argue about whether she should try to find gallery representation in Chicago during our upcoming holidays with her parents. I tell her that her hard-edge airbrush paintings inspire awe in everyone, including fellow artists, who're normally a critical bunch.

She reluctantly agrees, but as the holidays unfold in Highland Park, I can see that she'd much rather be home, watching TV with her football-crazed dad, than trying to promote her paintings. Even though I accompany her, hovering outside galleries like the parent of a trick-or-treating child, she's anxious. While she garners plenty of interest, none of the galleries offer her representation.

When we return home, Sharon uncharacteristically goes to a worknight party with people she got to know during her brief stint at the Chem Department. I spend the evening installing a doorbell to our interior space so visitors can alert us when they arrive at the locked front entrance of our sprawling Warehouse.

A few days later, when Sharon gets home from work, she states, "Forgot to tell you, I'm starting an evening class at a camera store." It makes sense, since we'd discussed leaving photos of her paintings with gallery owners who might want to revisit her work after she leaves. I inform her that Lee, back in Marshall after his breakup, and his friend Skip Henderson will bring fresh crab from Skip's restaurant to our space Saturday night.

"I'm not thrilled," she says. "It'll be messy."

"I'm sure they'll bring bibs," I quip, but Sharon just stares at me.

We end up having a wonderful time with Lee, Skip, the Orsics, and a Warehouse couple, Greg and Nancy. Skip regales us with stories I haven't heard about his cousin, Joan Baez. This makes me think of Ira Einhorn. *I wonder how he's getting along, since Hogan's last report was that his only ever live-in girlfriend had left him.*

At sunset, light enters our high-up saw-toothed roof windows at a perfect angle, enhancing a magical evening...delicious in every way. As we bid everyone goodnight, I overhear Lee and Ric talking about a grand jury report accusing Synanon of child abuse and Dederich of profiting from the cult he reinvented as a nonprofit church. Ric says he and the *Light* continue to track Synanon.

****

On a late afternoon in January, I'm shocked to come home to find Sharon has kicked and destroyed a two-foot cube, an airbrushed piece that took weeks to paint. Initially, I think selfish thoughts. *How dare she? I constructed the cube—that sits on one side, displaying five paintings*

—*out of masonite.* Then, after calming myself, I find her sitting in our sleeping loft and ask, "Why?"

"Wasn't good enough."

"What d'ya mean? People love your masonite panels."

"I'll never be a precisionist, like Charles Sheeler."

"Sure you will. You've got the chops."

"Wrong! I'm a perfectionist instead. And a failed one at that because I cheat—I write my perfect grocery lists using a ruler."

"C'mon, honey," I say, smiling, "you're a cubist, if nothing else."

"Not funny! Anyway, perfectionism's a bitch! So is precisionism." She throws herself on the bed.

As she broods, I think, *Maybe perfectionism's why Sharon doesn't paint people. Humans are imperfection personified.*

I let the destroyed cube slide, though I know selling it and others she envisioned would ease our financial strain. Reflecting on Sharon's perfectionism over subsequent days, I realize I've got a perfection problem too. One example: it keeps me from understanding gray areas in criminology, like justice being a process and not a goal. And similar to probating a will and life in general, justice is imperfect.

My perfectionism likely comes from the fact that Dad encouraged me to build perfect toy models, and Mom, to write perfect "thank you" notes. Although I'm not sure the causes of Sharon's perfectionism, I'm hoping the messiness of the Warehouse, and its lifestyle, will rid both of us of its scourge. Like work deadlines which force one to submit an imperfect project, the industrial grit and artists that surround us might help us let go of perfectionism.

A couple of Fridays later, as Sharon and I awaken, I kiss her on the cheek and tell her we've got a great weekend in store.

"I'm afraid I won't be around for it."

"Why not?"

"A troubled friend in my photography class needs me. Wants me to walk and talk with her at Stinson Beach."

"That's odd. You nev—"

"Make plans with the Orsics. I'm spending the night at Stinson."

After smarting a moment, I say, "You've been away a lot lately."

"No more than you, with your ride-alongs, conferences, faculty meetings—"

"Just doing my job."

"It's never-ending!"

****

A few days later, I can't find our van outside the Warehouse. I call Sharon at work, frantic. She's taking a long lunch.

When she phones back, she says, "I parked it down a bit from our usual spot near the entrance."

"Then it's stolen! Thought maybe you'd left it at your photography class and gotten a ride home, given you were tipsy late last night. Can you report the van to the cops?"

"No time now."

"Whaaat? I gotta get a cab or bus now. You took the VW today. I can't be late to class."

"Okay, okay. I'll report it," she says. "Guess we'll have to share the VW now. Not gonna be fun, given your odd hours on campus this term."

The next night, I wait up for Sharon, although I've spent the day at both the Oakland and San Francisco PDs proposing research projects. Sharon returns at 2 a.m. While sitting in bed with a book, I nod awake and smell alcohol as she enters the loft.

Sharon blurts, "I wanna divorce!"

My sleepy eyes widen, and I ask, "What?"

"I'm not happy with you, the Warehouse...I don't love you anymore."

Blood rushes to my face as I scramble out of bed, my PJs trying to keep up with me. "B-B-But...I don't understand. Not happy here? We talked endlessly about moving here."

"And art's not my thing anymore."

I reach for her hand, but she backs away. "You've been into art since I met you."

"It's only because of you, pushing me to do art, be productive."

"Huh?" I say, not hearing well because blood's pounding in my ears now.

"I'm moving this weekend. Got somewhere to stay. Need to get away...from you, the Warehouse."

"I can't stop you, but we gotta talk, fer Chrissake."

"Not now. I'm sleeping on the couch."

My eyes follow her as she descends the stairs, pillow under her arm. I return to bed, wondering, *What the hell did I do wrong? Thought we had a perfect life. Questions swirl. Should I stifle my anger or should I express my fear of rejection, always present for a cleft-affected person?*

CHAPTER 20
An Executioner's Story

He spotted the blue Mercury sedan, parked where the guy said it'd be, on a side street with trees and bushes everywhere. Approaching the driver, he asked, "Y-Yan?"

"Yeah. Hop in. Ride shotgun," Yan said, chuckling about the fact that he wasn't in the least a wordplay kinda guy.

He knew Yan was driving to a more secluded area, but he always had trust issues — whether buying or selling. In truth, he needed a gun so he could trust more readily. Be more confident.

Yan parked and uncovered a few handguns wrapped in a jacket "How'd you get my name?" Yan asked, wheezing a bit. "Maybe you told me when you phoned?"

"Friend of a friend."

"You can do better 'n that. Even my go-between can."

"No names! The guy's done hard time. Never wants to go back."

"I only brought snub-nosed guns, as you asked."

"Good! I need one for a jacket pocket …in case deals go sour." His face flushes. "Never wanna be pushed around again. Suppliers can be bloodsucking loan sharks."

Yan smiled, stopped, and wheezed. Then he said he'd recommend a .38 Special, which he handed to him with the revolver cylinder flipped open.

He closed the cylinder and spun it.

Yan called it "the Off-Duty," the detectives' favorite — the perfect concealable gun because it has five shots, and so is lighter, narrower than a six-shot. He elaborated, "While cheaper 'cuz Charter Arms is a new manufacturer, you'll love the Off-Duty's enclosed hammer design. Means snag-free firing from your pocket...when you're surprised."

"You can really shoot from a jacket pocket?" He reopened the cylinder, inspecting it carefully.

"New to guns?"

"Naw. I'm a vet," he said. "Know my way around what the Air Force used to issue."

"Protected hammer makes it super-reliable," Yan said as he swapped it for a Colt, also opened and without bullets. He explained this one was heavier, a tad longer, and $400 more. "But it's a Colt!"

"So what're we talking total, pricewise?" he asked.

"Both guns're brand new and untraceable because my go-between bought 'em without paperwork. So $700 for the Off-Duty. Eleven hundred for the Colt."

"Holy shit," he moaned. "Confidence comes at a price!"

"You've shopped around," Yan said. "You know grey market's always triple sports store prices. And sure, black market's just double, but you never know if the gun's been used in a crime."

"Any way you can knock down the price?"

"Remember, the Off-Duty's probably the smallest, most reliable .38 Special out there. It allows a clean-cut guy like you to deal discreetly, with confidence."

"Well, I, uh—"

"Look," he said, "I'll throw in fifty rounds of ammo. You choose which gun, and I'll drive you a mile further to a deserted place where you can fire it."

A pause: only Yan's slight wheezing punctuated the silence.

"Okay," he said. "The Off-Duty."

Yan started the car.

CHAPTER 21
The Warehouse Burns. Fire Turns to Ice

Berkeley – February 1978

Sharon's off to work before I can talk to her. I'm stuck at the Warehouse, since she's taken the VW. As the day progresses, I can't concentrate or be productive, so I fix a nice dinner and have it waiting for Sharon when she returns around 5 p.m.

Midway through dinner, I ask whether alcohol or the late hour caused her outburst last night. She says she meant everything...and even held back about the Warehouse. She's hated spending money on our space ever since Yulia started trying to convert the money artists paid for their spaces and improvements into shares or some community currency.

"Don't blame me for Yulia's Marxist ploys," I say. "I do agree, money's been tight –paying to fight Eve and to upgrade our space."

"Yeah, I hate Eve...Your family...You!"

"Jeez, you hate everyone!"

Suddenly, someone outside our door shouts, "FIRE!"

A microsecond later, another "FIRE!" and "Get out! NOW!"

We jump up, grab our cat, and run the short hallway to the front entryway and outside to safety. We join dozens of others standing in the street, watching smoke rise from the rear of our sprawling single-story building.

Scorching fear then cold chills take over my body. But soon, immense bright yellow-and-red flames overwhelm my senses. As best as I can tell, the fire is mostly coming from spaces that are far beyond ours. Sirens wail in the distance, and an acrid smell permeates the air.

Sharon and I shift from foot to foot to stay warm while the flames mesmerize us, as twilight—really smoky haze—turns to darkness.

Artists who see their spaces start to burn scream or drop to their knees and strike the pavement with their fists. Not many pray, however.

When screams and shouting firemen finally spook our cat, I put him in our VW station wagon a block away, out of harm's way.

I return to see many in the crowd sobbing or wringing their hands, but not Sharon. A knot forms in my stomach as I realize that even if flames haven't reached our space, water from the firehoses has. I put my arm around Sharon, who stiffens her back then relaxes after a bit. The physical contact comforts me.

After an excruciating length of time, firemen move less frantically. I ask one who passes by how it's going. He thinks they're close to containing the blaze.

Yulia's been circulating among the crowd, telling everyone, "The nearby Holiday Inn will put you up for free tonight, but no pets."

I say to Sharon, "I'd rather stay with the Orsics anyway. They love our cat. I'll call 'em from the gas station payphone. Should we keep quiet about your wanting a divorce for a while?"

She nods.

****

Returning to the Warehouse the next morning from the Montclair district of Oakland where the Orsics live, we're stunned. The fire structurally damaged twenty studio spaces, but not ours. With borrowed boots, we wade ankle-deep into murky water in our space, repulsed by the smell of smoke and wet charcoal. Our once-white immense walls are black and tan.

I tear up, but Sharon shows no signs of anguish, even when she sees damage to many of her canvases. They survived the onslaught of water but succumbed to gashes from shards of glass flying about when high-pressure streams from firehoses broke countless small windows in our saw-tooth roof.

Sharon actually permits a long consolation hug after we slosh around assessing our losses. Though there's damage to clothing, kitchenware, and furniture, my books and lecture notes in my enclosed office remain unscathed.

We sit a while on wet dining chairs, not talking. We then roll up our sleeves and start salvaging what we can, making notes of losses since, unlike most residents, we have insurance.

Meeting assembled residents in an artist's loft across the street, Yulia states that the cause of the fire remains elusive. However, she's suspicious of the oil-spill cleaning company that stores oil-soaked stuff behind our building. She also wants fire inspectors to see if residents with gas heaters installed them properly. I whisper to Greg, a photographer who's in law school now, "I hope inspectors see if wood-burning stove residents followed codes too. You're our legal beagle now."

Greg whispers back, "I doubt Yulia held wood-burning folks to the same code standards as us. She thinks we gas-heater folks are rich."

Yulia then says she's got a $500 city-grant to speed up the restoration of utilities and phone lines to the twenty intact spaces. After this, she'll coordinate the rebuilding of totaled spaces to let newly-homeless artists return to the Warehouse. The rest of us must pay to fix any minor or cosmetic damage to our spaces.

Someone objects, saying Yulia should pay for cosmetic repairs since she's been claiming she owns the increase in equity as tenants upgrade their spaces.

She responds, "Take it up with the building's true owner. I rent from him just like you all rent from me."

Sharon shouts, "That's BS! Now that the fire's ended your capitalist equity grab, you're back to being a Marxist."

An anonymous voice from the assemblage shouts, "*Facts* matter, Yulia. You're a shrewd businesswoman, not an artist. No one's ever seen your art."

I say to Sharon and Greg, "*Words* matter too. . . and rarely as much as in debates with Marxists over property and ownership."

Returning to the Warehouse's entrance, Sharon and I see a telegram taped to the row of mailboxes which stand amid a proud hodgepodge of doorbell buttons, a tribute to the individualism of Warehouse artists. Sharon rips open the telegram from our insurance agent, and it says he'll cover per diem room and board except alcohol, until our place is habitable. He'll also cover cleaning, repairs, and replacements over our deductible...pending adjusters' approval. I smile, but Sharon huffs and continues to our space.

My smile soon disappears after I open a business letter from a publisher. I read it aloud to Sharon:

"Wallsworth Publishing regrets to inform you it must cancel the contract signed with you for business and professional reasons. Your editor will soon phone you to explain, as far as he's legally allowed, the specific reasons why."

I enter our space and splash through water and climb the steps leading to our sleeping loft. Sharon's removing the water-soaked fabric that enclosed the four-poster bed I built to keep us warm. I tell her the publisher's decision.

"Life's tough, Karl. You should know that. Seems like it's time for a good stiff drink...or two."

"Okay by me."

"Rusty Scupper? No one will see us."

At the bar, I ask Sharon, "What else can go wrong this week? I've lost you, my home, my van, and now a book contract."

"You've hit bottom," Sharon says with a quirky smile.

"And before that, I lost my mother, my father, and my sister—in spirit if not in body."

Sharon pats my free hand. My other grips the stem of my martini glass. She smiles mischievously, saying, "Did'ya remember to lock the VW just now? We're in Oakland now."

I smile, then frown. "That editor at Wallsworth's a jerk. He knows better than to sign a contract then renege."

"Maybe he just contracted with you to prevent you from signing with another publisher. Or he took your ideas to another prof and offered a contract favoring Wallsworth more. Publishing's a business,"

"Maybe, but don't care at the moment." I crane my neck to see night light playing on the water in the distance. After steeling myself, "Know your mind's made up, but how 'bout staying 'til we reclaim our space, replace our stuff?"

Sharon looks down, remaining silent.

I finish my drink, thinking, *Got nothing to lose.* I take a deep breath. "Remember all our talk about open relationships a while back?"

"Yeah, when the O'Neills' *Open Marriage* came out."

"Lotsa couples, even friends, tried it. Maybe we should...now?"

"That might work," she mutters, raising two fingers for the bartender to see.

"As I remember, open marriage frees people to pursue what they're missing in their relationship."

"That appeals to me."

"So you won't leave right away?"

She agrees.

I mention the O'Neills' claim that open marriage can deepen communication, even revitalize relationships. We argue about this. But oddly, we don't argue about their claim that jealousy can be prevented if couples hammer out rules to follow. So we start brainstorming rules.

"Write down what we come up with, Mr. List-Maker," she says. "We'll forget everything in the morning at the rate we're drinking."

I write our rules: No dating mutual friends. No overnights. No falling in love. No blabbing about the arrangement. And the must dos: Tell each other everything. Give each other precedence over any newcomer.

We keep drinking until a sedating fog rolls in, just as it does now on nearby Jack London Square. We eat to sober up—as if we could—and drive very, very carefully to our new place, a close-by hotel.

****

Next morning, I'm hung over but still able to sort through the wreckage of my Warehouse life. In the afternoon, I tackle the wreckage of my emotional life. I need to know why Sharon no longer loves me. I approach it indirectly. Dumping a broken table lamp on our growing debris pile, I ask, "Why d'ya hate the Warehouse after just six months?"

"Gotta deal with too many people."

"Didn't bother you before we moved."

"Just painted in my little space. Ignored people. Living here, we socialize more than before."

"We've made some new friends, true. And old friends love visiting the Warehouse."

"People don't energize me."

"But you thrived as a sorority girl, and we see your relatives all the time."

"Well, I'm aloof now."

"Your aloofness, even to me sometimes, makes you seem haughty, superior."

"Leave me alone."

Though wanting more, I move away from her and busy myself, in deed and in thought. *I like people, and admittedly, our academic friends outnumber our art ones. But we've got lots of other regular friends, even ones we both grew up with.*

As the sun sets, I shout to Sharon across a real darkening chasm between us since we're without electricity, "Remember the portable radio the Orsics loaned us? Wanna listen to Cal basketball?"

****

Sunday morning, we phone friends and relatives from our hotel. After telling them about the fire, but not about the domestic one engulfing us, we return to further clean our space. Around mid-afternoon,

Sharon seems in the mood to talk. I ask, "Why don't you love me anymore?"

"You're always writing articles, papers for those alphabet-soup conferences."

"That soup bit's clever, but I gotta attend the ASCs, ASAs, SSSPs. Professionalism—"

"Conferences, books, work¬—"

"It's publish or perish."

"Well, you're publishing, but your marriage is perishing."

"But I still don't know why—"

"God! You always wanna know why. You're never home!"

I find I can't focus on cleaning, so I enter my office to think more clearly. *Yes, I travel to conferences, but I'm home more than 9-5 husbands, and home over winter and spring breaks and summers. I don't understand...*

****

On Monday, insurance adjusters promise that Sharon'll get compensated for damaged canvases and, because we make a stink, we'll finally get a loaner for our stolen van. On Tuesday, I'm so busy supervising workers removing soot from our walls that I forget it's Valentine's Day until I crawl into bed at the hotel. Sharon said she'd be home late due to office work she'd let slide since the fire.

When I awaken at midnight and Sharon's still not back, I worry she's out with someone, testing her open-relationship wings already. We've long since stopped doing anything special on Valentine's, but I feel pangs of jealousy. When she comes to bed at 1:30 a.m., I don't confront her, knowing it'll keep her up even later. She'll struggle as it is to awake in time for her job.

After dinner together at the hotel Wednesday, I share my Valentine's night jealous feelings. Sharon doesn't respond. So I explain that I'm okay with the O'Neills' feminist notion that women need to lead meaningful lives, given that both our mothers struggled to find meaning after their kids left home. "But really, these late nights—"

"Sorry it's tough on you at home while I'm out at night, but I was home lots while you studied cops at night."

We have a shoot-out over the double standard that gives men more freedom, especially at night, than women. When Sharon pauses to reload, I say, "Just remember, feminists rarely admit it's easy for females to get male attention when they want it; they ignore that most males have to work hard for female attention."

"Guess that's just how the world works," she fires back. "Young women may have power, but lose it when they start families. Even childless women lose their power as they age."

We argue some more, then I remind her that the O'Neills believe open relationships require as much communication, trust, and emotional work as monogamous ones. "If we don't talk, honor boundaries we set, and share our feelings with each other, our new relationship won't work."

Sharon says she's tired and, changing into PJs, states that despite the bad news the mailman brings, she's glad he still delivers to our half-burned-out building. She repeats what she's said before: she'll keep writing the checks for the bills that come in. "I like doing that at work, paying expenses that faculty run up for research and travel."

"That's fine," I say. "No bills today. Just insurance forms."

Sharon crawls under the covers of the rollaway bed she had the hotel set up, over my objections.

The next morning, Sharon says she'll stay on campus for dinner. Worried that she's shutting me out, I mention we've committed to a dinner party Saturday at Scoma's in Sausalito and zing her with "Remember, an obligation to a spouse trumps those to others."

"Yeah, I know," she says, heading out the door.

At the Warehouse that afternoon, glaziers replace the broken small saw-tooth windows, allowing me to stop worrying about rainwater in our space. But I still worry, increasingly so, that, contrary to research findings, adversity hasn't brought Sharon and me closer together.

****

Despite romantic evening trips across the Golden Gate to and from Marin Saturday, plus Scoma's great food, Sharon is emotionally distant. As we begin to pack our hotel clothes on Sunday, she tells me she's been invited to go away next weekend and I should make plans to be with someone else then.

"Plans! It's not like I can snap my fingers and find a date like you can. You're a beautiful woman."

"Go skiing with Greg and Nancy."

My heart's incessant pounding forces me to ask Sharon who invited her away. When she refuses to say, I ask, "Should we do couples therapy?"

"No way."

"Divorce courts usually advise counseling–"

"Cross that bridge—"

"Glad you really want to save our marriage."

We each resume packing our stuff because we get to return to the Warehouse tomorrow. The city has finally turned on the electricity to all the studio spaces.

****

En route driving to her job, Sharon drops our several suitcases and me at the Warehouse and informs me she'll be working late again tonight. I scowl as she drives off, and scowl again, realizing I'll be stranded even longer since buses and cabs avoid our industrial zone. I wonder, *When'll we get that damn loaner?* Resigned to being stuck, I unpack, organize the kitchen, and do insurance paperwork. I manage to finish a couple of academic projects too.

The loaner appears the next day, allowing me at last to meet my classes more easily. Sharon continues to come home late and leave work early for the next few days. We're ships passing in the night. I arrange to go skiing over the weekend with Greg and Nancy, but I'm starting to yearn for female companionship. Since I have neither the time nor energy to get intimate with anyone other than Sharon, skiing's a good distraction. And for the money, it's much better than visiting one of the full service massage parlors that surround the Berkeley campus, something I did once, long ago out of curiosity. Back then, I settled for talk and a traditional massage.

Friday, I have my first session with my one-on-one counselor since the fire. I ask him if I'm an idiot to let my young wife stay out late with people I've never met. He's noncommittal, but we explore my feelings about Sharon and other assertive women in my life like Yulia, Eve, and Gayle. As a result, I resolve to stand up to them more often.

We also dive into how Sharon resembles my mom, likewise a beautiful, sensitive artist before she died, who was often unable to articulate her needs. I count myself lucky to have a counselor's help understanding women as well as matters around my adoption of progressive delusions of the time, like the O'Neills' dismissal of jealousy and Zero Population Growth's ballyhooing of "childlessness."

****

When I get our Warehouse mail after my session, I open it all as a way to avoid having to get down to work on a directionless Friday afternoon. When I open the credit-card envelope, I don't put it in the stack with other opened envelopes. Instead, I pull out the bill since it's unusually thick. An entry for Borg's Motel in Monterey jumps out at me.

"January 25?" I read out loud. "What the hell!"

I see charges also for Martino's Café and Bentley's Bar on a couple of Wednesdays in January when I thought Sharon was at her photography class. I see a charge for the Metropole Bar and Grill from a few nights ago as well.

I stare at a huge freshly painted white wall, not believing what I've just seen. I get angry, thinking, *No wonder Sharon wanted to pay the bills herself.* I recall her unfaithfulness when we dated years ago, running off with a Greek guy after a Mediterranean cruise instead of meeting up with me in Europe.

I stew and seethe as I await Sharon's arrival home from work.

CHAPTER 22
Confrontation, Mystery, and an Emotional Desert

Berkeley – Spring 1978

As Sharon unlocks the door, I leap from the kitchen table, waving the credit-card bill in her face, shouting, "How could you cheat on me and then lie about it for a month?"

"W-What're you talking about?" she asks, pulling back from my flailing arms.

"This. THIS!" I slam the bill on the table. "Borg's Motel in Monterey!"

"Show me."

I point to "January 25" on the bill. "The weekend you supposedly went to Stinson Beach to help Linea."

"Calm down! We changed our minds. Went to Monterey."

"Bullshit! You're lying. Linea wouldn't give you flowers at work."

"You're making no sense."

I pull a florist's card out of my pocket and read, "Sweetheart, lovely as these flowers are, they cannot express what I feel for you, Eduardo."

"You've no right going through my clothes—"

"We've both been inspecting clothes for fire damage lately. Found a seashell you kept with the floral card. You cheated before asking for a divorce, before the fire, and before our open relationship!"

"Who are you, Perry Mason?"

Raising my voice again, "You were my wife in January, right?"

"Uh...yes."

"Damn straight. You not only broke your vows but later pretended your new relationship was casual, open. Instead, it was serious. Why else save mementos?"

"You shoulda just asked about Eduardo when I came in the front door."

"Thought you'd confess when you saw me waving the bill. How long's this been going on?"

Sharon's shoulders droop, and she puts her coat on the back of a chair. "Honest, just since the photography course in January, though I met him when I switched from Chem to City Planning. He's my supervisor at work."

"Your boss? That's a step backward. If you think I control you, he's paid to control you."

"He's impressed with me. Gives me emotional support. Never pushes."

I clench my fists. When I can't bear it anymore, I shout, "Get out! Go to Eduardo."

"But I need to pack, phone him."

"Get your toothbrush. Call him from the gas station."

"But it's getting dark...and cold."

"Time to act like a grown-up now!"

She grabs her toothbrush and coat, and as she walks to the door, I say, "What gets me is you had French food on Valentine's. You and I could never afford the Metropole."

She slams the door behind her, but not before I yell, "You've tossed ten years of marriage."

Sinking to the now-dry concrete floor, I tailspin into a depressed funk.

****

The next morning, I barely make it to Greg and Nancy's on time, though they're only a studio space away. It's good I did, though. They let me vent all the way to Gold Rush Country and the entire two days we cross-country in Bear Valley.

At one point, I say, "Sharon and I didn't handle conflict well. I knew she hated it, but I thought from all my study of conflict resolution, I could deal with that."

"People with knowledge can't always apply it," Greg says. "Law school's teaching me that."

Nancy laughs. "Understanding behavior—your own, let alone someone else's—doesn't mean you can change it."

At another time, I venture, "My guess is Sharon avoided conflict by caving, then drinking afterward to console herself."

"Bet you thought you could change that," Greg says.

"Well, I thought art, painting might. I felt I could have a perfect relationship, surrounded by perfect friends—"

"Greg and I. Perfect as they come." Nancy chuckles.

"Perfectionism made me a striver, not a lover," I say. "A fact guy, not a feelings guy."

"From my psych training," Nancy says, "Sharon sounds like she's got some antisocial disorder."

"Yikes. Been too close to notice—"

"Narcissism, shallow emotional life¬—"

"Not now, Nancy!" Greg interjects.

****

When I return home, I notice a message on the answering machine that old-roomie Ned loaned me. (He's invested in a company that makes these devices with receiver and transmitter indentations to nestle the phone handset.) My machine has good news—the Oakland Police Department has found my white van and I can come claim it.

****

Over coffee on Telegraph Avenue, Scott says he's still looking for full-time carpentry. I summon up courage and reveal Sharon and I have separated. When I describe her affair, he's amazed she could change partners so suddenly, unless she met Eduardo years ago when her studio was in Wurster, the same building where Eduardo worked.

After a bit, Scott and I decide we miss having a mother to help us understand women. Scott concludes we're *both* without partners, one's without work, and *one's* without a home and a book contract.

"And without a van 'til yesterday," I add.

"You got it back!"

"The thieves are still at large, though."

"Kids, I bet," Scott says. "Just joyriding."

"Not likely. They left a shotgun in it. Cops think they used the van to commit a crime."

"Well, your van's a bourgeois luxury."

"You Marxists got that wrong. In California, cars are often a necessity. If you've got to drive to work, your car thief steals your job too. Also, steals your freedom—"

"Conservatism's metastasizing in your brain, Karl."

"Yours too. We've tried to claim our inheritance, and that's a no-no to Marx."

"Just trying to teach Dragon Lady a lesson."

****

Since Sharon left, my days fly by, but not my nights, when I sleep fitfully. I think about suggesting reconciliation when Sharon and I deal with insurance or other financial matters. But she often says or does something that angers me and kills thoughts of getting back together. As months go by, most of our mutual friends stay in touch with me, not Sharon, even though we never ask them to choose sides. Oddly, their appraisals of Sharon and our relationship support my decision finally not to seek reconciliation. Some use the term "narcissist" to describe her.

****

I'm thrilled when grad-school buddy Hogan calls me. After hearing about his thesis setbacks and love life, I provide a blow-by-blow account of how Sharon quit our marriage. Hogan tries cheering me up, saying, "Our friend Ira's in worse shape 'n you...since Holly walked out last fall."

Hogan explains the problem was Holly kinda walked out on everybody else too. Her parents felt it odd, though, that she'd fall off their radar. So they pressured Philly cops to investigate by asserting that someone who regularly checked in with them couldn't just cease to exist. Some of Holly's friends and Saul Lapidus in New York agreed, adding, "An attractive woman doesn't simply disappear. People notice."

Hogan continues, saying Ira told the cops, just as he's told all of us who bump into him and ask, that Holly just went missing on September 10. She said she was going to a store to buy tofu and greens for dinner...and vanished.

"Oh yeah," I say. "It's coming back now. I heard somewhere the cops gave up searching for her last December. Considered her just another missing person then."

Hogan resumes his update, explaining Holly's parents then hired two retired FBI agents to keep looking for Holly. Hogan asserts Ira had a weird gray pallor back then. Blamed it on sadness and a need to get out into nature. He bounced back and convinced most of us he never knew where in hell Holly went after their many break-ups over the years, saying, "She always disappears."

Hogan points out Ira's energizing his so-called network that links together his many, many contacts in science and pseudoscience, including paranormal stuff and UFO sightings. He's also promoting computer conferencing, even teaching futurist Alvin Toffler how to use this leading edge technology.

"Quite the hustler, as usual," I say.

"Oh, and he's organized Sun Day in Philly."

"Heard about that. Not a pagan Worship-the-Sun thing, but a real event celebrated in other cities."

Hogan agrees, saying President Carter preached solar panels in Denver while actor Robert Redford and activist Barry Commoner pushed environmentalism in NYC and D.C. Ira did work harder for Sun Day than he did for Earth Day, and so people weren't so flustered by him taking credit for it.

Lastly, Hogan surprises me by saying Ira just finagled a teaching gig with the Kennedy School at Harvard, teaching a one-off seminar about creating networks to spread New Age ideas.

"About time he earned some legit money." I chuckle.

**

With summer coming, I decide to follow up on a long-deferred dream—to produce documentaries as my dad once did. Citing my writing and ever-increasing radio-and-TV involvement, I apply to UCLA's Broadcast and Film Department to learn doc writing, directing, and narrating. I'm admitted for the summer term but must take two prereqs concurrently with my classes. The prereq for the narrating class is an acting class, which requires auditioning for admission.

Los Angeles – Summer 1978

After subletting my Warehouse space to Joan's cousin, I drive to Los Angeles, free of past cares but facing new ones. I prep for a scary audition, filmed with three cameras, by memorizing a scene from *Barefoot in the Park*. Somehow I pass, and over the weeks, I get to know many impressive faculty and students. On my first weekend break, I leave Westwood for Glendora to see Mom's sister, Ruth. On my second, I visit Glendale, closer by twenty-five miles, to begin producing a film about their police department's groundbreaking use of computers in patrol cars.

**

Early in the summer, Sharon and I correspond about insurance, finances, and, of course, our relationship. Regarding the latter, I write, among other things:

You pushed for equality in all things, and I may've fallen short, but I tried to treat you as an equal regarding our respective careers, household chores ....

I don't understand why you cheated, then continued to deceive me—before and during our open marriage. You're such a realist and perfectionist, how could you fall in love so easily?

She writes back:

The clash between your ambition and my ambivalence for my art career motivated me to find someone new. You—well, really, society—pressured me about art and babies....Now, having dealt a lot with Eduardo's kids after work, I'm even more certain I don't want babies. ...

On July 13, she sends me a tenth-wedding-anniversary card with a cartoon of an unhappily married couple on the front. Inside, she writes:

Take some gorgeous L.A. bunny to dinner and have a good time.

A few weeks later, she mails a short note.

I'm offering to do the paperwork for a simple DIY separation and divorce. If you agree, I'll divide our assets fifty-fifty. No spousal support. I'll keep the van to haul paintings, and you keep the cat.

I respond:

Considering my limited options, I accept your proposal.

She sends another note:

I've moved in with Eduardo. His ex comes to their house to care for their boys while we're working, and she often eats food I've bought for myself. Pisses me off...

Eduardo's a super-parent, but I hate being awakened at night when a kid's afraid of the dark or has to pee.

Also, I get angry and shout at Eduardo, even throw stuff. He's had to coax me back after I've stormed out of his house.

I put the note down for a moment and blink in disbelief. Sharon's gone for good! Her life's changed drastically. Although I'm happy her misery's over, and happy for me too, in a confused and confusing way, I'm sad as well.

Utilizing insights from my therapy sessions, I try to honor my recurring sadness and grief, though I'm alert about not letting things morph into depression. I try, too, to honor my need for intimacy and a relationship. That's why I decide to go out with a couple of older students, who like me, live in Rieber Hall, UCLA's high-rise dorm.

****

I date a wannabe actress a few times who says she's thirty-something. Things go well initially, but I lose interest when she talks incessantly about Hollywood and does astrological charts. She did mine, but I never asked her whether it revealed compatibility with hers.

I then pursue a freckled-faced woman in Rieber Hall. At first, during long phone calls, I sense she doesn't like me because she goes silent for seconds at a time. But when she finally admits she's having petit-mal seizures, we bond over outsider stories. She's an epileptic and, like me, was bullied as a kid.

Freckle-Face says she's thirty-five-years-old like me. Even though her work and college stories suggest she's a true age-mate, her face and skin let her pass as much younger. For this reason, she tells me, she's really not interested in me, but is instead really into a twenty-six-year-old hunk in Rieber. She's not bothered that he's already got plenty of female admirers.

So, like Freckle-Face, I delude myself and go after a twenty-something would-be model. I delude her too by acting as if I'm mainly interested in having her narrate my Glendale PD documentary. After a few dinners out, this gorgeous "L.A. bunny," to use Sharon's phrase, agrees to do the on-camera narration for me. But soon, it's clear work and pleasure (with me) don't mix for her.

****

After finishing the documentary, other coursework, and a written proposal to work with the Glendale PD on a future project, I feel I'm due a vacation before heading to Berkeley. Because I learned from hitchhiking around the world in 1966 that solo travel can be lonely, I decide to travel to Club Med resorts in Puerto Vallarta and Cancun, Mexico. Although I'm attracted to several of the Club women I meet over a couple of weeks, I find they're from places in Texas, New York, and France. I put on the brakes, therefore, since I discovered over a decade ago that "geographically undesirable" romantic relationships can be difficult.

San Francisco Bay Area – Fall 1978

Upon returning home, I start frequenting the over-thirty singles bars on Union Street in San Francisco. (My evolving politics has ruled out "hippie chicks" in Berkeley, causing me to trade my collarless Gandhi shirts for coats and ties.)

Fortunately, I've started to work at AudioVideoResources in S.F on days I'm not professing on campus. After finishing work at AVR's production house on Broadway, I usually dash from its quaint used-brick building to another one housing a fern bar near the Marina District. En route, I economize by grabbing fast food, knowing well the steep price of eating at Perry's and other trendy bars. Ditto drinking at Perry's: I generally order the best bar value I know—the courage-in-a-glass martini.

Tonight, I chat with a woman sitting next to me. She tells me how lucky we are to have barstools since the after-work hordes usually grab 'em early. She's able to duck in from her mother's apartment nearby to take a breather from studying for the bar exam and caring for her three-year-old.

I carefully clink my martini glass with her lemon-drop glass, saying, "I'm impressed. Not a lot of women lawyers in the city."

"I only went to Golden Gate Law at night, but if I pass the bar, I'm opening up an office with a sign 'Divorce—for Women Only.'"

"Already got a business plan!"

"Damn straight! My ex and his chauvinist lawyers cheated me left and right...You a lawyer?"

"No. This yuppie outfit's not really me. Just wore it to meet ad-agency bigwigs today."

Her eyes light up. She finishes her drink and deadpans, "Buy me another."

I slap a twenty on the bar and, as multitudes suddenly swarm us, clasp my half-full glass, not wanting it to spill.

"You an ad man, then?"

"No, a prof in the East Bay."

Her eyes dim, and almost shut. "That's where my jerky ex wanted to drag me," she says. "No way. Too crazy, too scary over there."

Just then, a woman I know, Karen, approaches with her roommate in tow, as usual. We three hug, and my new barstool-mate turns away to admire a faux-Tiffany lamp against the wood-paneled bar.

"Hey, where'd ya slip away to last night?" Karen chirps. "Off to a third job to support me someday, I hope."

****

Driving home, I conclude I've been looking for love in all the wrong places. Yuppie bars and Club Meds aren't working for me in the great singles' desert. I've been looking at all the wrong faces too. Women my age tend to have kids I can't afford to support, particularly if I someday add in my own. And these women tend to distrust men, especially newly single guys.

I like meeting women impromptu and following up if attracted, but I don't meet enough women this way. So, throwing spontaneity out the window, I try newspaper personals. I labor over a thirty-word ad for the San Francisco Bay Guardian, pitching a few qualities, but emphasizing my wish to find love and start a family. Satisfied with a good, but not perfect, ad, I submit it and wait.

****

Finally, what Scott and I have been waiting for: Dad's estate to settle in Seattle. On my birthday, November 28, our Oakland lawyer summons us to his wood-paneled office to update us. Unfortunately, the Court rejected our petitions for a fairer distribution of Dad's estate. But it did decide to divide up the Palo Alto house proceeds now, to prevent Eve from investing them poorly. Our attorney hands us a document filled with numbers, which Scott examines in detail as we stop on a landing of the iron staircase in our attorney's vintage building.

"Sheesh!" Scott exclaims. "Eve got her entire legal and other expenses paid off the top, before the final distribution. You and I end up with less 'n $9,000 each."

"What the hell?" I exclaim, looking at the document. "We get next to nothing. Eve gets almost everything, and she's been in the family barely six years!"

I put my forehead against the stairwell wall, letting my arms hang limp, and think, *Is Eve another woman in my life with some sort of emotional disorder?*

Scott asks, "Wonder if Eve will ever give Mom's jewelry to Gayle, or family heirlooms and photo albums to us?"

The only answer is the loud clanging of our footsteps as we descend the remaining flights of metal stairs.

CHAPTER 23
Shocking News

Berkeley and Philadelphia – March 1979

"Ira's been arrested. For murder!" Hogan shouts into the phone.

"Nooo. Not Ira!" I shout back. "Can't believe it. Einhorn?"

"Who'd he kill?"

"Holly."

Wha-What? Holly? It can't be true," I say, raising my right hand reflexively. I almost tangle my hand in the always twisted cord between the receiver and the phone on my desk in my Warehouse office.

"It's true. His arrest pushed the Three Mile Island meltdown off Philly's front pages."

"Yeah. Just heard about the nuclear meltdown. Guess Philly newspapers can't get enough of Ira." I fuss with a gadget which amplifies my phone ring because of the basketball-court size of the studio.

"Right, papers are now calling him 'the Unicorn Killer.'"

Mr. Nonviolence has his flaws, but killing Holly?"

"Ira maintains Holly just left him one day back in September of 1977. Said she phoned him and others afterwards, saying she'd started a new life in New York City."

"I remember."

"But get this. Cops now say Ira mummified her body, then lived with it—slept feet from it—for eighteen months!"

"Christ, Hogan! This can't be. He's crazy smart, not crazy stupid. Why would he do that?"

"Ira denies everything. Says the CIA killed her and planted her body in his apartment."

"Why?"

"To frame him because he knows too much about their high-tech war plans."

"Je-sus."

"Gotta run, Karl. Sorry. I'll update ya later."

"Okay. Thanks, Buddy." After Hogan hangs up, I'm at a loss and all I can do is dangle the receiver by its cord and watch it rotate in an effort to untangle itself.

I'm sad for Holly and especially her loved ones. Sad, too, that cops think a champion for nonviolence has killed someone, a guy so kind and unusual people considered him a unicorn. I'm not convinced he's the culprit.

Over the next few days, I read Philly newspapers at the campus library and follow the national media. Like so many others, I can't get enough of this sensational story, yet it's personal for me. I call other Philly friends and discover Ira's got plenty of support, including the Quaker City's former top district attorney and ambitious politician, Arlen Specter. Ira hired him, and Specter used his clout to broadcast Ira's claim that the CIA sneaked Holly's body into a trunk he'd used to store documents to send to his growing network of subscribing scientists, business men, and cutting-edge thinkers.

Ira had continued to let friends, repairmen, missing-persons investigators, and fellow Sun Day organizers come to his place during the eighteen months. Everyone who knew Ira agreed he'd never be so stupid as to keep a decomposing body at his apartment and still have people over. David Ehrlich, who once owned dumpsites, said Ira knew where Ehrlich's landfills were and could've dumped a body there anytime. No one would've ever found out.

Ira's research associate, Tom Bearden, trumpeted that the frame-up meshed with a string of unexplained calamities befalling their colleagues of late: the arson of a paranormal researcher's house where Ira frequently stayed, the plane crash death of a biomedical pioneer, and the stroke death of a psychokinesis scientist.

Also, Ira's fans dismissed any suggestions of a common domestic-violence motive, jealousy. They argued that the times Holly left Ira before, he had always remained nonviolent, even accommodating. Ditto for the motive of money. Ira hadn't touched Holly's bank account since 1977, estimated at $20,000 due to an inheritance, even though he had access to the account.

San Francisco Bay Area – April 1979

Even though I get a trickle of responders to my personal ad and have disappointing dates with some of them, I still arrange to meet Colleen Higgins. She's a paralegal at a downtown S.F. firm, and meeting in Golden Gate Park, she lives up to the photo she sent—a medium-height blond, fashionably dressed. We go for coffee nearby, and I learn she and her siblings grew up in San Anselmo, a Marin County town her ancestors helped found. She graduated from Dominican College, a small Catholic school in San Rafael.

After talking for hours like lifelong friends, we return to the park to explore. We eat at a small restaurant, where we share stories until they boot us out. As we walk to her apartment, she blurts out a doozy: "As a criminologist, you'd be interested to know my dad sustained a shotgun wound to his side,4 below his ribcage, when he was seventeen."

"Holy smokes! And he survived."

"Barely. Back in his day, all doctors could do was put vinegar-soaked sponges in the grapefruit-sized hole!"

"Must've stung horribly! So who shot him?"

"No one. An accident, but it did keep him out of WWII."

****

Once at Colleen's Victorian apartment building, I kiss her, knowing the partly enclosed porch gives us some privacy.

She returns the kiss, leading us to make out in earnest. Somehow, though, we both sense we should leave things in a fevered state, and since it's a work night, I drive back to Berkeley, a smile on my face.

We talk on the phone the next day and agree to dinner Friday. I bring up Ira, his alleged crime, and how I got to know him through his fascination with Baez. I explain Ira knows scientists, businessmen, and celebs, whom he chases like he chases skirts.

"Sounds too busy to be a vengeful boyfriend."

"Insightful of you! Moreover, Ira boasts he's into non-exclusivity, open relationships."

"Hmm."

"He's a paunchy paragon of peace, a philosopher and a physicist into psychokinesis."

"An alliterative mouthful about a paranormalist. Ira must know of Uri Geller, the spoon-bender!"

"Yup, he's friends with him. You know about paranormals?"

She blushes. Whispers, "Yes."

"And it is all about 'p's—Ira also hangs with a parapsychologist named Puharich, an expert on Soviet psychotronics as mind-control weapons."

"And...Puh..." she struggles.

"'Puh' is okay...Ira and Puh talk about ELF waves, ESP mind-reading—"

"Since I can't read minds, where would you like to have dinner in San Francisco? BART's too far away for me to ride to get to the East Bay Friday."

****

I keep trying to make sense of the news filtering in about Ira. I like that he peacefully submitted to arrest, but not that he showed no emotion when Detective Chitwood opened the trunk, finding a body and a god-awful stench. Granted, Ira may've had an impaired sense of smell, possibly explaining why he rarely bathed, but really...

****

I wish I'd been back in Philly the year leading up to Holly's disappearance. It would've been 1976, during America's 200th birthday. Its birthplace, Philly, underwent a facelift during my grad years there for the Bicentennial, making the city dusty and noisy. During 1976, communes still flourished in Powelton Village, just as art co-ops did in the Bay Area. If I'd been in Philly, I would've known Holly joined a commune in the spring of 1976 to get some space from Ira¬ even though she'd had short and long separations from him, going to Tyler when he was away in Canada and Europe.

I'd have known too, that Holly's beauty gave her the ability to start and stop affairs almost as easily as Ira the charm warrior could. In their open relationship, Holly dated other men, such as Larry Liss, who had an open marriage with his wife a lot. Ira bedded all sorts of women, but he didn't like any of them very much.

****

During my dinner date with Colleen, I tell her of the celebs and hotshots Ira courted to broaden his network beyond hippies and yippies in the '70s. Many will testify at his upcoming bail hearing. They'll vouch for Mr. New Age's character.

"How d'ya feel about that?" Colleen asks.

"I'm trying to reconcile the man with the murder…at least the man I knew."

"Cognitive dissonance?"

"Lots of us feel dissonance, conflict regarding Ira. He championed kindness, nonviolence But I never liked his need to be the center of attention, the smartest guy in the room."

"His need to dominate doesn't square with nonviolence," Colleen says.

"He broke lotsa real-world norms as he proselytized for other-world utopias…but hey, let's talk about us."

"Fine! I'm looking forward to our time after dinner."

"Me too." I reach for her hand and squeeze.

December 1978 – January 1979

I joke that my life's in Scott's hands, but it really is. We're out in the San Francisco Bay in a small sailing dinghy Scott's borrowed. I'm risking my life to support Scott's renewed interest in sailing as he dips his toe into bourgeois life after rejecting it throughout his college years. He hopes to build a dinghy like this one, the type he learned to sail in as a teen.

Amid frequent cold splashes that leave my lips salty, we lapse into discussing Ira. Scott's been following Ira since before his recent arrest, and so I ask him if he thinks Ira felt jealous whenever Holly left him. I ask him because I felt jealous when Sharon left me for Eduardo.

Scott suddenly loses control of the dinghy and it lists ominously. Scott shouts, "I thought I was the only one battling jealousy.7"

"Oh?"

"Yeah, my girlfriend Mandy insists on seeing her estranged hubby. Eats me up."

After commiserating for a bit, we agree that Columbia anthropologists who raved about mate-sharing in Polynesia got it wrong. Yale psychologists probably got it right, though. Salovey and Rodin recently found people get jealous mainly over what matters most to them.

Scott sums up, "Ira may've been bothered more about Holly getting serious than getting sex. Romance was more of a threat." But Scott doesn't like the term "competitive" applied to romantic rivals. Scott thinks only capitalists are competitive but understands my notion that most of us envy smarter, more attractive, more productive people than ourselves, making us all competitors of a sort.

While driving home, we get real about buying a house in Oakland. When we split, we shake hands on pooling our inheritances to invest in a city losing its battle against crime. I'm still idealistic enough to want to keep the U.S. from moving toward two societies, one Black and one white, separate and unequal. The Kerner Commission's call-to-action resonates with me.

****

After Colleen and I plan a getaway to the Calistoga hot springs in Wine Country, we discuss the news that "Son of Sam" Berkowitz just admitted he faked hearing voices in his sanity hearing. We wonder if Paper Bag Bill heard the news. Colleen then reveals that the Zodiac shot and killed one of his victims, a taxi driver, near her apartment.

"You never told me that."

"He then walked right past my place here on Cherry Street, and later, three teens across the street helped the cops draw the famous sketch of the Zodiac."

"You'd think with that composite—"

"And all those coded clues, the cops would've had him by now," Colleen says.

"Detective Falzon is trying his damnedest."

Colleen then asks about the latest on Ira. I explain that his attorney got very specific yesterday, saying the CIA framed him because he knows too much about MK-Ultra. It's a super-secret project I know about only because the *Daily Pennsylvanian*, and many of us protesting Penn's complicity in war research, sued to access Ultra documents. Turns out the CIA tested psychedelics like LSD on both young and old civilians, trying to develop mind-control tactics to fight Russia and the Soviets

Colleen and I agree this new Ultra info is potentially helpful for Ira.

****

Chatting with Ric a week later, I mention that Ira added Moscow's notorious KGB to the mix soon after attorney Specter's Ultra announcement. Ira asserted that KGB agents helped their CIA counterparts frame Ira because the Soviets also don't want the world knowing about mind-control weapons. These, called psychotronics, involve beaming extremely low radio waves, kinda like EMFs, at people's brains. It's stealth warfare. Cheap, simple, and hard to detect and defeat.

"Not sure I buy into the KGB bit," Ric says, "but Ultra came up in my consulting work with the *Light* during our Synanon investigation. Some of Dederich's drug nonsense extends back to when we were in high school and Dederich's mentors fronted for Ultra and LSD. It's a small world when it comes to kooks and nuts."8

"Incidentally, Ric, I've got a life besides Ira...And I've been meaning to thank you and Kath for it. Having me to your house a lot has blunted the loneliness of my Big Box space at the Warehouse."

"You had a constant life partner for the last ten years...Anyway, Kath's motive's been," Ric says, half smiling, "to figure out what went wrong with you guys. You seemed so compatible."

"We weren't," I say, explaining a few issues and our inability to resolve them. I then add that over the final months, something went terribly wrong. I describe how Sharon distanced herself from me, then shined me on by agreeing to an open marriage after she'd betrayed me.

"But you may've missed something."

"What?"

"That Sharon may've sent signals to Eduardo before you two tussled around her career, getting a gallery–"

"What d'ya mean?"

"She could flirt. She knew how to use her sex appeal."

"Christ, Ric! You think they were an item for a long time?"

"You never know. Women do have advantages in the battle of the sexes."

****

As Scott and I set out to look at another duplex to buy jointly, he tells me Gayle revealed, sheepishly, that Eve has moved back to California.

"Jesus!"

"To a pricey town just miles from Palo Alto!"

"Belying her assertion that she couldn't live in California."

"Thus completing her highway robbery!"

"I'd like to know if she's a Machiavellian—testing high on the MMPI and PRI for manipulation."

Scott draws a blank until I explain these traits are additions to the famous 1950s characterization of psychopaths as manipulative, guiltless liars. Scott smiles, then tells me what he recently heard from our two Seattle cousins who first dubbed Eve Dragon Lady. Before moving south, Eve invited them to cross the bridge to Kirkland. Over dinner, she asked them to consider remodeling her home pretty much at cost ...so she could rent it out. They politely declined, feeling she'd be paying them with their Aunt Laura's, Mom's, blood money. Even if she'd served them steak rather than spaghetti, they still would've declined. 1960s through 1980s

CHAPTER 24
Beauty, the Beast,
and Deteriorating Relationships

Greater San Francisco Bay Area – *1979*

From info gleaned from friends, reporters, and my own journals, pieces of the Ira and Holly story began to fall into place. Apparently, Ira became enamored overnight by the graceful Holly, who'd atypically mastered both ballet and cheerleading routines in her youth. She'd escaped Tyler to attend Bryn Mawr and RISD in the Northeast and had just graduated when she met Ira. She'd evolved since Texas from a fresh, blue-eyed ingénue of sorts to being a mildly hip women's libber, and defying all logic, she fell quickly for the hulking, unkempt Ira. She soon moved into 3411 Race Street with him.

I summarize this boy-meets-girl story for Colleen during another outing on the Bay, this time in Colleen's friend's sailboat. (Luckily, Scott's outing taught me port from starboard.) I also explain how during five turbulent years together, the odd couple travelled widely—always attracting attention as a lithe Beauty alongside a paunchy Beast. They even traveled to Tyler at one point to meet Holly's parents and four sibs. Ira irritated Holly's ultra-conservative parents: his antiwar diatribes and unbridled pacifism particularly put off Holly's dad, a proud WWII veteran. Still, Holly's parents tolerated Ira, devout churchgoers that they were.

I tell Colleen that attorney Specter ensures the media knows that, prior to his arrest, Ira had finished a teaching fellowship at Harvard and flown to Yugoslavia to help officials arrange a centennial bash for native son Nikola Tesla.

"The Tesla Coil, wireless-transmission guy," she exclaims.

"Wow, Colleen!" I exclaim. "And coming home, Ira met the Shah of Iran's nephew in London to talk ecology and spiritual issues. Specter informed the media further that just days before his arrest, Ira won a five-thousand-dollar grant, met with AT&T hotshots, and dashed to D.C. for a congressional confab on the future."

"Definite overachiever, but not a criminal yet," Colleen says. "We constantly remind ourselves at the law firm—innocent 'til proven guilty."

"Yup. Let Lady Justice do her thing."

Spring 1979

Thanks to timely detailed reports in newspapers at the university library, I feel like I'm back living in Philly. Although campaigning now for the U.S. Senate, Specter surprises everyone at a pre-bail hearing by requesting Ira's next hearing be postponed because of search warrant irregularities and a delayed coroner's report. Additionally, Specter says he'll call an array of professionals and community pillars to testify as to Ira's character at that hearing. When Judge William Marutani asks for more details, Specter answers: CEOs, attorneys, and scholars as well as icons of the '60s, including rock star Peter Gabriel and Timothy Leary's colleague Richard Alpert, who knows lots about Ultra.

The judge grants a continuance, allowing Specter time to gather an even more impressive group of witnesses. This delay gives the media the impression that Ira's got such powerful friends that the State's looking foolish trying to demonize such a well-connected, nonviolent hero.

At the actual bail hearing, Specter emphasizes Ira's no longer a hippie-like guru promoting counterculture values but a sought-after interpreter of his generation's values to the mainstream Establishment. His foremost expertise, which'll be attested to by collaborators and scientists alike, is his knowledge of global cutting-edge research into mind control via psychotronics and mind-altering drugs.

Specter asserts Ira's not an offender, but a victim of the secretive CIA and KGB. They framed Ira by planting Holly Maddux's body and belongings in a closet on his enclosed balcony to take Ira out of play.

Judge Marutani nods to Prosecutor Joseph Murray, who seems distracted by a courtroom full of Ira's supporters. After promising the State will give specifics at the trial, Murray says, "If nothing else, Ira Einhorn's just like many men guilty of domestic violence. He can't handle rejection. So forget his New-Age zeitgeist when he states, 'I was soaking in the bathtub one evening, and Holly told me she was going to the store to get tofu and greens.' When she never returns, forget his Zen-like 'She just walked off into the sunset.' And forget the smokescreen of Ira knowing about cutting-edge uses of LSD and psychotronics for mind control. None of it is true."

Marutani then okays Specter's parade of witnesses, reminding them they're under oath to be truthful. First, a corporate attorney and childhood friend of Ira who says Einhorn has exhibited excellent character his whole life. Next, an Ivy League adjunct professor. "I've nothing but praise for the man." Then, an Episcopal priest known for his work in the peace movement. The reverend says, "Einhorn's a man of nonviolence. That's the way he's known in the community." When Specter asks each of them whether Ira might be a flight risk, they answer no.

The raves continue: from a playwright, a scholarly economist, a Bell Telephone executive, a bureau chief for the *Wall Street Journal*, and on and on. Marutani tries to get each witness to moderate their glowing reviews, and Murray tries to poke holes in various claims. But Specter, always combative, helps witnesses counter every point.

So many prominent people want their turn, that when the judge moves to curtail the testimony, Specter has them all stand to show how many people came to praise Ira's character.

Prosecutor Murray then asks the judge for a minimum of $100,000 bail. But Specter stridently insists on $5,000, saying Ira's not rich and whatever defense funds he might raise will have to cover bail, investigation costs, and attorneys' fees. The judge struggles and finds an acceptable way forward, saying, "Sounds like flight isn't a risk. And if the charges against Mr. Einhorn are true, then they constitute domestic violence, overwhelmingly a crime of passion. As such, the defendant doesn't pose a threat to the community because there's less chance of recidivism than there is for, say, burglary or robbery, which allow defendants to earn a living."

Marutani sets bail at $40,000, a remarkably low amount for a murder case. To minimize the outcry his decision's sure to provoke outside the courtroom, he adds, "In all my years on the bench, I've never seen such an impressive parade of character witnesses."

****

As expected, Ira's out of jail in no time. A Canadian friend of his, Barbara Bronfman, who married into the Seagram's liquor family, pools her money with Ira's parents' to pay his bail. Out in public, Ira tells anyone willing to listen that he's completely innocent. He questions all the facts of the case, even whether the body in the trunk belongs to Holly. After all, the CIA can fake dental records.

However, when prosecutors at last reveal forensic lab results during Ira's arraignment, he realizes he must ratchet up his PR campaign. Accordingly, he picks sympathetic reporters he knows, and spins the facts to buttress his argument that he's being framed because what he knows threatens worldwide security.

May-September 1979

Colleen and I talk most evenings, visit each other alternate weekends, and take trips together. At one point, we drive to Marshall, along with the Orsics, to meet Lee. Straightaway, Colleen regales Lee, a Marin County history buff, about her Marin ancestors, while Kath, ever the social worker, attempts to check on the welfare of the kids at Synanon. Ric and I talk about the latest developments in Ira's and Jed's cases.

Regarding Ira, Ric agrees we must let justice take its course since so much that we know in the case we've heard second- and third-hand.

Ric's way more judgmental about our colleague Jed Drell. He's very angry that campus higher-ups have just promoted Jed to a deanship. We wonder, as usual, if they kicked him upstairs because he's a lousy teacher.

"What bugs me most," Ric says, "is the news Angela's reconciled with Jed. She's gotta be the only fool ever to drop divorce proceedings against her would-be killer."

"Wrong. Happens every day," I say. "Confused, irrational behavior among victims—especially those enmeshed with their would-be killers—occurs a lot. Moreover, Angela's now the classic, financially dependent victim who, likely as not, will soon take her girls along with her to the new house Jed's bought, not far from their old one. I do blame Angela's attorney for not attaching Jed's salary, her relatives for not insisting she avoid Jed, and her social worker for not pushing her to upgrade her job skills so she can survive without him."

I tell Ric Jed's definitely not a typical heat of passion family violence offender, given his pre- and post-scheming around his murder attempt. This manipulativeness, coupled with his smarts and white-male privilege, let him keep landing on his feet compared to the minority offenders I see in court or in the field.

"He's still a total ass!" Ric says. "A psychopath."

"He's definitely Machiavellian. I call him Mach-o-Man sometimes."

****

On another house hunt with Scott, this time to check out Ric's neighborhood in Oakland, we examine several fixer-uppers, the only properties we can afford after pooling our inherited pittances. Given Scott will be the carpenter, he nixes the Tudor-style house we like best, explaining how costly remodeling will be since we shouldn't compromise its Tudor-ness. I muse, *He's still got Schonborn perfectionism in his veins.*

As our house-hunting continues over the months, I sense a hesitation to commit on Scott's part. When I finally confront him, he says he's still conflicted about owning property due to residual Marxism. When I counter that we thirty-somethings should be investing and that stocks seem like a bigger Marxian no-no than real estate, he says, "You're right, but I think I've just come up with a better investment for me: getting a master's in architecture. In fact, I've decided, right now, that that's what I'm gonna do. Invest in myself."

"Congrats!" I say, concealing disappointment.

"I've been worried of late about outdoor work—skin cancer, falling off roofs—just like I write about in my OSHA safety columns. Need to do architecture now. At a desk. Indoors. Sorry to abandon you."

****

Without Scott's funds, I have to house hunt in cheaper, rougher parts of Oakland now, ruling out where many of my progressive-liberal, as well as Black-radical, colleagues live. They've insisted on moving to safe neighborhoods like Montclair and Skyline, where Ric and Jed live. I wonder, *Unwilling to fight for declining neighborhoods in Oakland, are they part of the problem, not the solution?*

Complicating things, Colleen wants to house hunt with me now, but has no money to contribute and dislikes that she'd have to drive to BART along with most Oaklanders who work in San Francisco. Walking to BART isn't an option since the neighborhoods next to stations often have poor schools. Moreover, Colleen doesn't want to quit her great job in S.F., and if she does, she wants to be a home-for-life mom. I think, *Reminds me of many women I met at S.F. singles bars... and Sharon too. A dependent lifestyle like this is a feminist no-no, and a trait often termed "parasitic" in some personality tests.*

****

One Friday afternoon, Colleen, Greg, Nancy, and I pile into my VW station wagon (technically a type-3-squareback) with our gear to head to Lake Tahoe for a weekend of skiing. As dark falls, my VW fishtails more and more as remote roads, kicking up memories of black ice in Minnesota, lead us to our rented cabin in Markleeville.

While unwinding with mulled wine, Colleen models a ski outfit and accessories she bought for the weekend. She loves fashion, hair, and makeup, transforming herself whenever she's bored with her look.

After a quick breakfast Saturday morning, we all dash to and from the VW, making sure it's got our downhill essentials. During one dash, Colleen swings a forearm in such a way that a quarter-inch-wide gold bracelet slips off her wrist, arcing high in the air. "Jeez Louise!" she shrieks, and we all come running. Amid shouts of "Not there, over a little," Colleen tries to direct a logical search, but to no avail.

Colleen guesses the bracelet's worth thousands of dollars since it's twenty-two carets and a family heirloom. "My mom'll kill me if I don't find it."

"Ski much?" Nancy asks.

"Know it was stupid," Colleen says, "but I wear it a lot. Even sleep with it."

"The kinda thing you wanna lock up," Greg teases, "but you're the criminologist, Karl."

"All I know is," I say, "we're wasting precious ski time."

"Go without me," Colleen implores. "Go now!"

"I'll stay and search," Nancy says.

"You sure, Nancy?" Colleen asks. "I'll reimburse your lift tickets. Know you bought yours in advance."

As Greg and I climb into the car, Nancy whispers to us, "I'm stayin' since she probably can't even light the gas stovetop to heat soup."

Oddly, skiing once a year reassures me that my heart has truly outgrown the scary condition that sidelined me from PE and sports in my youth. Because my gear gets little use and replacing it is costly, I stick with old boots and skis. They've begun to attract stares.

Greg says, "Time's a tickin' " while watching me examine tiny bits of plastic falling from one boot as I slip it into its binding beside the lift line. I hesitate to enter the line, fearful that aging plastic—not wear and tear—will cause my boot to fail. But Greg and the mountain's allure propel me forward.

I make it down our first run without incident, but realize I'm skiing too cautiously for Greg and suggest we split up. He agrees, then a thought crosses my mind. *Will Colleen and I split up too? Have birth perks made her irresponsible?*

Despite the beauty of Tahoe and mesmerizing snow-laden trees, I soon stop for a break and enter East Peak Lodge. After drinking an overpriced hot chocolate, I notice more shredded bits of plastic falling from my troubled boot as I get up from the table. A Lodge staffer notices, shakes his head, and points to a wide, road-like trail as the easiest way down the mountain.

Even though I'm skiing slowly, my bad boot suddenly splits in half, freeing its ski. I tumble end over end and shout obscenities as I watch the freed ski slide down the trail.

After untangling my limbs and righting myself, I retrieve my runaway ski, my sock foot getting ever colder. I detach the ski from my good boot, place it next to its runaway mate, and sit down on the narrow sled I've created. Shoving off with one hand, holding my poles over my shoulder with my other hand. I descend the mountain the same way I did in the '60s after Lee "tried to kill me" on a Black Diamond run.

It takes an hour to sled down to the parking lot and another hour or so waiting for Greg, before heading back to the cabin. All the while, I ruminate that my relationship with Colleen will shred like my boot. Even though I help Colleen continue looking for her bracelet the next morning while Greg and Nancy ski, Colleen's forced to leave a note for the owner of the cabin. She tells me she hopes he's honest when the spring thaw comes.

****

Over subsequent weeks, I try to sort feelings from facts. I can't believe my mind's rehearsing breakup lines. *You limit where I can buy a house since you dislike driving or using BART.* I find myself asking her, "Why don't you want a career?" She answers, "Maybe because as a kid, I never had to do chores or work summers. Maybe that spoiled me. Who else can say, 'I'm going to leave my body to science since I've never eaten at McDonalds?'" I laugh out loud but cry inside.

Another concern roiling in my head: Colleen's makeup skills and superb fashion sense make me wonder "What version of her will I see today?" and "Am I truly attracted to her?" Trying to be more in touch with my feelings than I've been in the past, I edge closer to a decision. Counseling has taught me to respect intuition after a lifetime of yielding to facts and rationality. So one afternoon at Colleen's, I blurt out, "I think it's best we not see each other anymore."

When she says, "I've sensed this coming," I'm taken aback. I think, *I've forgotten how sharp and insightful she is.* However, I plunge ahead.

I reveal the feelings I've wrestled with as well as the geographical challenge of living twenty miles apart given her aversion to both driving and BART.

I edge closer to her on the couch to face her directly. "We grew up so different—You, comfortable, privileged—Me, hardscrabble, life's a challenge!"

She tears up and mumbles, "Possibly."

"I hesitated committing to Sharon, but years ago, I didn't know that hesitation meant my gut was saying, 'Don't.'"

"Then we shouldn't drag this out...for sure," she says.

We both cry, recount our good times, and say we'll miss each other, hugging many times before I slowly leave.

Once again, I'm destined to wander the relationship desert.

CHAPTER 25
Three Psychopaths

Point Reyes, 1979

Months later, while driving to see Lee, the Orsics and I discuss the fact that two Synanon members, as well as Dederich, were found guilty of conspiracy to commit murder. The two put a rattlesnake in the mailbox of an attorney suing Synanon for holding members against their will. Though hospitalized for six days, the attorney survived his snakebite. The two men got jail time and Dederich probation, where he's free but monitored sporadically.

Kath relates the saga of Synanon's numerous acts of violence that had triggered the attorney's suit. Although courts actually assigned teenagers to Synanon for drug rehabilitation, staff beat many of these youths, causing them to run away. To cope, outsiders and ex-members set up an underground railroad to return runaways to their parents.

Ric notes that after Dederich rebranded Synanon as the Church of Synanon for tax-exempt benefits, he erected buildings without permits and created an illegal landfill dump and airstrip. He also ignored locals' complaints that Synanon's tin roof glinted in the sun, ruining the ambiance of Point Reyes.

Ric apologizes to me after all these stories, saying, "As if you need to hear about another psychopath, Karl."

"No worries," I respond. "Like you, I knowingly signed up to be a social psychologist, and we study individual behavior in group contexts. Dederich was raised in a dysfunctional family group, like many psychopathic killers. I bet you'd agree, Ric, that he is different from them mainly because he seeks power in a similar group, the family-like cult he created, whereas they don't."

"I agree," Ric says. "Like Bill Hanson, their path to psychopathology may be similar, but they express it differently."

Once we arrive in Marshall, Lee takes us to the Tavern to celebrate that the *Light* has just won a Pulitzer Prize for its articles exposing Synanon as a cult. We toast to the *Light's* editor-owners Dave and Cathy Mitchell, and to Ric, who helped them throughout the process.

East Bay, California – 1979-80

On campus, I teach grad students to produce "soc-umentaries," a word I've coined for my attempts to put sociology articles and research into video form to publicize their ideas and findings beyond just social scientists. Soc-umentaries belong to a growing discipline known as visual sociology. My students and I produce *The Plight of Migrant Farmworkers*, about migrant and seasonal farmworkers in California.

I also act as a scriptwriting consultant for *Fitz and Bones*, a TV crime series starring the Smothers Brothers as an investigative reporter and an offbeat cameraman in San Francisco. Orsic and I bite off part of a nationwide study of how American cities responded to crime over many decades. We write a chapter about Oakland in *Crime in City Politics* and the process, fortunately, helps me identify safe neighborhoods in Oakland as I continue house hunting.

This during a time when house prices and interest rates are climbing rapidly under President Jimmy Carter. Oil prices have killed U.S. growth, and former nuclear sub expert Carter refuses to support nuclear energy after Three Mile Island. When I try to buy a home as rates briefly dip below 16 percent, others outbid me.

This setback and a feeling of aloneness causes me to accept Gayle's overture to reconcile. I find she's needy too. Chastened by Eve's duplicity and an inability to find a professorship despite being a newly minted female PhD, she resigns herself to working in Silicon Valley, where she's moved.

Philadelphia, Pennsylvania – September 1979

After professional meetings in Boston and NYC, I head for Philly to spend time with Hogan. At a cheese-steak place on South Street, he fills me in on Ira, saying he brings the same intensity to helping attorneys prepare his case as he's brought to most everything else in his life. For instance, he helps pitch that his plight is a global cause, something affecting everyone. Hogan shows me part of a letter Ira wrote for his legal defense fund, pointing to the last three paragraphs.

"I am very conscious of the general shock and pain that my arrest has brought about. Due to the nature of the legal situation, I am not able to talk about the facts of the case.

"However, I can share with you that I am sick to heart at this interruption of work that I have slowly and patiently created over a period of many years. The psychological shock of such an abrupt transition has left me dazed and totally without a context. I feel as if I have lost my home planet. It would be so easy to give up or disappear.

"Yet I know that I must not desert at such a critical time, for the transformation is accelerating rapidly and must be understood if we are to survive...Peace, Ira Einhorn."

Hogan continues, explaining Ira's got many fervent supporters in Philly, and none more so than colleagues into the same kind of psychic mind-control research as he. They allege his arrest is part of a grand scheme to limit the release of information about psychic warfare. They cite the suppression of books such as *Mind Wars* and *Psychic Discoveries behind the Iron Curtain* and sympathetic articles in the *Washington Post* by esteemed political columnist Jack Anderson.

Turns out too that Ira effectively counters both friends and skeptics alike who question him in person. When they ask, "Did you do it, Ira?" he marshals his self-confidence—his best and worst trait—and says, "No," and proceeds to counter every allegation. Overwhelming and mesmerizing, Ira then hits back with his own questions: "Do you know me as a violent person?" "Why would I kill Holly, the woman I loved?" "Even if I did kill her, aren't I too smart to keep a body in my apartment?" and "Wouldn't the CIA and KGB rather frame me than kill me and make me a martyr?"

Hogan concludes with, "Very few people who engaged Ira's intense blue eyes in these encounters came away thinking he was guilty."

All this is why I visit 3411 Race Street, in addition to the fact that I'm never able to reach Ira by phone. I want assurances from him in person, but no one answers his doorbell. Hogan says it's understandable since Ira's away a lot, traveling cross country, and even out of the country, to rally his friends and raise money for his defense.

Before leaving Philly, I visit Bryn Mawr College to channel Holly. I learn of the dread some people had when they thought back to when their naïve flower child went missing in West Philly.

East Bay, California – Fall 1979

I return home to find a house I can afford. The interest rate's dropped from absurd to terrible. In late September, I bid and counter-bid on a duplex that'll allow me to collect rent to help with a still-insane mortgage payment. I win the contest. Just after the deal finalizes, rates spike to 18 percent. Real estate isn't for the faint of heart.

My duplex near Mills College sits next to an immense quarry, which scars the Oakland foothills, but once provided the crushed rock to build East Bay roads. My realtor says Fundamentalist Christians live in many of the houses in my neighborhood, hidden from a nearby freeway and most of Oakland by trees. Stay-at-home moms in full-length dresses, required by their faith, keep their eyes and ears peeled, alert to crime.

I immediately rent the downstairs unit. A taxidermist moves himself and his stuffed owls in… and then out right away for some reason. Maybe he's a stuffed shirt, didn't like that he'd have to patch the walls upon vacating if he displayed trophy mounts. So I rent to a wonderful Dutch woman, Olga, who stays a while.

Just before moving from the Warehouse, I throw a Farewell-Bon Voyage party in my space, featuring a live band. Scott borrows bags of sand from a jobsite, and we create an artificial beach on the floor. We add life preservers and unlit tiki torches to enhance the tropical vibe. I invite friends, students in my classes, and fellow Warehouse residents: partners optional, modest beachwear and flip-flops mandatory.

Over the course of the evening, I meet a woman named Lynn Lawson, the friend of one of my students. She likes to dance, talks a lot, and plans to teach school after her master's. We don't have much time together because I'm busy supplying drinks and food to revelers while, at the same time, reminiscing and saying farewell to artistic friends. The next day, Scott and I re-bag the sand and leave the space spotless. Inspector-General Yulia is coming to collect my keys.

****

After the holidays, I phone Lynn, and we meet for wine in Berkeley. She's got a slightly older sister, a younger one, plus two half-brothers. We share general info about our parents, upbringings, and places we've lived. (She's essentially lived in one area, the East Bay town of Alameda, her entire twenty-two years. I've lived in eight areas in thirty-six years.) When Lynn declares children are her passion, my eyes widen, having dated many women who're ambivalent about having kids. Hearing a few of Lynn's stories, I dub her the "kid whisperer." I'm also attracted to her blunt, straightforward speech. I think too, *Unlike Sharon, she's a talker who doesn't stifle her feelings. Could she then possibly withhold info and deceive?*

Upon parting, I realize Lynn stirs my heart as much as my head, which I'm not giving much credence to these days. She's also easy to look at and a natural blond with sky-blue eyes.

Regrettably, I'm so busy, that as a follow-up, Lynn and I go on a working date—filming street prostitutes at twilight for two soc-umentaries I'm doing. I ride in the passenger seat of her VW Bug in Oakland and have her pull over and park whenever I see a prostitute soliciting a john. I ask Lynn then to scrunch down in her seat too, like I do so people can't see my two-foot-long broadcast-quality camera. When Lynn threatens to report me to the police, I tell her I've already filmed Oakland's police chief and Alameda County's sheriff and top district attorney for the films.

We have coffee afterward. Lynn tells me her stepfather's like me: olive-complected and knows fancy cameras, since he films TV news for the NBC affiliate in San Francisco. Unlike me, he's fathered two kids and pretty much wreaked havoc for nine years at Lynn's house before her mom kicked him out, demanding a divorce.

Not long after the second date, I suggest a third—another film shoot. This time, it's interviewing scientists at TransTime Cryonics. I ask Lynn, as with the Unicorn Killer facts I've shared, to have an open mind about frozen brains. When finished, we get a tour but don't actually see quick-frozen heads, let alone bodies, which cost way more because tall liquid-nitrogen-filled stainless-steel canisters don't come cheap.

Driving home from the shoot, we laugh, recalling the hero in *Sleeper*, awakened from cryogenic sleep, who turns the ignition in a two-hundred-year-old VW Bug, which starts!

I then broach the wrinkled elephant in the room. "Do you worry about our age difference?"

"No! I welcome your maturity," Lynn says. "My first boyfriend was my age, but really an immature guy. On swim teams his whole life. Spent too much time in the water."

"Hadn't learned the social skills needed for dry land?"

"Yes. And I've somehow attracted immature girlfriends, who required rescuing."

"For example?"

"Well, Judy constantly got into jams as one of the few white girls at Oakland Tech, across the estuary from lily-white Alameda High.

And Sarah, as nutty as they come. So these days, I prefer older people, older guys."

"Looking for a father figure? Or a sugar daddy?"

"C'mon! Don't need either. I've been paying my own medical, dental, car insurance, and tuition since sixteen."

"But you still live with your mom?"

"I'm not stupid. Rent's crazy-expensive now."

"So you just need a mother figure?"

Smiling, "Not really. She's more a pal...even when I was growing up. My grandparents were probably the only real adults in my life. My dad got into drugs and abandoned Mom and us girls early on, showing up only for our birthdays and Christmas. Mom then married the cameraman who overdid the parenting role. He was okay with his two little boys, but way too strict with us stepdaughters. Tried to control us as teens, dictating who we could date, be friends with—"

"A looker like you probably needed some rules—"

"He'd pick me up after every shift at McDonald's when I was fifteen. Lied about my age to work there, knowing he'd cut me off financially at sixteen."

"Ouch."

"He had a great network-TV salary but burned through it. Wasted it on alcohol."

Oakland, California – February-March 1980

I finally have the chance to spend some extended time with Lynn and show her my new place. During the house tour, she literally backs me into a corner of my sparsely furnished office, insisting that I explain my failed marriage. I manage her rapid-fire "who, what, where, when" questions, but stumble on "why" when she asks.

My short answer flops, so I go long. "Remember I told you I traveled the world solo?"

"Of course. Your courage amazed me."

"Well, I started in Europe as a true innocent abroad—staying in hostels, making new friends, entertaining people who gave me rides as part of a hitcher's quid pro quo—"

"So?"

"I remained idealistic 'til Sharon, my girlfriend at the time, showed up and then ran off with a Greek guy. I chased after them to Greece, then Cyprus, where she gave me the slip. Outta money, I had to work my way back home via a tramp freighter—"

"Your point?"

"A decade later, 1978, she gave me the slip again."

"You must be glad she's gone."

"Yes. She's outta my life for good now. Just married a guy from Guatemala. But our marriage at the end mimicked my parents' marriage at the end."

"Meaning?"

I tell her about my parents' fatal dysfunction after we sibs had left home. And when she wants the latest, I say I'm equally ashamed about Eve's financial dysfunction. My wonderful family self-destructed in effect.

When I finish, Lynn hugs me, saying, "Your mom's suicide makes me sad."

I murmur "Thanks," almost tearing up, as I often still do when talking about Mom's death.

"Coupled with Eve's treachery, you've been through a lot."

To get off the hot seat, I ask, "So what about your relationships after the swimmer?"

"Well, there was a guy ten years older, Chip, who was a hardcore partier like my dad. Then a manager at McDonalds, even older than Chip."

Wow, to think, Colleen never ate at McDonalds and Lynn immersed herself in the franchise.

I'm slightly relieved after the tour to prepare dinner, my famous rubber chicken.

****

To get to Lynn's house, I take the next freeway exit heading north to Berkeley, and shoot straight down the Oakland foothills to Alameda, home to a still-active Navy base. Lynn's Spanish style house is just a few blocks after I cross the High Street bridge, the one Lynn's sister Valerie jumped off once, on a dare. Though structure's a low-to-the-water drawbridge, Lynn says she'd never do such a thing because jumping's forbidden. "I obey the law. I'm not a risk-taker like Valerie."

Lynn's attractive, young-seeming mom, Carole Conde, sits me down right away in her dated kitchen, plying me with cookies and questions. Satisfied I have no horns, Carole shows off her antiques-filled home, including the remodeled basement where her young boys sleep. Lynn whispers during the tour that a grandmother bought the house for Carole to help her cope with having three daughters, a drug-addled ex, and only a few college credits at age twenty-two. I realize, *That's Lynn's age right now.*

After walking around the neighborhood and pushing one another on the swings at nearby Lincoln Park, Lynn and I return to her house. Directing me to sit on a sofa with chintz coverings, Lynn brings over two photo albums to show me her family. Right off, she points to pictures of her brothers, who're away visiting their dad, Carole's second ex.

As Lynn names people in other photos, many artsy stills that her cameraman-stepfather took, I say, "I'll have to meet everyone to remember all these names."

In the second album, when we get to pictures of Lynn in her teens, she says, "Here's that first boyfriend, the swimmer. And here's Chip, the slacker, stoner.

"And here's Mitchell Lewis, my longest, most serious relationship."

As she flips through a couple of pages of Mitchell, I comment, "Doesn't smile much."

"Yeah, but he did love imitating comic Steve Martin in *SNL's* 'Two Wild and Crazy Guys' skits with Dan Aykroyd. Mitchell didn't do one-liners or kid around like you." She grabs my hand and squeezes it.

After another page, I say, "He looks menacing with that moustache."

"Well, he did frighten some people."

"Oh?"

"Worked as a bartender upstairs from me at a place called Sophie's. I worked as a hostess and waitress downstairs at Spider Healy's. Met him in 1974. Both restaurants looked out over the water near Jack London Square."

"Oh, yeah. The Square near the Rusty Scupper, where Sharon and I got drunk after the fire."

"Small world! My co-workers, including Mitchell, walked to the Scupper after their shifts and spent their all their tips."

"Easy come, easy go?"

"I didn't like him spending so much on cigarettes."

"Kinda dumb?"

"Few of those people went to college. Mitchell didn't even finish high school...in Tampa. Thought he was too smart for classrooms."

"What'd he do instead?"

"Joined the Air Force to fly but couldn't. Bad eyes. After being stationed in Macon, Georgia, came to Oakland, where his dad and two siblings lived."

She flips a page.

"Whoa. Piercing eyes!" I exclaim.

"Yeah, Mitchell has an intense stare."

Flips another.

"Here're some touristy shots," she says, pointing to Mitchell and her, plus her brothers, at Alcatraz.

"In this shot, behind the steel bars of a cell, Mitchell looks sinister."

Mitchell's fascinating, I think. *Need to learn more about him.*

And learn more I did.

CHAPTER 26
Einhorn's Defense. Lawson and Lewis.

East Bay, *1980*

Lynn and I take a break from bike riding to snack at a cafe overlooking the Bay. As we're finishing, Lynn gestures toward a middle-aged couple with wedding rings who've hardly spoken a word during our time there. We agree we'd never be like that, given Lynn's need to get her words out and my tendency to ask why.

Back at Lynn's place, she reaches for a photo album and resumes her show 'n' tell. After a few pages, I ask why so many photos of Mitchell include her brothers. She explains that Mitchell actually lived at her house a few months between apartments.

"Thought you hated smokers?"

"Made him smoke outside."

"Why didn't he just quit?"

"He tried but said he was hooked. So, yes, numerous photos. He did lots with my brothers—wrestling, video games, stuff. Was patient usually, but screamed at the four-year-old once for dawdling and grabbed his arm, yanking him out of his VW bus."

"Ouch! Did Mitchell sleep in your small bedroom?"

"Nope. Slept in the always-cold basement. I'd never sleep there. But enough about him, What was wrong with Colleen?"

"In a word, spoiled, like Sharon."

"Weren't you too? Palo Alto, the Ivies?"

"Only on paper. Bullied growing up. Always had chores, summer jobs. Not privileged."

"Outta your league, then, with Sharon, Colleen?"

"Not really. Just hard to live with 'em. Been bumping into privileged people my whole life. Even dated a newspaper heiress a while back, one of Tiffany's best customers, but I knew it wouldn't work out."

****

Lynn keeps busy, and I'm in no hurry to rush into another relationship. Still, I do like her a lot and feel us connecting more deeply as time goes on. She stays at my place more often than I at hers. It's nice that Carole's bedroom's at the other end of the house, particularly when I share the latest Ira news with Lynn. I'm still embarrassed that people I've known, like Bill and Jed, have committed heinous crimes.

My Ira news comes mostly from Philly friends who call or send articles and clippings. Not Hogan, though, since he's having trouble finishing his thesis because he suffers, like Ira, from being more a talker than a writer. From the materials I receive, I'm becoming an expert on all-things-Ira. For example, a long-delayed, then quickly sealed, coroner's report concludes Holly sustained six blows to her skull.1 This info requires lukewarm Ira supporters like me to wonder if the CIA or even KGB would ever be so brutally amateurish.

The report puts to rest a plausible explanation and result I'd entertained: what if Ira had lost his temper and whacked Holly's head? (My research teaches me anything's possible among intimates.) If this blow caused her to fall, hit her head on the bathtub, and again on the floor, then Ira might've only committed involuntary manslaughter. He could confess, do brief time for the crime, then resume saving the world. He could even, as yippie-turned-yuppie Jerry Rubin suggested, say that male hormones briefly subverted his nonviolence, do minimal time, then start an institute to study male-testosterone offenses. But six blows...

I then learn, and pass along to Lynn, that there's forensic info that counters the coroner's report. Follow-up tests on Ira's floorboards, the rugs beneath the trunk, and the plaster ceiling of the apartment below the trunk all come up negative for human blood or tissue. Ira immediately uses this new ammo in an interview quoted in the *Philadelphia Bulletin*:

"If I did it, why is there no blood in the apartment? The skull was supposedly fractured...multiple times. You can't tell me blood didn't squirt all over the place. And no matter how careful you are, you wouldn't be able to get it all up!"

Ira says the new tests also belie the claim he mummified Holly. "If so, where'd all her blood go?" Ira doesn't stop with the *Bulletin*. He trumpets the results of the follow-up tests to anyone who'll listen.

I also tell Lynn about new info the Madduxes' PIs have discovered. They found signs of Holly's emerging self-confidence, like her tossing her diabetes Med-Alert bracelet because she learned she could manage her disease through diet and mindfulness. More germane, though, she was applying what she'd learned from assertiveness training and increasingly stood up to Ira.

According to the private investigators, Holly had often suggested to Ira they separate for a while, and—getting nowhere—lobbied the woman who'd let Ira and her stay at her home in London. Though the woman was the companion of Ira's close friend and benefactor, Puharich, she realized Holly needed support and became a co-conspirator. Together they hatched the plan for Holly to leave Europe ahead of Ira. The woman even arranged for Holly to stay at her Fire Island home and introduced her to wealthy friends and associates there. This likely contributed to Ira's falling out with Puharich.

Months later, after finding out, I tell Lynn of a rumor that Specter recently tried to get Ira to plead insanity. Ira resisted the idea vehemently, arguing that that would be exactly what the CIA and KGB would want. They'd want citizens to believe psychotronics was insane so they'd remain blissfully ignorant of the mind-control tactics they planned to use someday.

Another rumor circulating suggested that Ira's refusal to plea bargain led Specter to quit his legal team. More likely, though, the demands of Specter's U.S. Senate campaign forced him to turn Ira's case over to a law firm associate.

****

Ira counters other rumors and growing skepticism about his innocence by publicizing that:

> He noticed his balcony windows had been tampered with the night before Detective Chitwood found the trunk. His enemies had obviously replaced the documents he'd stored in the trunk with Holly's body, drained of blood and mummified by KGB scientists who'd preserved Lenin's body.

> He'd bought the trunk and locks when evidence surfaced that CIA agents felt increasingly nervous about the classified psy-warfare documents that experts sent him. Agents knew he knew ELF transmissions, Soviet jamming techniques, and other psychotronics were potentially as dangerous as nuclear weapons.

> The trunk and locks allowed him to leave his apartment for his recent trip to England and Yugoslavia. He and Holly routinely stored their belongings in the balcony closet whenever they sublet their place during summers away from Philly.

Overall, new info, reports, and evidence, either for or against Ira, mean more pretrial motions and hearings. Since both sides argue over everything, these delay Ira's trial. Therefore, I continue to wait, along with countless others, for Ira's day in court.

****

When various people ask why I still give Ira the benefit of doubt, I spout some—or all, when pressed—of Ira's accomplishments:

> A huge mailing list that allowed him to send—on Bell Telephone's dime—cutting-edge pamphlets, articles, and books on physics, psychology, and New-Age topics to key political and cultural influencers in twenty-two countries.

> A political resume, including candidate for Mayor of Philadelphia and mayor of Powelton Village, where he mediated neighborhood disputes and fights with city hall.

A book, though as obscure as its ISBN title *78-187880*, published in 1978 by Doubleday.

A friendship network of relationships—including actors, futurists, paranormalists, counterculture stars, and respected investigative reporters.

A column, even if eccentric and irregular, entitled "The Unicorn Speaks" at the *Drummer*, Philly's underground newspaper.

A fellowship at Harvard, requiring he teach New-Age networking, the theories of Marshall McLuhan, and more.

****

Lynn and I keep up our phone conversations, but she frequently cuts them short because she's busy. So I make sure we meet often to enjoy one another's company since we've got chemistry despite our differences. We talk over coffee, visit antique shops, and go to the beach near her home. While waiting for a barista to filter our coffee in Berkeley one day, I ask, "Whatever happened to Mitchell?"

"A few years ago," she says, "he missed a coupla days' work without anyone knowing why. I visited his place, but my key no longer worked. So I looked in a window and couldn't believe my eyes. Empty. No furniture. Nothing."

"Quite a shock, I bet."

"Yeah. And it hurt a lot...after two years together."

I take her hands in mine. "He send you a letter?"

"Didn't even call."

"Any idea why? You fought?"

"Nope. No fights. I called his sis. She had no clue either—no crisis with their mom or sibs back in Florida. She guessed 'Maybe some girl from his past.'"

"That must've hurt."

"Yeah. Still does, after four years."

"Any signs of drug use besides alcohol or weed?"

"Well," she pauses, "when I'd sleep over and wake up at night to pee, he'd often be pacing back and forth. Said he couldn't sleep."

"Sounds like cocaine."

"Nah. Said he just got wound up working nights."

"Or maybe nerves from dealing drugs? You said he rented furniture. Typical of dealers. That way, they can get outta town fast."

"Jeez. Never thought of that."

****

I continue getting updates about Ira and his endless pretrial hearings Because of the cost of these hearings, Ira keeps soliciting defense donations, without much success, as well as shopping a book idea for a six-figure advance. However, he gets no bites from publishers, who suspect his book will flop as *78-187880* did. Why? Because Ira refuses to write anything other than an "I'm innocent" book.

What's interesting is how Ira manages the stress of being a hero-turned-villain in many people's eyes. Not to mention, if true, keeping a grisly secret for eighteen months while sleeping next to Holly's body. One theory holds that drugs explain his upbeat attitude, except for a coupla months' depression after Holly's disappearance.

For instance, there's a rumor that he's using ketamine, a cutting-edge drug, which induces a trance-like state while providing sedation, pain relief, and memory lapses. Ric Orsic tells me it's a sister drug to PCP, which he's researched, but more dangerous because it creates dissociative anesthesia from one's environment. This effect may explain Ira's fascination with out-of-body techniques, which he teaches to some, including the women he allegedly asked for help dumping the trunk. May explain, too, his ability to deny an act totally at odds with the nonviolent person he professed to be.

Since out on bail, Ira's traveled to California and found solace staying with a friend on a Sausalito houseboat, lunching in nearby Mill Valley, and meditating while hot tubbing at the Esalen Institute in Big Sur. I'm amazed to find he's also lunched in Palo Alto with a UFO expert, spoken to a group in San Francisco, and attended a conference in Berkeley. All this was while I was away on a trip, so I wouldn't have been able to get together with him.

Ira's also traveled out of the country several times, erroneously assuming he was free to go anywhere out on bail.7 And despite his judge confiscating his passport, Ira's managed to get a new one and fly to the U.K. on occasion. Interestingly, he drives to Canada via artsy Woodstock on one of his visits to the Bronfmans in Montreal.

Ira also begins seeing a woman the Bronfmans introduce to him, a quiet twenty-two-year-old from Virginia, Jeanne Morrison. He moves from Race Street, to avoid more 'n' more awkward encounters in Powelton, to a modern high-rise at the edge of Philly a mile from where he grew up. Jeanne soon moves in with Ira, and her deference to him reminds people of Holly, scaring many, especially Jeanne's parents and friends.

In the summer of 1980, Ira takes Jeanne to Nova Scotia and tries to rent a vacation place, as he and Holly had often done. Cape Breton islanders, who've heard of his troubles, reject his bid to rent several places. Ira does manage to rent a cabin, where he keeps busy with correspondence and articles. The couple returns to their apartment in Philly in the fall, and Ira works with his lawyers on his defense for his upcoming trial, set for January 1981.

I continue to be increasingly conflicted about Ira's guilt.

****

Not long after my downstairs tenant gives notice, I show the unit to a young, very pretty woman who's the only applicant responding to my newspaper ad. Crista Dahl says she's new to California, and so I waive the usual references.

Instead of using a cashier's check for her first-and-last rent, she pulls out a wad of cash and peels off several hundred-dollar bills. I don't think of it again until much later, dazzled in the moment by her fresh, sexy looks.

CHAPTER 27
The Making of a Psychopath

East Coast, *1981*

Ira cuts and runs just before his murder trial.

This ends any remaining indecision I felt about his guilt.

When Einhorn fails to appear in court January 14, the judge replacing Marutani, Paul Ribner, immediately issues a bench warrant for his arrest. A week later, Ribner angrily summons both sides to court. Norris Gelman, who's replaced now-Senator Specter as Ira's lead lawyer, is stunned by Ira's flight, as is Prosecutor Barbara Christie, a petite but tenacious woman who packs a heavyweight's punch. After both sides claim to know nothing of Ira's whereabouts, Ribner growls that the court's been made to look foolish. He warns anyone assisting Ira, including prominent people, will be charged and prosecuted.

Though all are galled an alleged murderer runs free, only Prosecutor Christie can do something about it. She orders Philly PD Sergeant Richard King, an extradition specialist, to pursue Ira. King tracks Ira and Jeanne to Dublin, but Irish extradition laws prevent the arrest of any fugitives.

****

Besides the shock of Ira's jumping bail, I'm dealing with the news that tests using best-practices techniques now find blood traces in the rug, floorboards, and plaster ceiling directly below Ira's trunk. This undercuts Ira's powerful argument that initial tests found nothing, but all that's irrelevant at this point. It's time for me to reassess my analysis of the Ira I thought I knew.

If Ira worried about getting open-minded jurors with an "I've been framed" defense, the worst thing in many jurors' minds is to jump bail. In my mind too. Regardless of mitigating circumstances if he killed her—like a jealous rage, a bad drug trip, whatever—I can't avoid feeling Ira's flight is an admission he straight-up killed Holly. I grew up with the notion that running equates with guilt...and the corollary one, "if you do the crime, you must do the time."

Bottom line, I feel by bolting, Ira betrayed his character witnesses, scores of supporters, and me. More importantly, he betrayed the best of the '60s: the nonviolent, loving-and-free aspect of the decade. Of course, he wasn't the only person to do so, since love and freedom allow people without inner controls to be self-deluding, indulgent, or even predatory. Ira's ambitious mother thought the '60s were perfect for Ira's gifts. Sadly, the '60s let him misuse those gifts.

****

As the days pass, I keep asking myself how Ira fooled so many others, including me. To begin with, words. Words, words, and more words. Ira simply overwhelmed most everyone he met with mesmerizing nonstop talk that likely numbed our critical faculties.

I bet, incidentally, as I search my memory, I'll find Ira spoke very few words that were truly original. Could he have just been a human time-delay tape recorder? Could he have remembered words from his voracious reading and simply regurgitated or recombined them in a way that seemed brilliant days later? He never wrote a graduate-level thesis or a real book. His *78-187880*, jammed with illustrations, may've been a comic-book portrayal of Buckminster Fuller's ideas, designed to win the architect's favor. What is clear: Ira spoke (and wrote in journals) untold numbers of words.

Could all of Ira's words have created a hollowness inside him, and a resultant rage because his head so thoroughly squelched his heart? Might this emptiness and rage have burst forth occasionally, swamping the external calm and nonviolence that was his calling card? To be fair, it was the calling card for many others of us too.

This all still begs the question; how did I in particular fall for his bluster, let alone his pseudoscience? I thought I had a brain back in Philly. It had studied at three Ivies and managed to write a doctoral thesis. Upon reflection, I probably wanted to believe in Ira's cult of nonviolence, a splinter off Joan's church of nonviolence. Why? Belongingness? In a big impersonal city like Philly, far away from the nonviolence community in still-small Palo Alto, I probably ached for a connection to a merry band of nonviolence enthusiasts.

****

In a nicely carpeted hallway at a sociology conference, I tell Snodgrass, who shared an apartment with Hogan in Powelton, that I blame Ira's flight in part on America's bail system. My increasing conviction is bail favors smarties like Ira as well as the rich. Knowing he'd ultimately flee, Ira managed to fast-talk witnesses—celebs, corporate types, community pillars—into helping him game the bail system, just as he'd hoodwinked us everyday folk with his gift of gab. Snodgrass agrees, adding, "Meanwhile, less gifted folk can't hire decent lawyers, raise bail money, or flee the country. Instead, they languish in jail."

"And," I say, "being a minority or a female multiplies these challenges."

"Unless, of course," Snodgrass snorts, "one's a super-athlete minority or an attractive female."

"I never bought in to Ira's overall perspective the way so many rabid fans did—psychotronics, mind control, all that. Only liked the nonviolent, environment stuff."

"I felt he used all that to attract, then seduce, women. Thought he was a phony, through and through."

"Hell hath no fury like this nonviolent warrior scorned. I'm angry at Ira for causing me to question what little is left of my faith in nonviolence."

"Hope you don't abandon it," Snodgrass says. "*Your* nonviolence actually helped Pepinsky conceive of peacemaking criminology. Not Ira's."

"Thanks....Hate to admit it, though, I'm close to advocating death for Ira."

"Again, hope you don't. Pepinsky wants to use his law and sociology degrees to overturn death-penalty cases someday. But, hey, let's hustle to the Penn Grad Reunion room across the lobby before it's time to catch the keynote address."

"Good idea," I mumble as I adjust my shoulder case and start walking.

Snodgrass and I agree that Ira spoke of nonviolence very persuasively but missed a key element of it: courage.

"He showed no courage in brutalizing Holly, a person half his size." I think, *God forbid that six-foot Ira brutalizes his current five-foot-two girlfriend, Jeanne.*

"And he showed no courage fleeing justice," Snodgrass says. "A conviction won't result in his execution, even if he's guilty of first-degree murder. It was back in 1977."

Snodgrass reminds me of the results of Pennsylvania's constant seesawing over the death penalty. "They voted no to death in '72, and yes the next year. No again in '77, reversing it to yes again the next year."

We arrive at a small room, decorated in Penn's red-and-blue. The fellow crim grad students we start talking to agree that Ira's a flawed New-Age philosopher who promoted himself brilliantly, winning countless admirers. He succeeded because, feeling entitled, he could make up his own rules and manipulate anyone to achieve his ends. According to one recent grad: in Robert Hare's psychopathy test, a score of 30 clinches the diagnosis of psychopathy, on a range from 0 to 40 with many non-psychopathic criminals coming in at 22. I argue that since Ira also possesses two rare psychopathic traits, promiscuity and a freeloading lifestyle (parasitism), he likely scores well into the 30s.

Everyone in our little circle nods in agreement.

Given our consensus around Ira's psychopathy, we then discuss the nature-versus-nurture origins of psychopathic criminal behavior.

Someone chimes in, "Psychopaths are usually antisocial personalities too."

After more discussion, I say, "To tie all this together, it's worth applying my favorite notion that nature and nurture conspire to create what we call 'personality.' From then on, personality interacts with nurture, the environment, to determine behavior."

I bathe in the smiles all 'round. Then Snodgrass says, "We'd better get on to the keynote address, guys."

I remind myself, *I gotta dig into Ira's upbringing to see how it contributed to his personality, his psychopathy.*

East Bay, California – 1981

When I return from the conference, I seek out news, articles, really anything, to reconcile Ira the murderer with Ira the man. I start probing his past and discover Ira's Russian-immigrant father, Joe, earned good money before Ira's birth in 1940. He sold jewelry, silverware, and appliances on the installment plan, charging hefty interest. Joe got a 4 -F health exemption when America entered WWII in 1941. After the war, he sold used cars, earning enough for his family to keep moving on up in Philly.

Ira's ambitious, outgoing mother, Bea, led the family's quest for better schools, increasing economic privilege, and higher social status. She also nurtured Ira's major gift, his high IQ. Coaching, doting, and promoting Ira became her passion. She taught him to read before his brother came along in 1944. After Ira started school, Bea continued tutoring him, supplying him books, and helping him develop a passion for reading. This obsession for books resulted in him often getting less than five hours sleep a night because he could get away with it.

While Bea disciplined the boys more than Joe did, she preferred rewards to punishments...or just ignoring the misbehavior of her favorite son, Ira. As he grew, she covered for him when he marked up library books, ripped out their pages, refused to return them, or got them wet while reading in the bathtub, flaunting his nude body oftentimes.

Bea pushed Joe to move the family often, landing ultimately in a quasi-suburban area in northwest Philly. Her goal, besides respectability, was to find academically challenging schools for Ira. Bea continued covering for Ira…when he acted up in school or became larcenous, as in ordering items from book clubs with no intention of paying for them. As Ira's fixer, cleaning up his various messes, Bea helped foster irresponsibility in Ira, a precursor to antisocial behavior.

As a classmate of Ira's said of him, when they started Central High, a college-prep public school, "Everything [surrounding Ira now] was for a good cause: to aid and abet the intellectual development of Ira." Bea considered Ira's genius (he claimed his IQ to be "upwards of 140") would take him far, especially in math and science. And it began to. His test scores got him into Penn, where he started in physics. But he soon switched to folklore and then literature.

With his lit degree, Ira continued on to Penn's grad school but started teaching at the Free U, where he indulged his counterculture appetite. Among his courses was one on marijuana, during which he and his students inhaled. Before long, Ira tired of being a conventional grad student, given his proclivity to hover around the flame of knowledge unbounded by disciplines. So he dropped out of Penn to be Ira full time. In some respects, he still straddled academia and hippiedom, just as he later would, the corporate world and the counterculture.

Some vindictive articles I've read claim Bea and Joe "got theirs" after Ira disappeared. Philly courts release defendants if ten percent of their bail is paid. But if defendants flee, the courts keep the ten percent (the Bronfmans lost their $4,000) and demand the remaining ninety percent. As a result, Bea and Joe had to sell their house for the $36,000 bail still owed the court. And after they paid thousands more that Ira owed his lawyers, they could only afford a small apartment. They were left pondering their son's behavior and why he accused their country of origin, Russia, of framing him. It's no wonder Joe died of a heart attack soon after losing their home.

Despite her losses, Bea steadfastly maintains Ira is innocent. I conclude he's guilty, not only of being a murderer, but of being a rat. A rat to his family and especially Bea, given all she's done for him. This is the thanks she gets for being his number-one fan.

****

Lynn's become even more interested in Ira now that he's skipped. It's kinda like he's joined Sharon and Mitchell, who skipped on each of us. (To defang them, she calls them Fatsy, Patsy, and Minus of The Three Mouseketeer's comics of her childhood.) One day, she asks, "Would Sharon agree with us—despite her running from your relationship— that people who run, like Ira, are guilty?"

"Yes, I think so. But she doesn't know Ira ran."

"You haven't told her?"

"No, she's been preoccupied with her baby—"

"A baby! Thought she didn't—"

"People keep surprising me too."

"Now I gotta meet her."

"Well, I gotta meet the rest of your family first."

This leads to Lynn inviting me to the next gathering of her extended family. I meet her look alike older sister Valerie, her younger sister Autumn, their boyfriends, plus two grandmothers and a great-grandmother who's one hundred years old. Oh, and an aunt, an uncle, and several cousins. Lots of people to keep track of, and lots of talk to process.

I enjoy talking to Valerie's boyfriend and now fiancé, Steve Holt, about his youth in New Jersey and his military service overseas. It's nice that Lynn's family will soon include other than just fourth- and fifth-generation Californians who've stayed put in the west. Steve goads Valerie into telling me her Maid-of-Alameda story. As I listen and observe, I think, *Valerie's a shyer version of Lynn since Lynn's an avid reader too.*

Valerie says the family pressured her into entering the annual Maid-of-Alameda beauty contest when she was sixteen. She more than held her own, in terms of poise and appearance, but her bookish nature didn't help during the interview when she spoke of enjoying Virginia Woolf. It became clear neither the interviewer nor the judges had ever heard of the feminist author. So Valerie came in second-runner-up to Debbi Sivyer, who soon married well and became the Mrs. Fields of cookie fame.

After the story, Lynn repeats one of her favorite sayings: "It's not how you look. It's your behavior."

****

A number of months go by and it turns out behavior *is* a biggie ... to Lynn's regret. While staying over at my place, she and I talk late into the night about Mitchell. Whether tired, wanting to unload, or loosened up by talk of Ira, Lynn says, "Mitchell's in prison now."

"Christ!" I shout. "I can't believe this!" After asking her to repeat her statement, I think, *Crime lands on my doorstep once again.*

"He'd called Mom while I was out with you a couple of months ago. Said he was doing time in Salem, Oregon."

"Jeez!"

"When Mom told me, she said, 'We should visit him.'"

"Of course, you didn't."

"We did."

"But why?" I ask, stuffing down the anger, exasperation, and jealousy welling up.

"To see why he skipped out on me."

"You coulda phoned him."

"Mom insisted we go. She'd never been to Oregon."

"Don't blame her."

"She can be persistent...Anyway, we drove up to the prison and met him in a stark room with people sitting at tables and guards everywhere. Without any pleasantries, Mitchell started describing prison life."

"And?"

"While it was interesting, he went on and on. When I couldn't wait any longer, I asked him why he ran out on me."

"And then?"

"A guard said, 'Time's up!' "

"'We just got here,' Mom objected, looking up at the guard.

"'Sorry, ma'am, twenty minutes, unless you're family.'

"I glared at Mitchell and asked, 'Why didn't you tell us about the rule?' He said nothing.

"'Then what'd you do?' I demand.

"He just sat there. And so did I, stymied. Then a guard grabbed my arm, forced me up, and said, 'Rule's a rule. You aren't family.'

"'Then, tomorrow?' I asked.

"'Nope, only one non-family visit a week.'

"I didn't say 'bye,' to Mitchell, sensing he was happy not revealing anything."

A bit confused, I ask, "And you never wrote or phoned Mitchell afterwards to get answers?"

"Right! I was so mad at him." She puts her arms around my neck. "Besides, I was falling for you."

Lynn tries to kiss me, but I pull away. I say, "N-N-No, please. I don't feel very loving tonight. I think you'd better go home now. I dunno. Chew out your mom."

After Lynn leaves, I'm overwhelmed by feelings. I wonder, *Are my nerves still raw from Ira's symbolic admission of guilt?* Disjointed thoughts pour out: I'm startled to see again how crime's impinging on me...the one who once believed in nonviolence for all, and of late, nonviolence for cops. Maybe violence touches us all, given the small-world findings that show only six people separate any two people on the planet. So much for my clinical, arms-length approach to studying violence. *Bye-bye, ideal. Hello, real.*

When I next talk with Lynn, I start by asking if Mitchell proves the fact that she and I come from different worlds. She explains that Mitchell's behavior shouldn't reflect on her, and I respond that my parents' generation taught that a partner's behavior does enhance or diminish one's standing. That's why folks usually interviewed the partners of ministers, faculty, and business associates they considered hiring. I muse, *I'll try to unlearn that, but it does show socialization for Lynn and me in the '50s and '70s differed greatly.*

After also thrashing out head-versus-heart issues with Lynn and learning a bit more about the dysfunction of her family, my newfound gut tells me I should go slow with her. So I push for a pause, a time to process all we've learned about each other. She agrees to a breather, going our separate ways, and even dating others. I realize I'm taking a big risk. She's special, and I know others will want to steal her away. It's happened to me before.

East Bay – 1982

My privileged killers keep forcing me to question the conventional wisdom in my field. And since politicians cite criminological findings to influence, even create, crim justice policies, my increasing doubts worry me. Since I've no inclination to date for a while, I've got time to write some opinion pieces and craft criminology class materials reflecting my newfound skepticism. As I tell students, questioning "received wisdom" requires knowing whether it's evidence based. So I ask my class to ponder science versus its antithesis, fake science, which likely characterizes parapsychology and paranormal endeavors, which I've shared with them regarding Ira's case.

After some student discussion, I argue that criminology's a soft science at best, and is fake science at worst. This is because crim findings range from experiments borrowed from other social sciences, to well-executed crime surveys, to analyses of flawed FBI data.

A student then asserts he's slumming it in my Criminology class as a physics major, eliciting a nervous laugh from all of us. He says,

"Hard sciences like geology and biology involve experiments with controlled variables and objective, mathematically expressed results."

I agree, saying, "A rock is a rock every time in geology. In my numerous premed and med-school courses, where the gold standard was also hard science, studies aimed to be replicable, with similar results every time. By contrast, soft sciences like criminology deal with complex human behavior and emotion."

A female student sums it up nicely. "One hypothesizes that girls are more likely than boys to be bullied. One samples girls and boys in certain classes in certain schools and then studies them. One finds girls are more likely to be bullied. But another person repeats your study elsewhere and finds opposite results."

"Correct," I say. "It's hard to isolate the variables that influence results. They could be the classes—the students, the teachers—the schools with differing socioeconomics, or unknown variables. Simply put, it's harder to control variables in soft versus hard science studies. Try figuring out your boyfriends or girlfriends someday."

Everyone laughs.

CHAPTER 28
Burglary, Rape and the Three Mouseketeers

East Bay – *1982-84*

Without a burning desire to date someone new, I fall in with a gang of weekly softball players through Warehouse friends Ethan and Melinda. I have the gang over to my place New Year's Day after too much fun the night before at the Roszaks', who now live in the not-so-counterculture Berkeley Hills as a result of Ted's bestseller. I also include Gayle and her boyfriend, but not Scott, who's stayed Los Angeles working on architecture projects. Gayle and I have put the probate battle behind us for the time being. Well, almost. After winning a color TV at an employee picnic sponsored by Hewlett-Packard where Gayle works, I joked, "Karmic, because you owe Scott and me big time." Gayle's not amused. Still, I enjoy getting to know Gayle's multitalented boyfriend better at the picnic, and we all enjoy ourselves days later at the wedding of a Schonborn relative in Sonoma Valley.

****

In a memorable criminology session, my students and I brainstorm bail reforms, with assigned readings of accepted, or received, wisdom as a starting point. After a creative give and take, designed to prevent both Ira-esque absconding due to wealth and languishing in jail because of an inability to pay, students hammer out this policy:

–Those charged with a gruesome crime like Ira's should be denied bail no matter what, as well as those charged with premeditated murder or mayhem.

¬Those arrested for other violent crimes like rape, robbery, and aggravated assault, or major nonviolent crimes, would have to undergo risk analysis. This would involve experts sorting defendants into low-, medium-, or high risk based on criminal histories and other criteria. Judges would be required to release low-risk defendants without requiring bail, and would maintain their usual control over high-risk offenders. Pretrial social-service specialists would decide whether to release medium-risk offenders or hold 'em for hearings.

–And those charged with minor nonviolent crimes would be eligible for release without bail within twelve hours of being jailed.

During their readings and this exercise, students discovered that bail processes, like other crim justice procedures, can be ripe for profiteering: to wit, profit-seeking bail bondsmen and bounty hunters. For these reasons, as well as the costly error of granting Ira bail, most students believe that reforms can and must be crafted.

Along these lines, I also help reform-minded students in my grad film class produce a soc-umentary titled *Guardian Angels: Police or Vigilantes?* Since I've conceded it's nigh impossible to disarm conventional police, I support innovative experiments like the Angels. They're teams of unarmed volunteers who don white-and-red shirts plus red berets to patrol certain events and big-city subway systems. They help reform-minded police chiefs who often request their services.

****

Apropos of film and visual sociology, when NBC cancels the Smothers Brothers' *Fitz and Bones*, it's back to regular scriptwriting for me. (My "Stop, Look, and Listen" script gets an agent but goes nowhere.) Relatedly, I change production houses, finding WrapUp Productions in the East Bay more convenient than AudioVideoResources in San Francisco. And it's fun sharing production tips with Ned, who films court depositions in legal battles over the international sale of museum-quality art. He's a fine-arts attorney who recently lost part of his inheritance via fraught investments. He's had to broaden his practice to include not only these filmed depositions but also filmed updates on recent changes in California law for everyday attorneys.

Besides professing and producing films, I do research despite increasing government regulations regarding the conduct of it and the publishing of results. I collaborate with Ric on the largest crim justice research grant in the US at the time. We both enjoy our task: looking at Oakland's response to crime during the 1948-78 period, part of a ten city LEAA project.

For sure, though, the thrill's gone around serving on committees to hire or to grant or deny tenure at department, school, and university levels. Ditto for committees to run regional and national meetings, though I agree sometimes to select papers and moderate panels for conferences.

Academia's requirement to serve the community is a different animal. I enjoy being on a community affairs board for a TV station, making promo videos for special needs kids, and so on. I also find it fun being interviewed and interviewing others on cable TV news programs.

I have lost my joy for yearly graduation ceremonies since separate affinity group and department graduations contribute, in my mind, to segregation and academic specialization rather than integration and interdisciplinary work.

****

Scott stops by my Oakland place just moments after I've discovered my place has been burglarized and turned upside down. I nod as I rush around trying to assess my losses. The scene paralyzes Scott. He's not seen, as I have on police ride-alongs, the chaos a burglar's search for valuables can leave. When Crista arrives a bit later, she finds someone's broken into and ransacked her place downstairs as well. Scott hugs the distraught-but-still-desirable Crista and drives off.

Oakland Officers Rullamas and Bilstein arrive an hour after my 911 call, merely giving Crista and me brochures and forms to itemize

222 · KARL SCHONBORN

our losses. I'm angry the police department can't afford to respond faster to property crimes but don't raise a stink because I know my OPD Family Crisis Outreach project needs the money more than any property crime detail. I'm also angry because I must absorb all of the burglary losses. This includes a two-month rent break I give Crista because she's uninsured, and I'm worried I might lose her as a tenant. She reciprocates by inviting me for a homemade pesto dinner, and later on, two other dinners. I enjoy her company but get a bit nervous because she also often entertains a big, muscular Black guy I wouldn't want to tangle with.

I spend a couple of weekends repairing the jimmied windows in both our places and mark my valuables with my driver's license number to facilitate their return if ever found. I also install doorscopes and double-deadbolt locks on the front doors up and down, adding guard chains on doorjambs for extra measure.

****

Whenever possible, I visit West-Coast friends—including the Greenes from med school, and of course, Lee, who's now with the *Gilroy Dispatch* in a valley town famous for its garlic festival. I also visit relatives—Schonborns mostly, since Stenersons still blame the family for Mom's suicide. At home, I hang with academics like Orsic, Noces, and Roszak as well as a few other friends. While I treasure all these people for their love and support, I realize I need a life partner to keep me happy.

For this reason, I try to listen carefully to my increasingly audible inner voice, valuing my intuition, feelings, and heart more. In so doing, I downplay the differences Lynn and I have in age, class, and cultural backgrounds. Bit by bit, I realize Lynn's a good fit for me, besides having many admirable qualities. Plus there's that chemistry between us. In other words, she's the one.

****

So I phone Lynn. After we share our thoughts and feelings about reconciling, we agree to start dating again. At a dinner at a Berkeley marina restaurant with glorious views of San Francisco, we catch up on news. Lynn's sister Valerie got married to Steve Holt in 1981 at a small church in Albany, not far from Sharon and Eduardo's house. The Holts rent the cottage in front of Lynn's grandmother's, off the next highway exit from my place. Autumn and her boyfriend broke up, but she's doing well, as are Lynn's half-brothers.

As the sun sets on S.F. and we start dinner, Lynn tells me that after she earned her master's, a principal in Alameda heard about her kid whisperer reputation and saw her stellar recommendation letters. He phoned her while she vacationed at Lake Tahoe, offering her a teaching position, sight unseen.

"Congrats!" I say, raising my wine glass to her.

"Thanks. I love kids but may need to become a principal to pay Bay Area rent."

"No way! Guys'll stand in line to do that!"

"So far, no offers. During our hiatus, I dated a bit. A dentist and the former quarterback of my high school class. Oh, and a bagpipe player. Only the dentist could've paid my rent. If he'd offered, I wouldn't have accepted. No chemistry. Not with any of 'em."

I smile.

During an after-dinner drink, I tell Lynn about my academic and film production efforts. At evening's end, her favorite story of mine has been my burglary, perhaps because she feels more vulnerable as a renter now, out of her mom's house at last.

****

Lynn and I date sporadically at first because we're both busy dealing with violence. Me: the arms-length kind, in class and in research. She: the real-life kind, in schoolyards. We do discover we still like each other a lot and soon become exclusive, spending nights at each other's places again. I like the pep in her step, to use one of the many phrases she spouts, and the simpler, "in the moment" life she tries to lead.

Nice counter to my world's need to always plan for the future: grants, classes, projects, conferences.

Lynn reintroduces me to her large family, birthday party by birthday party. We double date with Autumn and her new boyfriend and do short trips with Valerie and Steve. I enjoy the countless stories the Lawson sisters tell, warts and all, of their childhood and youth.

Oakland – May 1983

One Friday after work, Valerie eases her car into the level driveway of the cottage below her grandmother's house, which is three stair flights up a wooded hill. Leaving the cottage's front door ajar, she dashes into the bathroom to clean a hard contact lens that's been bothering her. She's planning to leave right away to join Steve at a party.

Suddenly, a young guy slips into the cottage, twist-locking the door after himself. He grabs Valerie from behind. She screams and struggles as he forces her into the adjoining bedroom. Knowing her grandmother and others won't hear her screams in the heavily wooded neighborhood, Valerie tries to reason with her attacker.

Soon, a frantic Steve calls me about the assault and says, "S-Somebody just attacked Val at our place."

"Christ! She okay?"

"Yes. Yes. Thank God. She's crying. Devastated. I just got here. Was at friends' nearby—"

"Anyone call the police?"

"On their way...H-He was younger than Val. As she got out of her car, she noticed him parked where the road has a shoulder. But he drove off, and she thought nothing of it."

"There's a widening in the road in front of my place too... where people park to make out." *I want to assure him that ignoring a parked car is normal, especially in a semi-rural area without sidewalks.*

"The bastard threw Val on our bed, tore off her blouse, got on top of her. Had her spread-eagle—"

"Horrible. Simply horrible! I'm *so* sorry for her. For you too, Steve."

"Val kept telling the guy, 'You don't have to do this. You can go. I won't tell.' Finally, he stopped fighting her, got off, and pulled up his clothes. He walked to the bedroom door. Then he hesitated. Val froze."

"And?"

"Nothin'! He left and drove away. So, she talked him outta hurting, raping her."

"Amazing. Did she get another look at his car, license plate?"

"No. She crept along the floor, beneath the windows, to the kitchen. For a knife."

"Smart."

"Then she ran up to Grandma's and they called the cops. She thinks the attacker's new at this. Hesitant. Frightened. . . Uh-oh. Cops are here. Gotta go."

"Okay. Have her call Lynn when she can."

****

On Saturday, Lynn and I visit Val and Steve to console them. After the sisters leave to climb up the stairs to visit with their grandmother, I face Steve squarely. I ask how Val's *really* doing. He says she's been quiet, but that's her nature. And I ask whether the cops've interviewed her again, arrested anyone. Nothing's happened, no investigation.

"The cops said they can't give much attention to her case because it was an uncompleted rape."

"Errrgh," I snarl. "Bet they called it an 'attempted rape.'"

Steve nods.

"That's such BS. And it allows the police department to slack off, conduct a halfhearted investigation. Criminologists consider attempted rapes as completed ones. Count 'em as such in their studies."

"Why?"

"Because rape's as much about power, the attacker's over the victim's, as it is about sex and testosterone. The victim's trauma, the sense of violation, and so on are essentially the same whether rape's attempted or completed."

"Lotsa talk about trauma during my military days," Steve says.

"Rape trauma is similar to military trauma. Can result in PTSD."

"I'll try to get Val to open up, talk more about it."

"Have her call Lynn again. And call me, Steve, anytime."

****

As a victim now of burglary and Gerald's gun threats and as an up-close observer of how people game the courts, I've become a victims' rights advocate. My zeal for nonviolence may've morphed into another kind of zeal. So I ask Brad Kerns, an acquaintance who's part of Oakland's Sex Assault Unit, to give extra attention to Valerie's case. He says okay, especially since she described her assailant well. Kerns will cross-check her description with that of other known rapists to develop leads.

I also ask Officer Rullamas, who's handling my burglary, to crosscheck the MO of my burglars—who knew our daily schedules—with other active burglars. When Rullamas balks, I counter, "There's software that can do that. Your chief rewards, promotes officers who use high tech."

A month later, in follow-ups with Kerns and Rullamas, they say, in effect, "These cases take time." Incensed, I threaten to kick ass—don't need to "take names"—when I'm next at police headquarters on Seventh. Months later, still nothing in either case.

****

Valerie and Steve soon move through the Caldecott Tunnel to a newer 'burb twenty minutes east of Oakland and Berkeley, which seem more like cities than the 'burbs they once were. The fleeing couple chooses refuge in an apartment complex known for its security. Soon, the Holts are featured in ads to attract other youthful renters. They'd moved on up from less-safe neighborhoods; they'd lived in a noisy, oft-sketchy apartment complex in Albany before moving to a seemingly safer cottage in Oakland. As kids, Valerie, Lynn, and Autumn had explored abandoned Leona "fool's gold" mines near their grandmother's house and cottage. Their anecdotal evidence about decreasing safety in the area confirms what Orsic and I found in our Oakland study.

Lake Tahoe, California – January 1984

One Friday, Lynn and I drive to the Donner Pass area of the Sierras to ski with Ethan and Melinda, friends from the Warehouse. As an architect, Ethan plans to enlarge the small house they just bought in tiny upscale Piedmont, bordered on all sides by Oakland. They're friends with a couple a block away on a border where one side of the street is Piedmont and the other Oakland. When I mention how quick police response time is in Piedmont, we discuss the huge difference the side of the street also makes regarding the quality of schools and city services. The couple's infant punctuates our long Friday drive with laughter, crying, and often annoying noises, much to Melinda's dismay.

On Saturday, Melinda stays in our Truckee-area cabin with her daughter, while I enjoy skiing with Lynn, a novice who keeps up with me in my ill-fitting rental boots. Ethan leaves us early on, though, in search of more challenging Sugar Bowl runs. Upon our return, Melinda complains, as she often does, about how difficult she finds this baby thing.

Knowing Melinda's frustrated and itching to ski, Lynn volunteers to swap places with her Sunday. I offer to stay behind too, but Lynn insists I ski with the others. She helped care for her infant half-brothers and doesn't really need Melinda's elaborate instructions about bottle warming, feeding, and burping.

Ethan takes me aside just before departing for home Sunday and says, "I heard Colleen lost her bracelet in the snow. I think Lynn's passed the ski-trip test with flying colors."

"No test, my man. But she is a keeper. Gonna ask her to move in with me."

****

Lynn accepts my offer to cohabit, but not until grilling me. "So tell me how you decided we should live together?"

"Well, you, and life lately, have taught me to trust my heart, my feelings."

"Could never fathom how you—most males, really—never learned to express your feelings. I mean beyond anger, envy, jealousy, the basics."

"Well, we weren't taught much about 'em. 'Tis why we're slow figuring out relationships, even life goals."

"Your main goal was to spread nonviolence, like Johnny Appleseed?"

"It's taken lotsa hits lately. Got new goals now—"

"To start a family?"

"Yeah, and to love you, and to caution people about misguided crim justice policy."

After moving in, Lynn's too busy to get to know Crista, but she sees her male friend come and go. Lynn's even encountered him a couple of times, but the guy just nods and moves on. She calls him "Mystery Man," and soon his mystery engulfs us.

PART IV – THE EXECUTIONER

CHAPTER 29
Deceptive Siren. Marriage.

Oakland, California – *1984*

Barely two months after the last break-in, burglars come again to our leafy, sunny hillside—ransacking again Lynn's and my place and Crista's downstairs. Two people for sure, because half-empty beers and two plates with food from our fridge sit on our kitchen table. The burglars know all three of our schedules since they've taken their sweet time eating. My new double-deadbolt locks prevented them from walking out with large items like my new color TV, but they handed smaller electronics and stuff to each other through broken windows.

As I'm boarding up Crista's window, I ask whether she's got a clue who the culprits might be. She doesn't but seems more interested in adjusting the tight top she's wearing than solving our problem. I try to look just at her eyes as I ask, "Does anyone know your daily routine?"

"I've only told a few people about my finally landing a job."

"Congrats on the Napa winery gig! D'ya think another tour guide might've figured out where you live?"

"Doubtful. But, as you know, I've had people over for parties, sometimes strangers, friends of friends."

"Might any have staked out the place to see when all three of us are gone?"

She balks at giving a straight answer and instead blurts out, "Scary!"

Stymied and caught off guard, I say, "Don't worry. I'm installing an alarm system."

****

I dig deep for the bucks to comply with what seems to be responding officers' mantra: "Alarm the place." But I'll be damned if I'll hire ineffectual OPD officers from Burglary who install alarms as a side business. Instead, I employ some other guys to hardwire windows and doors so they'll trigger an exterior alarm if breached. They also leave handheld remotes to sound the alarm if someone is outdoors and is confronted or in need of medical help. Rather than having a company monitor the system 24/7 for an outrageous fee, I trust the neighborhood Fundamentalist Christians will call the cops if the alarm sounds.

Soon after our talk, Crista surprises me by giving notice and breaking her lease. Though I still suspect she's withholding info about the burglaries, I decide not to risk charging her breach fees. Anger plus her narcissistic sense of entitlement means she might retaliate by match or by muscle. Since I've survived the Warehouse fire and the equivalent of punches to the face—six cleft surgeries—it's okay to start an investigation rather than a fight.

I begin by sketching a composite of what Lynn and I remember of Mystery Man's face and estimate his height around six feet and weight, two hundred pounds. I show the sketch to students and friends who follow sports to see if they recognize the face.

I finally get enough feedback from my sketch that I figure out he's the second string for the superstar running back for a Bay Area pro-football team. My informants say he has a wife and kids who live in Alameda.

I theorize Crista's been a kept woman by this man, who, from the git-go, gifted her a roll of cash, which she used for her rent and first-and-last deposits. He's likely to have also paid her board as well as room, and more importantly, given her cash for cocaine, which has surpassed alcohol as the drug of choice for Bay Area pro-athletes.

Crista, and maybe he, probably bragged to someone about the what and the where of their recreational drug use. The word spread. The burglars likely wanted Crista's cocaine, which they thought she'd stashed in her apartment or upstairs in mine. Even though I give this info to my friends Officers Eberhardt and Kyle, who have burglary and drug expertise, the OPD is unable to crack my case.

****

When creating the syllabus for my current Crim course, I added a segment on burglary, to which criminologists don't pay much heed, despite being the most common crime in the U.S.. In class, we debate paying higher taxes for more police attention to burglaries. Radicals and Marxists predictably say consumer stuff isn't worth cops' time. Others counter with the "Broken Windows" theory I've taught, like the student alleging, "You radicals wanna turn burglary into a petty crime. But if you did, it would degrade people's quality of life and create a climate where serious crime would flourish."

Students express a range of concern regarding burglary, and we analyze who feels vulnerable and why.

****

Bringing my work home, I ask Lynn if certain crimes trigger feelings of vulnerability for her. She says she's afraid of burglary and rape, given what's happened in our neighborhood and her grandmother's. Since there's been no further trouble with Crista gone, I convince Lynn my inside job explanation is probably true, and she can relax about burglary. We talk about her rape fears at some length. When I finally point out we lock doors religiously, unlike Val and Steve, she realizes she's probably not going to be victimized by a so-called opportunity rapist like Val was.

Lynn then changes the topic while correcting worksheets from her second graders. "Hope you're still willing, after we cohabit a few more months, to marry and start having kids?"

"Well...ahhh."

"Has something changed?"

"Got my own fears, like a fear of messing up the second time around."

"Fear of failure?" Lynn asks.

"Yeah. And I may have an even bigger challenge, 'fear of intimacy.' If I've got it, may stem from being abandoned for weeks at a time for surgeries as a baby."

"I thought your mom brought expressed breast milk to the hospital to hold and bottle feed you every day."

"No idea how long nurses let her hold me. Was before Harlow's infant monkey studies."

Lynn says, "Mitchell reawakened *my* fear of intimacy...when I found he'd left me. Kicked up memories of when Mom sent me to Aunt Sally's when I was three."

I still her hand with her red pencil, saying, "These things may've taught us that intimacy results in abandonment."

"I'm also afraid to commit to us for a related reason," she says.

"What's that?"

"Because you say 'Stop phoning your mom so often'."

"You've gotta cut the cord sometime! No pun intended."

Refusing to laugh, Lynn says, "Mom 'n I have been best friends forever—"

"But you've got a new best friend now...me."

"I know." Pausing, then, "Maybe we should see a therapist to deal with our fears of intimacy, of marriage."

I think, *Sharon never wanted therapy; this is too good an offer to ignore.* "Sure, let's," I say.

"Great! I'll check with a friend who swears by her couples counselor."

Berkeley, California – Winter 1984

Dr. Nanette Swartz greets us in her business-like, sparsely furnished office. After we're all seated, she pages through forms we filled out in the waiting room. She puts them on a table next to her and peers over her reading glasses, saying, "You do understand my forte is brief, not long-term, counseling?"

We nod.

"Then let's start with you, Lynn. Karl wrote he thinks the blaming you do when fighting hurts your problem-solving efforts as a couple. What d'ya think?"

"I agree. I've wrestled with why I fight so differently from him."

"And Karl's style of fighting is...what?" Swartz asks.

"He's cool and analytical, while I blame...and yell."

I interject, "I *am* trying to be more emotional and feelings oriented."

"That's right," Lynn says. "And I'm trying to blame less."

With a frank but caring voice, Swartz helps us explore our fighting styles and why we bicker so much. I'm dying to take notes, but that's what counselors do.

Wrapping up our brief exploration, Swartz says, "Be glad you're both fighting and verbalizing your needs. You do seem to meet in the middle often, which means one of you isn't always the good guy, the other the bad guy."

"That'd be boring," Lynn says.

Swartz says, "As I understand it, the main reason you're here is you guys alternate being committed to the relationship. Rarely both at once. Correct, Lynn?"

"Yes."

"I noticed you wrote you've done counseling around your fear that intimacy will lead to abandonment, loss."

"Yes," Lynn says. "Karl also has similar fears that—"

"Don't worry about him, Lynn," Swartz says. "What about your intimacy fears? What's caused you to pull back lately?"

"Well," she pauses, "marriage scares me when I realize I'll lose my closeness to my mom."

"Karl notes you only phone her once a day now. Sounds like you're making progress."

"Yes, I'm trying hard to pull away."

"Moving from a known relationship to an unknown one isn't easy," Swartz says, "but I'm confident you can do it."

After probing my commitment issues—involving abandonment feelings around my mom and Sharon—Swartz sums up, saying, "Like Lynn, you must've realized that there are necessary losses in life that are part of maturing." She studies us for a moment and says, "A colleague I know would call you both dance-away lovers. He just published a book about clients like you—one moves toward commitment, the other dances away. Then they reverse roles."

"My analogy," I say, "is we're pilots afraid to land our planes on an aircraft carrier bobbing on stormy seas."

Swartz smiles, shifts in her chair, then clears her throat. "So let's get real and figure out who wants to land on the heaving ship of matrimony. Karl, you say you're trying to listen to your gut now, giving up weighing the pros and cons of Lynn as a life partner—"

"That's been my way: lists, balance sheets—"

"So, do you want to marry Lynn? 'Yes' or 'no.' "

I sit up straight, look down at the floor, then look at Swartz, and say, "Wow. You said you do brief therapy, but—"

"But what?" Swartz asks.

"Don't know." My mind spins. *Be decisive. But past relationships. Sharon. Mitchell. Arguing. Bickering.*

Swartz breaks my reverie. "Answer my question, Karl. Yes or no?"

I collapse back into the softness of my chair, and from deep within my soul, I hear the answer. "Yes! I want to marry Lynn."

We all collectively catch our breath.

Swartz now faces Lynn, asking point-blank, "Do you want to marry Karl?"

Lynn looks at me, then reaches for one of the glasses of water on the table in front of us. "I drink eight glasses every day, you know." She drinks, smiles, and then says, "Yes!"

The three of us look at each other, a bit dazed by what just happened.

An eternity of silence.

Swartz breaks it and says, "This isn't the first marriage I've brokered in this office."

We all laugh.

Swartz uncrosses her legs, drinks from the glass at her side table, and stands up.

****

Lynn and I hold hands as we walk out of Swartz' office and don't speak until we're out of the building, since something sacred has occurred.

"I think I need to formalize this," I mumble. I stop and get down on one knee, in the parking lot. *Bye, bye, ideal. Hello, real. No more Hollywood perfection.* "Will you marry me, Lynn?"

"Have you thought this through?" she asks, chuckling.

"Yes, and we should do it anyway," I answer with a wry smile.

"In that case, yes."

We embrace and kiss, longer than we usually would in public.

Then we talk nonstop about whether to announce our news, when to get married, and where to honeymoon. We conclude we're both still anxious about this big commitment. So, we decide to keep quiet about it and have a small wedding in front of only our relatives. We send out a handful of invitations for a ceremony over Memorial Day weekend in our living room in Oakland. Because Lynn hasn't been to Europe, we decide to honeymoon there early summer before having a delayed wedding reception with all our friends.

Oakland, California – May 25, 1984

My new downstairs tenant, a professional photographer, agrees to document our ceremony and reception in exchange for a month's rent. Our ceremony includes Lynn's relatives, ranging from her twelve-year-old half-brother to her ninety-year-old great-grandmother, who lives with Lynn's Grandma Conde above the cottage. No one gives Lynn away since Carole refuses to invite either of her ex-husbands. Representing my side: Scott, Gayle and her new husband Don, plus my mom's sister, Ruth. Everyone seems to enjoy the ceremony except Carole, who doesn't cry, laugh, or emote.

After dropping my Aunt Ruth at the San Jose airport to return to Los Angeles, Lynn and I continue south to Monterey for our wedding night. The next morning, Valerie calls us to say, "Didn't want to tell anyone and spoil your day, but Grandma Lawson died yesterday, just before your ceremony." Lynn takes this news hard. She admired Lawson very much, following her into teaching. Lynn never blamed her for not being able to rescue her only child, Lynn's dad, who got into drugs after Lawson's husband split.

****

By the time our honeymoon trip to Europe rolls around, we're good and ready for our respective school terms to end. Lynn and I enjoy the early summer weather in Europe and pack a lot into our three weeks. The trip's a cultural eye opener for Lynn and a wonderful replay of past edifying and pleasurable times I've had in Europe.

Berkeley, California – August 1984

Our delayed reception at the historic Hillside Club building in Berkeley proves to be fun for all, except Carole again, who seems aloof and unhappy. Ric, Lee, Ned, and some of my relatives—plus a mix of Lynn's friends and relations—give wonderful toasts. We dance to the same band I'd hired for my Warehouse farewell and eat hors d'oeuvres and a salmon buffet prepared by my friend Tina, once a close sorority sister of Sharon. She and I puzzle over the fact that Sharon's ended all contact with former friends and stopped painting.

****

In the fall, Lynn dives into her teaching responsibilities with gusto but grows to dislike the congested freeway and tunnel to Alameda she has to endure twice daily. She's reverted to phoning her mom more often these days.

Out of the blue in October, Lynn says, "A three-day weekend's coming up. What'dya think of me going to Reno with a few teachers?

Kind of a girls' weekend away? You and I have been underfoot a bit of late."

"Yeah. Our place is small, and marriage is work."

"We'll fly to Reno. Know it'll cost, but one teacher's got a timeshare, so no hotel fees."

"Food and drink—your only expenses as long as you don't gamble like your dad."

"Never would. Was his downfall. Another teacher'll get us to and from the airport."

"Sure. Go. Maybe I'll drive down to Gilroy on Saturday and visit Lee. He probably doesn't get many freeloaders anymore, 'cept at garlic festival time."

CHAPTER 30
Betrayal, Sexual Assault, and a Power Struggle

October 1984

When a fellow teacher phones for Lynn early Saturday morning, I tell her Lynn is in Reno with other teachers. After the caller questions that, I phone Lynn's airline and find she wasn't on any Reno flights. I phone Lee, canceling "because something's come up," and then distract myself with yard work. I'm weary with worry by the next afternoon, when I hear Lynn's key in the door. She says she's back early because two girls got sick. I wait for her to unpack, freshen up, and enter the living room where early evening shadows underscore a cloudy day. We sit on the sofa.

"You sure you went to Reno?" I ask.

"Of course I did."

"But you didn't!"

"Why wouldn't I?"

"C'mon? A teacher phoned for you. Said she hadn't heard of any girls' trip."

After hesitating a bit, Lynn breaks down in tears and turns away.

"I-I went to Portland...wh-where Mitchell's on parole."

"He's outta prison?" I yell as I jump up from the sofa.

"Since September," she mutters, bent over, staring at her hands.

"Holy crap! But why visit?"

"This last month, Mom's been on me nonstop to go."

"So that's why you changed topics on the phone whenever I got near you?"

"Mom all but demanded we go—"

"Why'd you give in?"

"She wouldn't let up—"

"But why?" I pace the living room, pounding my right fist into my left palm.

"To get closure, find out why he abandoned me."

"After eight years?"

"You know abandonment freaks me out. Never told you or Swartz, that besides sending me away as a toddler, Mom sent me and my sisters away when I was five."

"Damn Carole! Sharon left me too. I get abandonment, but for you to lie—"

"I shouldn't have. Know lying was wrong too."

"We're still newlyweds!"

"I'm so sorry, Karl. I truly messed up." She grabs my hand and pulls me to the sofa.

"So, why did he leave you?"

"Unlike Mom, who had no reason to abandon me, Mitchell did."

"And?"

"People were threatening him. He owed money. He likes nice things. Fancy watches—"

"Jewelers don't threaten, but dealers do. Was he dealing?"

"Don't know."

"Likely was. Wouldn't clear out his Alameda place unless lotsa mad customers."

"He's vague about stuff. Always has been."

I sit down, stymied, and then ask what they did. Lynn says Mitchell met her flight, and they took a bus to Portland State where he'd just moved after time at a halfway house. While playing outdoor miniature golf next to the campus, Lynn demanded to know what landed him in prison. He wouldn't say, but at the snack bar, he treated her to a sandwich and talked her into a beer. The midafternoon beer caused her to let down her guard and agree to see his dorm-room on campus.

"Jesus, Lynn!" I cry out.

"It was really small, and we had to sit on his ratty couch. He said the chair he used at his table to eat and study was broken."

"I bet."

"Yeah. He lied about studying. Told me later he missed the enrollment deadline. Anyway, he opened two beers from a mini-fridge and started to guzzle his. I didn't touch mine. In fact, I got up to pee soon 'cuz of the lunch beer. When I returned to the couch from the dorm bathroom down the hall—"

"Did you ask if he's allowed to drink on parole?"

"No. I was too busy answering his barrage of questions...about you, about Europe." She hesitates. "Suddenly, he grabbed my face and kissed me on the mouth."

"Damn it, Lynn!" I jump up again and start pacing.

"I didn't encourage him. I swear."

"And?"

"He put his arm around my shoulders, and I almost wrenched free."

"Sheesh!"

"I yelled, 'Stop it! I'm married. I love Karl.' He then asked, 'Why're you here, then?' and I asked, 'Why'd you go to prison?' He was holding my shoulder so tight that I could barely move. With his free hand, he started pawing, groping me."

I stare at Lynn's eyes—my mouth open, heart exploding in my chest. I then look at my hands.

"I struggled free enough to hit him. He kept warding off my blows, saying he loved me and pawing me. I finally broke his hold, stood up, and grabbed my stuff as I raced out his door. He chased me down a coupla flights of stairs–."

"Jesus, Lynn!"

"I ran, zigzagging to a nearby street, losing him. I got a taxi to the hotel Mom had reserved for me. I hid in my room and eventually moved my return trip up a day. Though I hadn't told Mitchell where I was staying, I hardly slept that night: worried he'd call Mom and track me down, worried about us, about you."

I look up from my hands and mumble, "I'm speechless."

"The hotel shuttled me to the airport. Mom picked me up, and I yelled at her all the way to Mountain Boulevard, where I had her drop me, shy of our street so you wouldn't see her car."

"Great," I murmur.

"Really thought I could just slip away, find out the truth, and return."

"All you had to do was lie to me...lie about Reno, lie about teachers?"

"I'm so sorry, honey."

"And jeopardize our marriage?"

"Stupidest thing I've ever done."

"And risk contracting a disease, even AIDS?"

"We didn't have sex, I swear. You gotta believe me."

"I'm trying to—"

"But there is one thing...Mitchell kissed me so suddenly that my mouth was relaxed. He pushed his tongue into my mouth."

"What the f—"

"It was so quick. I forgot to mention it—"

"That kinda kiss means saliva!" I yell. "And it can transmit AIDS if there are open sores."

"Oh, Christ, I had a canker sore or two."

An eerie quiet envelops us.

With tears streaming down her face, Lynn asks, "So what should we do?"

"Don't know."

"I'll get an AIDS test," she sobs. "I'm so, so sorry, Karl. Don't hate me."

"You gotta wait six months to take it. AIDS takes time to develop—"

"We can put off trying for a kid."

"I want to believe you didn't contract AIDS."

"I did ask Mitchell when I arrived if he'd had sex or injected drugs—in or outta prison."

"I'm sure he said 'no.'"

She nods but grabs my hand, pulling me back to the couch.

"I wanna make it crystal clear, he's history. Was the day he left Alameda." She puts her head on my shoulder.

I tense up momentarily, then relax.

****

The next day, I ask Lynn how exactly Carole persuaded her to visit Mitchell, knowing Lynn can recall conversations like a tape recorder.

"Mom first broached the idea during our Tahoe trip last August. Mitchell had been phoning her since April, when he learned he'd probably be paroled in September. Mom told me, 'He's still in love with you.'

"'I'm married!' I said. 'Anyway, why should I care? He left me.'

"'You've always wanted to know why. He says it wasn't another girl and he's been thinking about you ever since. I've kept the letters he's written you.'

"'Burn 'em. Don't want 'em.'

"'I'll pay for your plane and hotel,' Mom said, 'Make all the arrangements. Karl won't ever know.'

"'He's not dumb. He's a criminologist. Knows about criminals.'

"'Fly up on the QT when Karl's away giving a paper.'

"'No! That's crazy. Anyhow, we're trying to start a family.'

"'Ahhh, I know...Tell Karl you're going to Reno with girlfriends.'

"'Mitchell's a criminal!'

"'He's a good guy. Maybe got caught with drugs. Your father used drugs too.'

"'Why're you so into Mitchell?'

"'I remember his time with us. He loved the boys. Kept us laughing.'

"'Karl's pretty funny too.'

"'Mitchell's turned his life around. He's getting paroled because of good behavior. All I ask, Lynn, is think about it. I'll arrange everything.'"

"I stomped away."

Blood's pulsing in my temples. My head's ready to explode. Lynn tries to hug me, but I resist. I stifle the urge to race to Carole's and scream at her, because I need to know more, since Lynn, not Carole, acted out the harebrained scheme.

Lynn tells me how Carole then continued pushing her, especially after Mitchell's release to the halfway house, where he could call Carole daily. When he finally moved from the house to the dorm, Carole went into overdrive, constantly phoning Lynn about Mitchell's plan to get a computer-science degree. Carole kept hammering away that Mitchell's upbringing matched Lynn's better than mine did.

Lynn admits she weakened at one point, telling her mom, 'Okay, okay, I'll think about it.' Her mom then became turbocharged, even lying by saying Mitchell had stopped smoking cigarettes. Eventually, Lynn says she gave up fighting Carole and yielded.

I decide to confront Carole soon, but first I gotta check in with Orsic.

****

Seeking out Ric on campus the next day, my face flushed, I tell him about Lynn's trip to Portland and the manipulative role Carole played.

"You're in a power struggle with Carole...over Lynn," Ric says.

"Yeah. I'm pissed at Carole but can't alienate her—she may be the only one who can keep Mitchell away."

"Don't let Carole off the hook. She's violated a basic norm. Marriage is sacred, no matter how charming she thinks Mitchell is. She's no different than Dederich, trying to wreck Synanon marriages."

"I'm pissed too, at the parole board that released Mitchell. 'Parole' is French for 'promise,' and Mitchell promised not to drink, not contact prior victims like Lynn—"

"He victimized her?"

"Stole from her when he abruptly left Alameda and his bartending job."

"Bet he dealt on the side," Ric says. "Probably thought some of the bucks he handled from big spenders at his bar were his. Must've been aware of the risks of dealing at work, though."

"My guess is he used cocaine too."

"If so, watch out. Studies show coke's a substance that users tend to relapse with."

"Hear ya. Mitchell's the one I'm really in a death struggle with. Lynn says he wants to come here. Win her back."

"If he does, don't challenge the idiot. You don't how psychopathic he is!"

****

That night, I drive to Carole's. I confront her in her foyer after making sure her boys are out of earshot.

"Why're you trying to wreck my marriage?" I demand.

"Don't mean to."

"You misjudged Mitchell, just like other men in your life."

"What do you know? And, for the record, I'm just unlucky in love."

"Don't talk to Mitchell again, or write him—"

"No can do!"

"You're putting Lynn and me in danger."

"Oh please. He'd never hurt anyone."

"A nice guy 'til he isn't. Lynn says he yanked your youngest's arm once, hurting him."

"Probably 'cuz he dawdled getting outta Mitchell's van," Carole retorts.

"That's no excuse. And it doesn't gibe with your belief Mitchell likes your boys."

"He included 'em in outings he took with Lynn. He made us laugh. Just last week on the phone, he imitated Steve Martin's Czech guy again."

"Still a cutup after years in prison! Bet you still don't know what he was in for."

"Doesn't talk about that. Not my business . . ."

"So, what do you talk about?"

"How much he still loves Lynn."

"Gimme a break, Carole." I shout. "Ask him why he sexually assaulted her Saturday." My patience gone, I open the front door, then slam it behind me as I leave.

Driving home, I think, *the old me would worry I'm being too harsh with Carole.* I mumble out loud to convince myself of Carole's absurdities:

"She had five kids and was divorced twice by age thirty-seven. Has managed to continue her dysfunctional ways ever since. She's the 'single head-of-household mother' progressive liberals fawn over. Yet she's irresponsible as hell. She's currently enabling a possibly dangerous ex-con who's had plenty of time behind bars to romanticize a relationship with her daughter...my wife."

CHAPTER 31
Kafka in Justice Land.
Sleuthing a Psychopath.

Fall *1984*

Now that Mitchell has sexually assaulted Lynn and might come to reclaim her, she and I need to know more than ever what sent him to prison and how dangerous he is. I phone Oregon's main state prison, in Salem; a sleepy place, I'd guess, like so many other state capitals across the U.S.

After hearing why I'm calling, the prison official I'm routed to says, "Ya gotta be kidding. Tons of inmates, last name Lewis."

"He's from Portland."

"Not helpful. Largest city in Oregon. Five times the size of Salem."

"Just need to know the guy's crime."

"We only know what inmates tell us 'cept unusual cases."

"Then guards could tell me if Lewis told 'em something?"

"Only if Lewis gave 'em written permission. And even then, guards are just too busy. Slammed here at the slammer!"

When I don't chuckle with him, he says with an edge, "Callers like you add to our workload. Too many inmates. Not enough staff."

"Should I try the District Attorney's office in Portland?"

Impatient now, he replies, "They're busier than we are. Anyway, you'll need much more than a name, son, to get anywhere."

"Like what?"

"Gotta end this."

"Thanks for your time—"

Click!

I stare at the phone. I know that as a prison inmate, Mitchell's a felon, not a misdemeanant, because defendants sentenced to more than a year need more services than a *jail* can provide. I ponder, *If he only dealt drugs, he'd be a nonviolent Class B felon. But I need to know if he's a violent Class A one. Gotta get creative here.*

I figure the prison, as is customary, released Mitchell to wherever he committed his crime. Guessing it's Portland, I phone their Community Corrections program because they typically run the halfway houses that smooth felons' adjustment upon release. The respondent is terse, saying, "Can't help you unless you have a case number. Try the courts for that."

All I get from the court secretaries routing my calls around is the realization that I'm wrong in assuming that Oregon's got the typical municipal and superior court system. A couple of annoyed secretaries try to explain the differences among Oregon's district-, circuit-, justice-, and specialty courts. Then someone's accidentally helpful, though dispiriting, "Be sure you absolutely know which court dealt with Mr. Lewis, then petition it for the case number, but it could take weeks to get it."

Phoning all sorts of courts, and then waiting weeks, will take forever. *Maybe,* I think, *we could ask Mitchell's relatives, but they might distort, withhold, or not know. Or we could even ask Mitchell.* Then I realize how irrational it'd be for us to enter the lion's den or actually stick our heads in the lion's mouth.

****

If I've got to continue slogging through bureaucratic muck, using still-expensive phone calls, I'd better be sure I'm on the right path. I consider calling Scott, who's winding up his M.Arch with time-consuming critiques of his and fellow students' building designs and architectural models. I hesitate calling Gayle at first because of our tangled past with courts, but I've got to share the jam I'm in and need a female perspective. By chance, she's got a reason to come to Berkeley tomorrow, so we meet at Caffe Med on Telegraph.

Upon settling in for coffee at the shop with an iconic blue and white striped facade, I thank her again for coming to my wedding and reception, knowing it took guts after so much bad blood between us. I then disclose an insight, that I may've opposed Eve because of distrust of adults, due to being "abandoned" by Mom and Dad for weeks-long hospital stays for each cleft surgery.

Gayle reciprocates by admitting she may've sided with Eve for exactly the opposite reason. She trusted adults implicitly and wanted one in the room, reluctant to become one herself once both our parents suddenly died.

Then we abruptly stop discussing the probate battle, as if a crime-scene crew had cleaned up most of the bad blood between us.

"I hope we can continue rebuilding our family," I say.

Gayle says we can. In fact, she is still a Schonborn, having decided to keep her maiden name for good after her divorce from Ben.

I pick up on her word divorce, to say, "The 'd' word's been on my mind lately."

When Gayle's eyes blink noticeably, I say, "Lynn secretly visited her ex-boyfriend in Portland who'd just been paroled."

Gayle's mouth gapes open. "Astounding."

"Her mom pressured her, just as she did when the two of them visited him in prison,

"Wha-what? She saw him before? Why?" In her astonishment, Gayle knocks the sugar dispenser over.

She cleans up the spilled sugar as I explain that Lynn didn't get closure on her relationship with Mitchell her first visit and tried again the second one, She claims she's freaked out by abandonment, having been left for months at a time with others by her mom at age one and again at five.

Gayle responds, saying, "Speaking as a woman, Lynn sounds reasonable, since knowing why relationships end is important for females."

I then tell about Lynn's report of Mitchell sexually assaulting her, concluding with, "But I must view her account of the assault with eyes wide open. Too soon to trust her totally."

"Trust is one of the challenges of second marriages," Gayle responds, patting the back of my hand.

"There's a lot I need to know about Mitchell," I say. "Like, is he dangerous? And if so, I'll need to act fast or lose my wife... maybe even my life."

After Gayle and I discuss various sleuthing tactics I can employ, she concludes our time together by standing up. "Just know I'll support any action you take, Karl. You're my brother."

****

I decide to try finding Mitchell's parole agent before calling courts of all types and stripes. As an ex-con, discharged from halfway-house supervision, Mitchell has to have a parole officer whose mandate is to protect society from him relapsing. Trained in social work more than police work, a parole officer these days should understand my need to know Mitchell's crime.

I phone Oregon's parole board to find names of parole officers in Portland. The state bureaucrat tells me counties keep track of parole officers in Oregon because they, rather than the board, hire, fire, and allocate them. (I know this is highly unusual but don't get upset because I'm getting used to crim justice runarounds now.) The bureaucrat tells me to call the Multnomah County human resources office, but when I do so, I'm told to contact a specific Portland city office. This annoys me, taking me back almost to where I started with community corrections. Very *Kafka-esque*, I think.

I finally zero in on the director of the Portland area parole office. His secretary says, "He's not in, but try him at 7 a.m. tomorrow." I think, *Not easy for me, given my early class schedule this term. But I'll comply.* Hearing at 7 a.m. the next day that the director's already out in the field, I tell his secretary I'm about to lose it and may soon be added to her office's caseload. She doesn't get the joke.

When the director finally calls back, he says, "You'll have to call the sub-area office where the ex-con lives." After giving me the phone numbers of the several POs working the Portland State subarea, he warns that, for privacy reasons, POs can only reveal if they monitor a specific person you name. *They* can't go through parolee lists looking for a name you give them."

I immediately call the first parole officer in the southwest subarea of Portland. He says he doesn't have a Mitchell Lewis in his caseload. I try a second officer: ditto. I waste precious time over several days playing phone tag, only to get the same "I don't supervise him." I begin to worry Mitchell's on his way to Oakland to reclaim Lynn.

Oakland – November 1984

When I finally talk to a certain PO Grady Nelson, I've long since dispensed with pleasantries and flat-out ask, "Are you Mitchell Lewis' PO?"

He startles me by actually saying, "Yes."

I identify myself and say, "I'm so glad to have found you...at last."

"We parole officers—a slippery bunch like our parolees," he jokes.

"I need to know why Mitchell went to prison."

"Can't tell you. Confidentiality issue. Only the Fourth District Court can."

"But I need to know. He's after my wife."

"Let me guess what this is about. You think he's screwing her?"

"Crudely put, but close to the truth," I say. "I'm battling to keep my new bride."

"All's fair in love and war."

"Bull crap! Not when an ex-con's already assaulted your wife."

"Mitchell scares you?"

"What the hell? I just told you he assaulted her in his dorm room."

"Her word against his, Dr. Schonborn."

"Seems like Mitchell's got little self-control, especially when he's obsessed."

"Doesn't surprise me. Most of my clients are obsessed, when it comes to sex, money, drugs."

"So why not deter 'em from these things? Or if that doesn't work, return 'em to prison?"

"The board releases clients to me. I supervise 'em. Simple as that."

"You haven't answered my question about deterrents —"

"Can't stop 'em. They're like teenagers."

"Look. Parole rarely works. Studies show so-called 'good risk' parolees mess up almost as much as inmates who serve their full sentence."

"Well, aren't we fancy, Doctor? You some kinda expert?"

"Help Mitchell get a job. If he's got one already, get him another. Research shows he can break the hold drugs have on him —"

"You are a know-it-all!"

"With all due respect, Mr. Nelson, you're not doing your job."

"Which is?"

"Protecting my wife, me, the community from ex-cons."

"Mitchell says he's following the rules: not drinking, not —"

"He's lying. Phone him at all hours, test him —"

"I know how to do my job, Doctor! I've had it. This conversation's over!"

"I'm dealing with your boss from now on!" I bellow. Then I hear only a dial tone.

I stare at my hands as they clench and unclench. *I hate that I now have to track down Nelson's boss. Hate that I lost my temper and hate I'm losing my fervor to liberalize crim justice.*

But Nelson did reveal a clue.

Oakland – December 1984

After a moment or two, I make another phone call.

"Hey, Stark! Been too long —"

"Schorny, you dog. Ya know why? We two be dragged down into the academic vortex."

"Yes. We should be igniting our students' fire and passion, but our departments douse ours with endless committee work."

"Sense you need somethin', man."

"Kinda. Lynn's ex-con ex-boyfriend wants her back. Just attacked her while she was trying to find out why he ditched her, years ago, splitting for Portland."

"Yikes!"

"So yes, need a favor. Need this guy's criminal case number to find out what he did."

"Lynn doesn't know his crime?"

"He's been evasive, tight-lipped for years."

"Well, you're in luck, Schorny! I usually visit Portland at Christmas, but I frontloaded my classes so I can go early to do research at Portland's Historical Society."

"Fantastic! You'll have to go to the Fourth District Court. We can only get the case number by an in-person hand search through the Fourth's files."

"I can do that."

"Look for Mitchell Peter Lewis,' but Lynn thinks he may've started spelling his name L-o-u-i-s or L-u-i-s when he split to Portland."

"Okay. I'll look at all felony files with those names and even Lu-Veis, Lu-ess, or Le-wess. As a scrabble-playing English prof, know my spelling options."

"Great! And I'd suggest looking at 1976 through 1983 files if need be. Sorry, but all we know is Mitchell had to have served at least a year's time during that time frame."

"Consider it done…and I'll stand by for future PI assignments." We laugh.

"I'll send a check for expenses, Stark. Thank God for friends like you!"

****

To better understand the crim justice hassle I've been through, I soon locate Oregon's 1859 state constitution in the Governmental Studies

Library to see if it clearly favors offenders over victims. Sure enough, it does, by idealistically declaring that crime consequences should be based on principles of reform, not punishment. I think, *It seems obvious that any well-intentioned attempts to reform or rehab Mitchell failed miserably, compromising public safety.*

I then look at recidivism studies, most of which are unscientific, and discover failure too in Oregon. I conclude, *The state's philosophy, and once mine, is flawed. It needs to protect victims and society better.*

****

Within a week, Stark calls from a payphone in a "dim, depressing building," as he puts it.

"Damn certain I got the case number for Lewis."

"Awesome," I exclaim.

"Only found the number, nothing about his crime, but his file does indicate lotsa pages for him in document storage. Here's the number..."

After jotting it down, I gush profuse thanks, which Stark appreciates because he says he imagined bad guys looking over his shoulder as he went through box after box of file folders.

"I'm paranoid. My old Madison High classmates always wanted to settle some score with me. Some still do. They run the gamut from hippies with rap sheets to drugged-out Vietnam vets. Oh, and a younger brother too. He did time at the Rocky Butte in northeast Portland."

"Sorry to hear all that. Your own research at Portland Historical should stress you less."

"Oh yeah. I'll be experiencing no paranoia there, just black-mold spores from musty journals and letters." We both laugh.

Within minutes, I'm talking to a woman at the court's storage warehouse. After she gets Mitchell's ten-digit number from me, she hesitates, then asks, "Who are you?"

"A criminology professor."

"Have you talked to the Research and Funding people at County?"

"Oh, this isn't professional. It's a private matter."

"I'll have to talk to a supervisor. Please hold."

Sweat breaks out on my forehead. I tremble until she returns.

"This case number is special. Contains a secret code in its digits, so you'll have to call the Credentials and Authorizations people in a different building. Here's their number…"

I grimace and curse, then dial the number. The receptionist puts me on hold for a moment. Then I get a man who says, "This case file is restricted, so I need to ask you some questions."

I respond "no" to each query—Newspaperman? Other media? Writer? Creditor? Relative of the defendant? Then he says wearily, "Relative of a victim?"

"Yes," I say, hoping I won't have to elaborate.

"Good! All we need now is a check to pay for photocopying and we'll start the process."

Hallelujah. There is a god!

"Oh, I forgot, if you want audiotapes of the grand jury testimony in this case, you'll have to call another department."

What might Mitchell have done to warrant a grand jury?

I call and order the tapes, hoping never again to talk to a crim justice bureaucrat.

CHAPTER 32
A Cold, Calculated Killing

December 1984

Signaling the end of a protracted battle, I shout when my mailbox yields a package from the Fourth District Court, State of Oregon. I rush into my place and rip open the package at our kitchen table, spilling out audio cassettes and an inch-thick packet of papers. A quick flip through the seventy-seven-page case file brings me to some pages of photographs. I gasp. My mouth remains open and I stare at one photo after another.

As the magnitude of Mitchell's crimes sinks in, I hear Lynn entering the house. She sees me leaning over the table, and I say, "Come look. Now!"

Bending over the photos, she draws a quick breath too.

"Oh my god! My god!" She drops her keys and two student files on the floor as she collapses into a kitchen chair. "He did all that?" she wails.

"Not sure. Looks grim, though. Maybe this tape'll help." I grab a tape labeled "Prosecutor's Re-enactment to Grand Jury," and say, "Get our cassette player."

After we're seated in the kitchen, I load the cassette, hit play, and hear a man introduce himself as 'DA Michael Schrunk.' He begins his re-creation of Mitchell's crimes by saying it's based on facts from reports by responding officers, detectives, and forensic techs including the coroner. Schrunk tells the grand jury he'll speculate along the way about Mitchell's motives and conversations, important elements in crimes. He then starts, saying:

"Mitchell Lewis awakens early Monday morning August 10, 1977. Normally, he sleeps in after a busy weekend bartending at Jakes in southeast Portland. A line of cocaine helps him fully awaken after his few hours of fitful sleep. He blames his poor sleep on the coke he'd done at the end of last night's shift."

I hit stop and ask Lynn if she's okay so far.

"Yes, but can we believe DA Schrunk?"

"I think so. His facts persuaded a supermajority on this grand jury to vote to indict. That is, they believed there was enough evidence to send Mitchell to criminal court to answer the District Attorney Office's charges against him."

"And obviously, Schrunk's facts persuaded a second jury because Mitchell got sent to prison," Lynn says.

She hits play and Schrunk continues, "Mitchell dresses and puts his snub-nosed .38 revolver in a pocket of his leather jacket. He's dealt drugs in enough dicey neighborhoods to know that packing heat's smart, a way to protect against thieves, competitors, or unhappy customers.

"Munching on toast, he drives away from his small house, which is hidden from the street by fences, overgrown bushes, and untrimmed trees on all sides, the perfect place for drug dealing. As he crosses the Willamette River en route back to Jakes, he reflects on last night's shift. He'd kept busy at the bar and enjoyed feeling the joy of the crowd that drank, danced, and hung in one of Bridge City's fun clubs. Snorting a line in the restroom during his break kept Mitchell energetic, and was no biggie for him in a restroom where drugs, and sometimes cash, exchanged hands often.

"Jakes had started raking in money Friday afternoon when the club's three pools, as he called 'em—two pool tables and a hot tub on the patio—drew early customers that day in August.

"Liking that Powell Boulevard is less busy now than usual, Mitchell trusts that Cynthia Gifford, a co-owner's wife, will be by this morning to pick up the cash stashed over three busy days. She's had family matters, which prevented her from making her usual rounds of the bars she manages. Mitchell intends merely to borrow some money, much of which had just passed through his hands.

"He didn't mind that losing this money might briefly set Cynthia and her husband back. They lived in Lake Oswego, one of Portland's affluent suburbs, and he needed the money more than they. His coke supplier had gotten very angry last week when Mitchell couldn't pay in full again. That's the problem with using product you buy to sell. You go into debt. Fast!"

Lynn fidgets in her chair, knowing Mitchell mismanaged money.

"Rather than expose his easily recognized van in Jakes's parking lot, Mitchell eases it behind shrubbery along Powell. He walks several blocks to Jakes and unlocks the back door to get inside. Normally, he locks up the bar around 2:30 a.m. after tidying up and depositing the register's cash in the slot atop the drop safe. This keeps cash secure until Cynthia shows up. Only she knows the safe's combination.

"After tilting the window blinds facing Powell to keep passersby from seeing in, Mitchell hides in the closet at the entry end of the long bar. He counts on predictable Cynthia arriving close to the time she estimated when she told him she'd miss the usual pickup. (He assumes he's the only one who knows of this change of plans.) Sure enough, Cynthia's on time. When he hears her drive up, he tenses and puts his hand in his gun pocket. When Cynthia finally gets to the bar, Mitchell cracks the closet door to see her put a money bag on the counter. She then steps to the far end of the bar and bends over the drop safe on the floor below the register."

I stop the tape when Schrunk pauses to drink water, and ask Lynn, "Wanna continue? I think the photos showed what's coming."

"Yes. But don't you think Mitchell's risking being identified, going without a mask?"

I nod and say, "Crazy stupid" as I hit play. DA Schrunk continues.

"Cynthia turns the safe dial to and fro 'til its door pops open, and a jumble of bills and checks fall to the floor. As she squats down to retrieve them, Mitchell pushes the closet door open, sneaks up on her, and wraps a large towel around her head, causing her to scream and flail. Keeping silent, 'cuz she'll recognize his voice, he restrains her arms and puts a knee to her back to push her face-first to the floor. Somehow he stuffs a counter rag in her mouth to keep her quiet.

"Kneeling on her now with his full 240 pounds, almost crushing her, he spots a phone cord running along the baseboard. With adrenaline-fueled strength, he pulls much of the cord free from its staples, cursing under his breath that he must cut it somehow. Cynthia keeps squirming and murmuring beneath him.

"He smiles when he finds a lemon-wedging knife within reach, but it takes both dexterity and strength to cut the multistrand phone cord without letting Cynthia wiggle free. He ties her hands behind her and fastens the cord to the legs supporting a sink so she can't stand up.

"Satisfied that she's subdued, Mitchell grabs the money bag and scoops up some cash and checks scattered around Cynthia's writhing body.

"And then! He hears a vehicle enter the lot! His heart pounds even more than it has during his struggles with Cynthia. But it slows a bit when he realizes it's likely just the janitor, Roberto Ramos.

"Leaving Cynthia still tethered facedown on the floor, Mitchell grabs a bottle from the bar and rushes to the back door. Standing to the side, out of sight, he waits for the door to open. When it does, he crashes the bottle down on the hapless janitor's head. He hears Roberto cry, 'Wha-th—' before collapsing to the floor. Mitchell checks to be sure he is out cold, then runs back to Cynthia. But she's managed to shake off the towel around her head. When she sees him, her eyes enlarge to saucers, and she screams, 'Mitchell?' through the rag in her mouth.

"Realizing she's ID'd him, Mitchell's face turns red. As he rewraps her head, he commands her to be still and shut up. With only a moment's quiet now to ponder his predicament, he comes up with a solution as Cynthia starts kicking at his legs.

"Deluded that he's thinking clearly, Mitchell decides to further hog-tie Cynthia to make it look like someone else, maybe Roberto, tried to rob the place. To keep Cynthia compliant, he prods her repeatedly with his gun, which he then puts on the bar 'cuz he needs two hands to remove his jacket. He's worked up a sweat.

"He rips more phone cord from the baseboards, and after binding Cynthia's ankles, untethers her from the sink supports and ties her bound hands to her bound ankles. He hears her muffled words, over and over, 'You'll pay.'

Then, exasperated, 'Goddammit, Cynthia! You're making me do this.'

He grabs his gun and shoots her in her head. She collapses fully but still twitches.

He fires twice again at her head. She's lifeless, unmoving."

Schrunk stops talking to let the grand jurors process the enormity of what's happened.

Lynn grabs my arm, exclaiming, "Oh my god." I pat her hand.

After a few seconds, Schrunk continues, "As blood oozes from Cynthia's head into a widening pool, Mitchell's eyes widen too. He leaves the bar area, leans against a pool table, and stares blankly at Roberto, who also lies motionless.

"Mitchell throws the money bag on the floor to make it more visible. Then, knowing his .38 has two shots left, he slowly puts the muzzle to the top of his left bicep and fires, grimacing from the pain. Not satisfied, he woozily aims the muzzle a bit higher, firing again. This time, he shrieks from the searing pain he feels as the bullet tears into his shoulder. He quickly tosses the gun near Roberto, hoping Roberto's dead so cops will figure he's the murderous robber. If Roberto lives, Mitchell will have more work to do, blaming the crimes on a killer who's escaped.

"As Mitchell's vision and hearing fade to black, his excruciating pain causes him to pass out, crumpling to the floor."

Lynn starts shaking, and I hit stop and reach to hold her shoulders a bit.

I whisper, "Violence always seems to be followed by silence, and that's as it should be. Violence is sacred as well as profane."

Lynn hits play when she's ready, and Schrunk resumes, "After a period of time, Roberto Ramos stirs. He sits up, feels blood in his hair, then stands and staggers across the room, only to find both Mitchell and Cynthia unmoving, on the floor. He's so dazed and frightened, he doesn't check the condition of either friend. Walking as fast as he can, but haltingly, he makes it to the bowling alley across the street. The owners call for help and tell detectives later they heard no gunshots—either because they arrived after the carnage or were testing their noisy bowling-pin machines.

"Paramedics revive Mitchell, and then, sirens blaring, speed to get him and Roberto to nearby Providence Portland Medical Center for critical care. The coroner joins homicide detective Phil Todd at Jakes."

****

I stop the tape recorder and scoot my chair closer to Lynn's so I can put my arm around her. She repeats several times, "I can't believe it." Then placing her head in her hands, she starts to cry. After a good minute, she looks up at me and—seeing I've cried as well—says, "I'm sorry to put you through all this. If only I'd known."

I try to comfort her and myself by saying, "I'm not sure for whom the tears flow, but some are for us."

"And to think I once loved that guy...and was with him in his apartment a month ago."

Lynn regains her composure and says, "We must tell Mom right away."

****

We drive to Carole's house, and Lynn asks her to walk with us to nearby Lincoln Park to prevent the boys overhearing what we've just learned. I start by telling Carole about Mitchell's plan to rob the bar where he worked to repay a drug debt. And then, unable to let the story unfold fully, Lynn blurts out the grand jury's four counts against Mitchell—Aggravated Murder, Attempted Murder, First-Degree Robbery, and Second-Degree Assault.

Stopping dead in her tracks, Carole demands, "What the hell is Aggravated Murder?"

"It's 'murder with depravity in Oregon," I say. "Probably 'cuz he killed after hog-tying his victim."

Lynn summarizes Schrunk's narrative and then asks, "Still think Mitchell's a nice guy, Mom?"

Carole throws up her hands. "All news to me. Didn't know any of it."

"Because you never asked him," Lynn says, "during all those phone calls."

"Aren't you shocked?" I ask.

"Just trying to absorb it all," Carole says. "Know you're mad, Karl."

"You should be mad too, Carole. For Chrissake, he sexually assaulted your daughter!"

"Aw, you're just jealous, Karl, because Mitchell's tall, handsome."

"You've got nerve, Mom, calling Karl jealous. You've been jealous for decades."

Lynn reminds Carole of her jealous nature. "Remember how you often had me drive you in my VW to the house of a guy you'd been dating to see if he was home? And how you once insisted I barge into a guy's office to see if he was at work or out of town on business as he'd said?"

Carole yells at Lynn, telling her she's an ungrateful bitch because she, Carole, had let her live at home all through college. Carole continues her rant, then finishes, saying, "Leave! Go away."

"Huh?" Lynn reacts.

"Go," Carole insists. "To your house in the hills. You too, Karl. Go!"

On the way home, Lynn says that Carole's obsessed with looks — her own and others'. Not sure of her own attractiveness, Carole changed her hair color with each man, going from blond to brunette to red-haired, depending on her partner's preference. Lynn thinks Carole got her "lookism" from *her* mom, Helene, who appeared in movies while growing up in Hollywood during the '30s, the birthplace of the American glamor machine.

Lynn says, "Helene was the first to point out the asymmetry of your face to me. I hadn't really noticed it before."

I mention another type of asymmetry I've suffered from recently — the lopsidedness between my idealism and life's realism. I explain how four murders in four years have occasioned a series of funerals where I've had to bury my idealism about changing the crim justice system. Sometimes I feel like a mourner compelled to wear black for years.

This and another thought I've been having were likely triggered by an article I'm reading about the ripple effect of victimization. *My four bad guys hurt around* twenty-five *families — those of the seven victims, the offenders own immediate families, their families of origin, and nine other families of their close relatives.*

I tell Lynn, "My four villains impacted over a hundred people racked by every emotion imaginable, including ongoing, sometimes fatal, conditions like depression and PTSD."

****

The article and Mitchell's brutal killing of his boss brings my syllabus to life once again and motivates me to share with students some tie-ins between the study of homicide and the relatively new crim subfield called victimology.

I start by asking students to guess which third-world countries have the highest homicide rates. Students shout out Colombia, Brazil, Mexico, the Philippines.

"You're on target," I reply, "but did you know America's right up there with them all, even though we're considered first-world?"

We consider the irony and reasons, then discuss too that homicide's one of the few crimes that's comparable—and thus, rankable—across countries. It's because all nations define death and count dead bodies the same way. That's not true with most other crimes.

I then ask, "What's the thing in surveys Americans say they fear most these days?"

Almost in unison, students say, "Crime."

"Yes, but not just any crime. It's violent crime, especially lethal violence like homicide, that we fear most."

Students perk up, and some start taking copious notes. "Our sky-high homicide rate of 6.1 per 100,000 in the U.S. comes to 15,500 murders per year. But even more staggering is the human cost of murders to victim families and other survivors. Incalculable, since it lasts a lifetime." I pause. "Guess how many relatives, close friends, neighbors, and coworkers are impacted by a single homicide victim?"

Students have no clue.

"Around ten people," I say, "And multiply that by fifteen thousand victims. That's 150,000 people impacted each year! Sure, some get over it, but one murdered woman I just heard about, Cynthia, left a seven-year-old daughter who may never be the same."

****

Mindful now of what Mitchell's capable of, I install a gadget—not commercially available, but loaned by a police chief—that reveals and records callers' phone numbers. After just one day of use, Lynn and I discover Mitchell's tried to call three times. *Someone's obviously given him our number.*

CHAPTER 33
Brazenness Talks, and a Court Listens

December 1984

I begin going through Mitchell's case file page by page. The first outrage I encounter is an affidavit filed on his behalf from his hospital bed. In it, he claims he can't afford a lawyer, despite making good money at Jakes and presumably even better money dealing. At the time of his crimes, Mitchell lived in a nice area in Portland in a house, not an apartment as he did in Alameda.

Perhaps because he's in a hospital—a private one at that, likely getting care superior to a county hospital—the Oregon justice system cuts him slack. He's *not* asked to officially swear that, because of lack of funds, he can't pay for a lawyer without substantial hardship. It's unlikely any officials checked his bogus claim to be indigent.

These exceptions to the rules may've resulted from pressure from his several family members, privileged enough to travel over 3,000 miles from Clearwater, Florida to be with him. Amazingly, Mitchell's able to get the court to hire a private attorney for him, not an overworked and underpaid public defender, who'll represent him at public expense. He gets an up-and-coming Portland attorney, Samuel Carr, to represent him the same day he's declared indigent.

****

I tell Lynn how I imagine the very first conversation went, after pleasantries, when Carr met alone with Mitchell in his hospital room a week after the murder. I do this to clarify in my own mind what I've read, but mostly because Lynn, as a gifted storyteller herself, prefers learning from stories, certainly not from lectures. She perceives lectures to be the default for profs in relationships.

Both men are face to face, Carr seated, Mitchell propped up in bed.

I start: Carr says to Mitchell, "First, the bad news. Soon as you recover, the police will arrest you on four extremely serious counts, one of them generally punishable by death."

Mitchell doesn't react.

Ending an awkward silence, Carr continues, "The good news. A voter petition last year to reinstate the death penalty failed to get enough signatures, so the ban on it was in effect during your incident at Jakes."

Mitchell sighs. "Thank god! I asked my family to research that, but no one could find out."

"That's what lawyers are for! But, be advised, even though Oregon banned the death penalty in 1964, courts will reinstate it soon, especially for aggravated murders like you're charged with."

"Yeah, I know Oregonians love capital punishment. They're gonna hate me—"

"You're lucky, indeed, that appeals courts overturned Oregonians' wishes." A wry smile flashes as he says, "You're already undergoing *corporal* punishment—hope your pain's lessening, Mitchell."

"It is, but I wouldn't advise anyone to shoot 'emselves...Uh, how'd the cops figure I did it?"

"Your ruse was pretty lame. And you screwed up in more ways than one."

"How?"

"Fingerprints, for starters. Most damning, the ones on your gun, the bottle."

"Shoulda worn gloves but was in a hurry. Didn't wanna miss Cynthia's rounds."

Drilling directly into Mitchell's intense eyes, Carr barks, "Remember, I haven't heard any of what you've just said. Understand?"

"Yeah. Gotta be more careful, I guess."

"Especially 'round family."

Mitchell nods as he glances about the large room, often filled with family and medical staff.

"We'll plead 'not guilty' at your first hearing. Mostly because I've gotta read up on a newish defense I've been thinking about: namely, 'coke addiction made you do it.' Gotta also find an expert witness or two. So, we must delay initial hearings at least three weeks. We'll have to waive your right to a speedy trial, but that's worth it. With a little luck, you might have a medical complication, a wound infection, say, that'll allow us to stall things longer."

With similar disregard, and no likely shame over Mitchell's main victim, Carr and Mitchell meet later at the exact hour Cynthia Gifford's friends and loved ones gather for her funeral. The two meet in the hospital to engineer further delays on a Friday when Gifford's husband, daughter, parents, sister, and others mourn her death at Sunset Hills Memorial Park. In lieu of flowers, the family asks for donations to the local Shriners Hospital for Children, which specializes in cleft-lip-and-palate surgeries. I make a mental note to thank the family someday for this.

****

After reading a few more case-file pages, I tell Lynn that Carr's infected-wound ploy worked. He and Mitchell were able to delay the initial hearing, typically held soon after crimes are committed, until October third. Lynn shows she's a human calendar by counting quickly in her head and saying, "That's forty days!" (She's also a human clock, keeping me moving and punctual.)

I go on to explain that Mitchell and Carr also filed an address-change form with the court. I figure Carr pushed Mitchell to distance himself from his secluded drug-den-like house to one located next to a small country-style church. Mitchell's new house is possibly the home of his brother, who's probably complicit in allowing Mitchell also to use his first name as an alias often, becoming Kenneth J. Lewis.

****

I keep updating Lynn because she's got no time to read the case file. We dine one night on my infamous rubber chicken (the secret is forgetting it's cooking) at our small kitchen table, surrounded by '40s sunflower yellow counter tile with sky-blue edge tiles. I describe the all-important initial hearing where the combatants couldn't be more different.

In Mitchell's corner, a decidedly mod Sam Carr, decked out in plaid pants and sporting longish hair. His casual appearance is deceiving, though. A graduate of Brown and Vanderbilt Law School, Carr's got a private practice, where some clients say he charges a lot and will take your house in the process. In the other corner, conservatively dressed, ex-Marine Mike Schrunk, the prosecutor whose grand jury testimony we just heard.

I say, "Carr and Schrunk had squared off three years prior as young attorneys in a highly publicized case where a thirty-year-old Native American male stood accused of killing a family of four, bludgeoning three of them with a hammer while they slept in their beds."

"Yikes!"

"Carr won the first go-around, but Schrunk prevailed in a retrial because he'd found a fingerprint that placed the suspect at the scene of the crime."

"Oh, good."

"Now with Mitchell's case: understandably, Schrunk prevails out of the gate, as the judge rules to deny Mitchell bail and shut down a few of Carr's gambits during the hearing. In retaliation, Carr files a motion to change judges."

"How does he do that?" Lynn, a fast eater, asks, putting down her silverware.

"He likely perused the court calendar, including vacation schedules, to find a judge friendlier to him and his client. This judge-shopping is common, and introduces bias in the refereeing judges do in court battles."

"So why isn't it illegal?"

"Shopping's hard to eradicate. Friendly–that is, biased– judges just happen 'cuz judges start out as young adults, and often know one of the attorneys they're refereeing from college, law school, or a law firm."

"But, don't they try to be *fair* on the bench?"

"In court, yes, but behind the scenes, their biases subvert the impartiality of plea bargain deals, which most felons choose over a trial. Friendly judges also perpetuate gravy trains for expert witnesses when they automatically approve state funds for costly hired guns like the psychiatrists in Bill Hanson's case."

"Perverting justice," Lynn says as she carries her dishes to the sink.

"And get this. Judges also sign off on what court-appointed attorneys, like Carr, can charge, not unlike what the judge did approving Dragon Lady's attorney fees and expenses."

"What a racket!"

****

Further reading of Mitchell's file the next day reveals the following, which I hope to impart to Lynn:

Carr asks the new judge for an extra thousand dollars to reanalyze Mitchell's blood and urine samples. Carr hopes that a different analysis will uncover results to bolster his theory that some kind of addiction to cocaine (which speeds one up) caused Mitchell's murderous rage. I ponder, *While people know 'speed kills,' don't they know that this refers to killing oneself, not another person? And that 'speed' refers to meth, not coke?*

What's surprising isn't that the judge grants the request, it's that he allows Carr to keep the results from Schrunk. That means the judge sanctions a rather pricey fishing expedition plus an unusual provision that Carr needn't disclose if they caught no fish.

Carr also files a petition pleading that Mitchell's "not guilty due to mentally-debilitating drugs." He asserts that Mitchell *suffered from* abuse "at an addictive level" of the drug cocaine. And in case the judge denies this, Carr also claims Mitchell's supplier adulterated his coke, so it's unclear what exactly addicted Mitchell. Carr hopes the reanalysis of Mitchell's blood will reveal a morphine additive—showing Mitchell had done a speedball combo of cocaine uppers with heroin downers.

Defense attorneys typically try an addiction defense any time a new drug appears or reappears after some time. Historically, though, this defense fails because the medical term addiction doesn't work well, just like the term insanity, within the legal system. And also because research has found most substances aren't physically addictive. But Carr's counting on one of his other notions, the idea of psychological addiction, being unusual enough to intrigue prosecutor Schrunk. Carr hopes Schrunk may budge a bit when negotiating with Carr if it comes down to a plea bargain. And if this fails, Carr expects his friendly judge may see psychological addiction as a mitigating factor when sentencing Mitchell.

****

That evening, when I tell Lynn all about Carr's strategizing and Mitchell's possible victimization by his supplier, she exclaims, "Even if Mitchell's coke were adulterated, he still chose to use coke in the first place."

"Yup," I say, "he's accountable for using illegal drugs. Like a drunk driver, he's making a choice in advance to possibly hurt someone."

****

To deal with unfinished business with Carole, we drive to her house, and Lynn confronts her in her small backyard, saying, "We know you gave Mitchell our phone number, Mom."

"I didn't."

"Then why does our phone device show daily calls from him?"

Carole shrugs.

"And in case you didn't believe Karl the other day, I'm telling you in person, Mom. I have no feelings for Mitchell. Hate him, in fact, so never want him near me again."

"I've told him that already," Carole counters. Then turning to me, "Mitchell says you're controlling Lynn."

"Ridiculous!" I declare. "Look, Carole, you've got to convince him. Lynn detests him. Repeat it often. He's had years in prison to romanticize their relationship. Lynn moved on years ago. Has taken marriage vows. She just made an honest mistake visiting him."

"End of story, Mom!" Lynn says. "Convince Mitchell. Then tell him never to call again."

"Not easy," Carole says. "He's hell-bent on getting back with you."

"Show some spine, Mom, for once!"

"No matter what," I add, "don't give him our address!"

Carole's lip trembles. "Too late. I just gave it to him."

"What's wrong with you?" Lynn shouts.

We both turn and leave, glowering.

CHAPTER 34
Fie on Experts, Plea Bargains, and Psychopaths

I continue reading Mitchell's case file and make notes. I share them with Lynn whenever we have some time to talk.

Luckily, Carr fails to get his friendly judge to dismiss charges on the grounds that Mitchell suffered from diminished capacity due to psychological addiction. In this twist on a type of insanity defense, Carr purposely conflates Mitchell's use of powder cocaine with rock or crack cocaine. He should've listened to Harvard Med School reports that powdered coke doesn't addict users the way crack does.

And luckily, Carr also fails to get his expert, Dr. Norman Zimberg, to rescue Mitchell.

But I ask Lynn later, "Why does Carr, using taxpayers' money, fly psychiatrist Zimberg cross-country to interview Mitchell when Zimberg himself has cast doubt on Carr's cocaine addiction defense?"

"Because he can?" she answers. I continue, saying, "Mitchell wears a suit and tie for his plea-bargain hearing before the new judge, Richard Emory."

Lynn retorts, "Mitchell's a chameleon and a liar."

"Carr coaches Mitchell not only on how to confess but what to confess to. He helps him craft a handwritten confession as part of the plea bargain whereby Mitchell admits to committing just one crime. And that one's a simple murder, not an 'aggravated depraved-heart' one, which it is."

"Holy smokes!" Lynn shouts. "The court's allowed to drop the robbery and attempted murder charges? Fudge the truth like that?"

"Afraid so, because a plea bargain goes in the win column for the prosecutors who also don't have to prep for a full-blown trial they may lose, though it's not likely here."

****

Lynn's off to bed, dejected. But I put another tape into the player to hear how Carr and Schrunk's plea-bargain deal went down in front of Judge Emory.

Prosecutor Schrunk opens with, "Your Honor, I trust you've read the reports of various expert witnesses in this unduly expensive case."

"I have," Emory responds.

Schrunk continues, "A high-priced forensic chemist wasn't able to overturn the State's lab results, though he found one new detail that's not exculpatory at all. Moreover, another expert witness failed to disprove the basics of the State's case against Lewis. And most damning of all, esteemed Harvard psychiatrist Zimring cast doubt on the very addiction theory Counselor Carr hired him to present."

Emory then asks Mitchell, "Are these reasons stated by DA Schrunk why you're dropping your 'not guilty' plea?"

"Yes, Judge. And I hope you'll accept my plea proposal."

Emory responds, "I've decided to."

Mitchell's nonreactive, but Carr utters a sigh of relief. Emory then addresses Carr and Schrunk, "I'd like to compliment you attorneys—"

"Your Honor," Carr interrupts, "I want to emphasize that the defendant didn't sleep for forty-eight hours before the incident due to coc—"

"Strike my compliment!" Emory snaps. "You're pushing it, Counsel. No excuse. Every criminal, and noncriminal, in America has suffered from insomnia. Anyway, Mr. Lewis has pleaded guilty."

"Understood, Your Honor," Carr says.

I pause the tape and think, *Cheeky bastard, that Carr. He's complicit in Mitchell's continuing self-delusion.*

Based on the official forms in his case file, Mitchell found ways to deceive himself and disrespect the court. He wrote, "I was under the influence of cocaine" on one form, but on another, "I wasn't influenced by any drugs or intoxicants at the time of my crimes." Regarding his health, Mitchell reported that it's always been satisfactory. This, despite asking to delay a hearing for forty days because of a physical disability (his self-inflicted shoulder injury), and also asking for a dismissal of his case due to a mental disability.

All this equivocation makes me wonder, *Did Judge Emory, acting on behalf of the state, really read through Mitchell's paperwork?*

****

I restart the tape and hear Emory announce that a court break has just concluded and that the defendant should rise. I assume the noise on the tape is sheriff's deputies helping the shackled Mitchell stand. Then, Emory says:

"The court finds you, Mitchell Peter Lewis, based on your own admission, guilty of one count of Simple Murder per Secret Indictment C76-08-3389. The court orders that the other four counts—first-degree aggravated murder, attempted murder, and robbery plus second-degree assault—all be dismissed. I'll sentence you, Mr. Lewis, as soon as I see your pre-sentence investigation report. This court stands adjourned."

I lean back, reflecting, *No wonder there are critics of plea bargaining. The leniency of plea deals like Mitchell's, the secrecy of negotiations among so-called opposing attorneys, and the acceptance of deals by judges in oft-private hearings...all run counter to Lady Justice's ideals.*

****

There are critics too, of the next step taken in most criminal proceedings: the pre-sentence investigation into a convicted defendant's past. These are conducted by probation officers, usually with social science degrees, who supervise "lite" offenders rather than by parole officers assigned to heavy offenders. I've just joined these critics who believe the reports coming from these investigations invariably emphasize redeeming traits and recommend judges go easy.

For Mitchell's report, the investigator interviewed him and relied on his and others' hearsay evidence about his financial history, military service, family and community ties, and so-called contrition. Mitchell's report notes that his parents provided a normal, stable environment for Mitchell growing up in the Tampa Bay region, specifically in an area known for sunny weather and Clearwater Beach, whose fine white sand helps it consistently rank among the best beaches in the world.

In this privileged setting, Mitchell had exposure to the restaurant-resort business, which he later entered, and to major league baseball organizations, including the Yankees and Phillies, who've made Tampa their spring-training home since the '40s.

The report also suggests Mitchell's family will continue to support him emotionally, just as they did in the hospital and in strategy meetings with Carr. There's no mention that taxpayers paid for hours of the family's time with attorney Carr or that no one in this large Irish family informed Lynn about his crimes or helped her retrieve what he stole from her. The report also appears to have accepted, without questioning, Mitchell's rosy promises to continue his education and obtain skills-training in prison.

The report concludes by playing the "he's too smart not to get a second chance" card. And it argues for an "average-length" life sentence so he can get on with living in eight years, Oregon's average life term for whites in the '70s. This leniency is no accident. Early settlers wanted Christian forgiveness to rule, and that's why they named their capital Salem, sourced from Jerusalem, where the historic Jesus allegedly lived, preached, and died.

****

Six months after Mitchell's execution-style killing amid an orgy of crime, Judge Emory sentences him to "indeterminate life," meaning Oregon's Parole Board can release him most anytime for good behavior. Compared to sentences given the same week to minorities in Portland, one of the whitest cities in the U.S., Mitchell got off easy.

Mitchell didn't grow up in a Black ghetto, like Darnell Hayes, who came from a poor community due north of downtown Portland. Darnell's drug-addicted single mother raised him amid gangs, pimps, and prostitutes. Darnell is still incarcerated seven years later as a felon for just selling cocaine.

And Mitchell didn't come from a barrio, like Ricardo DeJesus in Portland, whom I also read about recently. Ricardo said, "Growing up, I saw drug users in my building's hallways and drug runners from my apartment window." Not surprising, then, Ricardo started making deliveries for dealers at a young age. "You could make $200 or $300 easy," Ricardo said. Like Mitchell, he went from being a person in the supply chain to a user. "I was my best customer!" DeJesus has served more time for nonviolent dealing and using than Mitchell did for his several violent crimes.

Mitchell also got away without *any* financial consequences. No full- or even partial- monetary restitution required for Roberto Ramos. For even the most indigent of offenders, judges and courts often craft a repayment plan for restitution and also for waived fines, jail fees, and such. I make a mental note, *Research the proportion of whites vs. non-whites saddled with such obligations.*

Mitchell's financial accountability is of more than academic interest. At one point, I tell Lynn what I estimate each phase of Mitchell's crime has cost Oregon taxpayers. A month-plus of private hospital care, hundreds of hours of fees for a private attorney and ancillary experts, seven years of prison room-board-amenities, followed by six months, and counting, of parole supervision. Lynn's facility with numbers lets her tally a total in her head. "He's ripped off taxpayers way beyond six figures!"

East Bay, California – December 1984

Once Lynn and I finish with Mitchell's case file, I feel compelled to tell Carole what we've learned. I clench and unclench my fists, waiting for her to answer her phone.

After saying "Hello," Carole moans, "What is it *now*, Karl?"

I explain the latest tape info, which she doesn't react to. I then say it's no wonder Mitchell hasn't learned, or shown, self-control since the crim j system let him off so easy for his crimes.

"So he's a spoiled kid?" Carole says.

"No! He's a grown man. And still dangerous."

Silence.

"Not been rehabilitated."

Silence.

I change tactics. "Are you reminding Mitchell that Lynn doesn't love him?"

"How can I be so cruel? He's still mailing love letters here."

"You must be kidding. He's a danger—"

"Only to you, Karl...his rival."

I take a deep breath, then ask, "Why do you hate me, Carole?"

She pauses a second. "You're not the son-in-law I wanted."

"Mitchell is?"

"He's good-looking, like Lynn's father."

"The father who abandoned her...and left you?"

"So?"

"Drugs wrecked his life just as they did Mitchell's."

"A little coke—"

"Lynn says it's ruining his teeth. Probably burning a hole in his palate."

"Just what I need—another cleft palate in my life."

I drop the phone. While retrieving it, I set my jaw, then say, "Truth is, Carole, you don't like my face."

"So what if I'm into looks?"

"Good-bye, Carole." I slam down the phone.

****

That night, I say to Lynn, "I'm beginning to think Mitchell's looks and charm have won over your mom just as they did Oregon's crim justice personnel."

"He's a pathological liar. That fact totally erases any looks or charm he may have."

Shifting gears, I remind her, "You know my main worry is his transmitting AIDS when he forcibly French-kissed you."

"I know…plus your worry that we had consensual sex. That's why I keep telling you, everyone, that I've hated him since he ditched me."

I don't speak, wanting to hear more.

"Learning the extent of Mitchell's lying and manipulation, and other problems, I've come to believe he probably injected drugs and had sex in prison."

"Yup, the two activities trumpeted as the main transmitters of AIDS—"

"I'm increasingly happy now that I agreed to AIDS testing. Not just to still your fear that we had sex, but to still mine that our babies might contract AIDS."

"Amen to that."

Although we held each other tight that night, neither of us slept well. A fatal disease without a cure scares both of us.

****

Now that I finally know Mitchell's crimes and the danger he represents, it's high time to call PO Nelson's boss. When Fred Willis's secretary puts him on the line, I get right to the point. "I'm trying to rein in a parolee in your office, but my talk with PO Nelson ended before it began."

"Sorry about that," Willis says. "Nelson's people skills sometimes—"

"He treated me as if I'd just crashed through police barricades."

"So, Mr. Schonborn. What can I do for you?"

"Get Nelson to protect my wife and me from Mitchell Lewis. He's after my wife and now has our address. Might come to Oakland to confront us."

"I'll do my best to stop him—"

"But your office hasn't even sanctioned him for drinking. You can revoke—"

"The parole board hates us revoking paroles. It takes away a key tool. The board even shortens the short sentences our most liberal judges give."

"So the board's to blame for paroling Mitchell so early?"

"Not that simple. The board claims prisons across the state pressure it to release good-conduct inmates early. They want the board to reduce overcrowding...Uh oh. Incoming call. Can you hold, Mr. Schonborn?"

While waiting, I think *The board's bringing about a warped version of the biblical dream of setting prisoners free. Overcrowding is partly due to underbuilding, which can be due to poor planning.*

"Got rid of that call," Willis says a minute later.

"That's fine. Was gonna say good conduct abounds in prisons, but only since it's rewarded by early release. Once released, offenders aren't rewarded anymore for good conduct. Sometimes prison terms need to be long."

"Don't forget, Mitchell spent six months in jail before prison."

"Not enough."

"You know, jails can be harder time than prisons."

I think, *I'm getting nowhere,* and so I wrap up with, "I know jails aren't set up to be country clubs with weight rooms, cable TV...but gotta go. Willis, just do my wife and me a favor, lean on Nelson to keep Mitchell out of our life."

"Will try as I said. But understand I got less control over my parole agents than they do over their parolees!"

CHAPTER 35
Arm-Wrestling with the Devil and Parole Officers

Soon as I have an afternoon on campus with some free time, I walk down the hall to Ric's office to update him on all things Mitchell, including my estimate of his cost to taxpayers. After hearing the estimate, Ric reckons Dederich must've cost taxpayers the same, plus the lost back taxes Synanon should've paid during its years of tax-exemptions due to its phony church status.

I say, "Both men burden society, and, in that sense are walking, talking, $100,000 manifestations of evil, a notion I'm toying with these days."

"Do tell." Ric's tone is half-mischievous, half-skeptical as he busies himself pruning and fussing with some of his exotic office plants.

I explain that in my youth, Unitarians never referenced evil, let alone sin. In college, I read Hannah Arendt on evil, but countless other writers on Hitler and the Holocaust didn't mention evil. Currently, our progressive-liberal politicians rarely use the word to describe, say, Uganda's Idi Amin, responsible for the deaths of three hundred thousand, or Cambodia's Pol Pot—behind the killing of two million of his own citizens.

"How do you define evil?" Ric asks.

"I'm beginning to see evil as shorthand for all that we don't understand about crime. Of course, most criminologists would never use the word since they worship science—they worry the field's not hard-science-y enough."

"You doubt the ability of your field to deliver?"

"Yes. Criminology presently can't think up, refine, and test serious hypotheses about the multiple and complex factors causing various crimes. Even worse, crim can't predict who'll recidivate or violate parole. Think Mitchell."

"So gimme examples of evil crimes," he asks as he grabs scissors to trim away stems and dead leaves of a couple of tougher plants.

"Forget the well-known, much-analyzed evil of all the Bay Area serial killers of late, and consider the incomprehensible, and hence evil, crimes of cannibalism and sexually perverse predation just beyond the Bay Area."

Ric nods when I describe Ed Kemper's admitted cannibalism, necrophilia, and terror in Santa Cruz. We agree on the evil of another guy, from Mitchell's hometown in Florida, who raped and chopped off the arms of a hitchhiker near Modesto, leaving her to die in a ditch. Ric winces at his recollection, saying that the sadist only got fourteen years, because his victim crawled out of the culvert and lived. We then add child molester Kenneth Parnell, who kidnapped two boys, keeping and raping one for seven years, to our list.

"But here's what shows vividly that evil is truly "live" spelled backwards, the antithesis of life. Many criminals claim they're motivated by the rush, the excitement of hurting others...and I'm not just talking about thrill killers."

"While we're brainstorming, be useful," Ric says, pushing his Parlor palm toward me. "Pick off the yellow and light green leaves... Social psychology will figure evil out."

"Doubt it, though as you know, I use a social-psych approach to crime. Much as I love Milgram and Zimbardo's studies of evil, they're not doing controlled, scientific work. For sure Scott Peck isn't. He combines the insights of both psychiatry and religion to probe the mysteries of human evil in *People of the Lie*, just out."

"And I suppose—fool that you are, Karl—that you'll say the devil is the source of evil?"

"I'm not such a fool that I acquire complex, high-maintenance office plants."

I then reply in earnest, saying some religions say this because they need an antagonist to fight. But I'm more in Peck's camp. He says evil's source is fear, a kind of fear that drives evil people to attack others rather than face their own failures.

Moreover, evil crimes can't simply be explained by some medical condition or be managed by medicating the doers. Legal defenses exploiting insanity, addiction, or other medical-field concepts push us to feel sympathy for criminals, just as we do for the genuinely ill. But this sympathy, applied to countless people, turns us into a society without limits or restraints on behavior.

"So you're not thrilled that Earl Warren's Supreme Court sympathized with defendants?"

"We've neglected victims' rights since Warren, the quintessential progressive, exploited the sensitivities of the '60s, tipping the scales in favor of defendants."

"Remind me how the Warren Court did that."

"Promoting reforms that eroded personal responsibility, minimized consequences for outrageous criminality, and eliminated serious forms of deterrence. So defendants and defense attorneys are having a field day, and criminologists, anxious to promote the progressive reforms of the day, are claiming their scientific studies prove the efficacy of reforms."

****

For over a week now, Mitchell has kept phoning us and leaving creepy breathing-and-background-noise sounds on our thirty-second message tape. Lynn's had it and insists I call Fred Willis again.

"Damn it, Willis!" I holler. " Thought you said you guys would force Mitchell to stop hassling us!"

"I instructed PO Nelson to do just that, Mr. Schonborn. How do you know it's Mitchell calling?" he asks with an edge.

"A gadget that detects callers' numbers. Police chief I know loaned it to me."

"Oh yeah. We had those at my police department too."

"So you were a cop, Willis? Knew I liked you. I've researched PDs for years."

"Call me Fred. A while back, I returned to college to finish my degree. Wanted to earn more as a parole officer....Anyway, Nelson said Mitchell claimed he'd stopped calling you."

"Mitchell lies."

"Not surprised. Many bad guys wanna stay bad."

"Nelson should visit Mitchell, yank his phone, check for a gun. He probably last saw Mitchell's digs when he was at the halfway house where guns weren't allowed."

"Guns...'cuz you think Mitchell's dealing again?"

"Otherwise, how's he paying for room and board plus lotsa long-distance phone calls?"

"I'm trying to get him trained for something besides bartending 'til he learns computers. Told me he learned roadie skills in prison."

"Yeah, setting up stages, speakers for bands. That requires shoulder strength. So did grabbing, assaulting Lynn. Proof he lied to doctors, DAs, judges about having a bum shoulder since he shot himself. So...get Nelson all over him."

"Will do, but Nelson's busy. Got a killer caseload, no pun intended."

"I don't buy that caseload excuse. Checked, and your county's got a better agent-to-parolee ratio than most."

"But my agents complain—"

"I complain too, Fred, when I get too many students in class...but I cope."

"Okay, okay. One of us will visit Mitchell—"

"Both of you should. Play good cop, bad cop." I snort. Then... "Can't believe I'm asking you guys to be more cop, less social worker. My mantra used to be the opposite!"

****

After hanging up, I face Lynn, who's listening at my office door. She says, "You've forsaken Joan Baez—"

"And the Bible, and those hymns about setting the prisoners free. Crim justice should protect victims and survivors, especially ones like you."

"Reminds me," Lynn says, "the radio just reported Jed Drell wants the new county jail to call inmates residents now and wants soothing music—"

"To think I once studied paint colors for jail walls …to reduce violence."

Taking my hand and pulling me closer, Lynn says, "Enough about prisoners. It's you and me now. Wish there weren't a six-month wait for AIDS tests. Wanna start our family soon."

"Me too. But be glad there is an AIDS test now. Scientists worried they'd never develop one…"

Lynn hugs me, saying, "You'll see, I'll test negative. That'll end all our worries about Mitchell."

"Hope so."

CHAPTER 36
Blackmail Escalates to Home Invasion

Oakland – *1985*

Great news—the Law Enforcement Television Network wants me to produce segments about Bay Area PDs. To promote me to journalists, LETN in Dallas wants info about my recent projects. I oblige, and one among my most recent is *Homicide Reduction*, a film about police efforts to reduce deaths in Berkeley and Richmond, used on campuses and by PDs across the U.S.

Others films, I note, feature B-roll footage Lynn I gathered on our first "undercover dates": *Prostitution Up Close*, featuring in-depth interviews of prostitutes, call girls, and brothel employees, explored three sex workers' feelings toward police, prosecutors, pimps, clients, and co-workers. It, and a companion soc-umentary with interviews of prosecutors, criminologists, and vice officers about sex workers— were sold and distributed nationally, as was another film examining how stigmatized people, like ex-cons and other outliers, "pass" and "cover" using coping strategies.

****

But just as I'm beginning to feel life's improving, I read "You and your TA Lynn are at risk. Do you want her diary, her sex history, made public?"

It's a faxed handwritten note my department chair has handed me. I'm speechless, paralyzed. My stomach knots up. I think, *Mitchell's escalated his tactics.*

"Student is a wacko," my chair says. "Got your TA's name wrong."

"Probably because I mention Lynn as well as Tonya in class." I say, purposely keeping him in the dark about Mitchell.

"So, this isn't some student's effort to blackmail you or Tonya?"

"Believe me, Tonya and I aren't having an affair. We're happily married to others! But we will look at our D and F students for leads. This guy probably hates us for grading tough."

"Pretty clever using a high-tech fax machine this way," my chair says. "The dean okayed this pricey gadget only if we shared it with other departments in the ivory tower."

"Ivory tower? Not for me anymore! First, it's Jed Drell. Now it's a crazed student."

"Keep your office locked. Have Tonya do the same. I'll alert the campus cops."

I nod but know it's not a campus problem. As soon as I get home in the late afternoon, I call Willis.

****

"For God's sake, Fred! Mitchell's threatening to make Lynn's sex history public now. He stole her diary back when he ditched her, but now he's faxed a note that my department chair and secretaries saw."

"Christ! Send me the fax," Fred says. "How'd he get your fax number?"

"Universities make all sorts of faculty info public—phone numbers, office hours, class schedules. Anyone can stalk us."

"Guess students are safer. Heard where schools hide students' info ever since kidnappers got Patty Hearst's address from a public Berkeley card index."

"Yeah. Mitchell could easily kidnap Lynn. He's over six feet. With a gun, he's ten feet tall."

"That reminds me, Nelson couldn't find a gun at Mitchell's."

"May've hidden it. But what I wanna know now, how'd Mitchell get access to a costly fax machine?"

"Portland Public Library?"

"Few libraries can afford 'em. Maybe Mitchell used your office fax on the sly?"

"Possible. Our secretary often leaves the front office, where parolees wait, unattended. Our fax is there. She leaves her purse behind too. Kind of a trust test."

"Well, it's a stress test for me!"

"Mitchell did come to my office today after meeting with Nelson."

"You're busted, Fred! He must've used your fax!"

Fred's silent until words leap from me. "What's keeping him from coming after Lynn, Fred?"

"Though he's admitted he's obsessed with her, he won't go to counseling. Can't get him to date locals either. Can't control his emotions."

"Forget controlling his emotions! Control his behavior! You got the power. That's your job!"

"He wants to leave Portland due to his notoriety. Wants to go to California. I told him he can't leave Oregon now. But, Karl, I can't keep him here 'til 2020, when his parole ends."

"Put an electronic monitor on his ankle?"

"Not possible."

"C'mon, Fred. You know that a judge uses monitors in Colorado. Another does in Florida."

"Monitors are expensive."

"Your office has the dough; you got a pricey fax. Portland's economy's booming!"

"I-I think—"

"Look, a hotshot criminologist just declared prison rehab's a failure, a joke."

I then note the high parole-failure rate in Oregon. Fred counters, citing low fail rates in Arizona and Nevada. I respond they're small states, that most populated states have sky-high fail rates. "Experts conclude most parolees should really be followed around 24/7."

"Then we'd only be able to afford to track a coupla ex-cons," Fred jokes.

"Ankle monitors can track the rest."

"Would require budget heroics, Karl."

"Then just get one goddamned monitor. For Mitchell! You can afford *one!*"

I hang up.

****

When Lynn gets home, she reacts to Mitchell's faxed threat. "Let him publish my frickin' diary! I've been open with you, honey, about my sex life. Started at sixteen. Then a coupla guys before Mitchell. That's it! He can tell the whole world!"

"Love your openness, Lynn."

"I think Mitchell's trying to get you to ditch me, Karl. Figures you'll decide 'Lynn's a cheat. Not mother material.'"

"Maybe he just feels you cheated on him? He did live with you once."

"No, no, he really didn't...in the usual sense. It was Mom's idea. She needed someone to do the lawn, do house repairs. Mitchell and I didn't sleep together at Mom's. Told you—our tiny rooms, his in a moldy basement that triggered my asthma. Plus, college and working double shifts kept me busy...and tired."

****

A few weeks later, I arrive home from an evening event on campus and find Lynn in tears standing in the bedroom. I embrace her and ask what's wrong.

"After it got dark, I dozed off while reading in the living room with the lights on. Had music playing. Then the doorbell rang, awakening me."

"Uh-oh. Mitchell?"

"I instantly realized whoever it was must've seen me through the front window gauze curtain. They knew I was home, , just a few feet from the front door."

I think, *Been meaning to replace that curtain with an opaque one.* "I froze 'til I noticed I'd latched the door chain above the deadbolt. The doorbell rang again, and I stayed in my chair, hoping the person would leave. Then a faint, possibly familiar voice said, 'I'm a student, selling magazine subscriptions to pay for school.'"

Not thinking, I blurt out, 'Really?'"

I grab Lynn's hand.

"A muffled male voice then said, 'Lotsa magazines. Only need a minute of your time...I go to the door. Look through the peephole. Mist dims the porch light, and I only see bits of the guy.

"I shout through the door, 'News magazines or women's mags?'

"'Everything.'

"'No thanks. Anyway, my husband's due any minute.'"

I tell Lynn, "That husband thing might've been the best...or worst thing you could've said." *The tension's killing me, and I just wanna ask, "So was it Mitchell?" But I know Lynn needs to talk, get the details off her chest.*

"'Open the door a crack,' the guy says, 'and I'll slip the price list through.'

"'Dunno,' I mumble, and then for some reason, I open the door the inch or so the door chain allows."

"Holy crap, Lynn!" I moan.

"The guy's tall, so he totally blocks the porch light now, preventing me from seeing him. He sees me, though, and growls, 'Let me in!' Suddenly, he wedges the tip of a shoe into the door gap and shoves against the door with his shoulder. The chain holds!"

I think, *Thank god I installed it right.*

"I scream, 'GO AWAY! GO AWAY!' as I try to shut the door. I push with all my might, but his shoe keeps the door ajar. I yell, 'I'm calling the cops.' His shoe slips out and he backs away a tad. As he does, I slam the door shut, twist the deadbolt, and catch my breath.

"'I'm gonna break your door down,' he yells as he slams against it with his shoulder. The house shudders."

I grab Lynn's other hand to comfort her as she continues,

"I notice the panic button on the alarm panel by the door and hit it just as I hear him crash against the door again, shaking everything nearby."

"You must've been terrified."

"For sure, but the door held. And as the outside alarm started going 'EEEEEeeeeee, EEEEEeeeeeee,' I felt relieved.

"I heard him say 'Fucking bitch' several times, and then he left. Sure sounded like Mitchell."

Lynn sighs and relaxes.

I guide Lynn to the edge of our bed. We both sit before we have a long, silent hug.

Then she says, "Neither of our neighbors must have been home 'cuz no one responded to the alarm. In between shrill sounds, I heard a car drive away from the top of the driveway. I stopped the alarm and locked myself like forever in the bathroom. Then I heard your car come down the driveway. When you shut your car door, and then turned your key in the front-door lock, I came out."

"You're one tough cookie, Lynn. You've been to hell and back."

"Thank goodness you're here. He could circle 'round."

"Doubtful. He's afraid of the alarm. Knows I'm due home."

We sit together in the dark for a long time.

****

"Should we call the cops?" Lynn asks.

"Of course, but we need to give 'em something to go on. You sure you didn't see anything distinctive—features, clothes?"

"I'm sure. Only heard his voice through the door...with music playing all the time. Certainly, it could've been his voice. And he's good at mimicking people, like a door-to-door salesman."

"So you'd guess it was Mitchell?"

"Yeah, 'cuz a similar-sized guy."

I call the Oakland Police Department and try to talk to Officer Ullema, who I know from Valerie's rape investigation, but he's off tonight. So a female officer takes the report from Lynn, getting all the details plus info about Mitchell.

When Lynn finishes, I suggest she ask the woman if there are any leads in Valerie's rape case and also if anyone's currently using a magazine-sales MO in our area of Oakland. The officer takes a moment to check her records, then says no to both questions..

When Lynn hangs up, she asks, "What do we do now?"

****

We sit down at our kitchen table to indulge in comforting bowls of ice cream, while trying to figure out how to prevent a repeat of tonight's terror. We agree that Lynn should never be alone in the house until things resolve with Mitchell. Our respective flexibility around work allows us to ensure this moves forward.

We also agree to pay an alarm company to alert OPD if and when we hit the panic button again. I rationalize finally subscribing to a costly service this way: *This means I don't have to buy a gun...and break with nonviolence totally. A relief.*

And, oh yes, we pledge to beef up our front door hardware and get a brighter porch light and an opaque front-window curtain. We also talk about long-term solutions. Tonight's terror represents a tipping point. Because of it and Mitchell's threats, as well as Valerie's rape and my two burglaries, we decide to relocate. We need a less-isolated neighborhood in a city where there's less crime, or at least more resources to fight it. We also know that in addition to safety, we want better schools for our future family.

"This change will be a big project," I say, having house hunted recently. "But it may distract us from worrying about Mitchell 24/7."

"It'll also be a chance to show the depth of my commitment to you."

"Since we worked through, via a freight train of words, your trip to Portland, I've tried to show my commitment to us too. For instance, I've never once asked to keep our money separate."

"Let's keep our house hunting a secret from my relatives, because, after all, Mom gave our address to Mitchell."

"Not gonna give it to Fred either."

****

The next morning, Lynn calls Carole about her night of terror, but isn't thrilled that she's unsympathetic and nearly unreactive. When she does react, it's to say she's amazed that Lynn is even talking to her, given that she feels we blamed her for Mitchell's faxed threat. Carole does tell Lynn she's burned Mitchell's recent love letters as we insisted she do.

By contrast, when I phone Fred about Lynn's ordeal, he sounds sincerely sorry to hear about it. I ask if he knows where Mitchell is at the moment, and he says he and Nelson just talked about this after Mitchell missed a required check-in yesterday. "Truth is, Nelson's not been able to reach Mitchell for over a week."

"Jesus, Fred!" I yell. "After all my pleading, you've lost track of him!"

"Sorry. He gave us the slip. Trust me, I'll find him and ask about last night. If appropriate, I'll revoke his parole."

"Fat chance," I growl. "I found it takes two hearings to revoke. Then appeals if—"

"Won't be easy in our bureaucracy, but I'll put a letter in his file that says something like...'This document reports on, and thus constitutes, the first revocation hearing for Mitch—'"

"Great idea!"

"I'll note that Lewis, Nelson, and Willis were present at the hearing; then describe each infraction—alcohol use, failing to check in, and finding and assaulting a former victim."

"Good! Be a bureaucracy buster. But ya gotta test Mitchell for coke. Carole hears Mitchell sniffling on the phone. Tell-tale, no?"

"Drug tests aren't cheap, Karl."

"C'mon? Recidivism costs way more. Surprise Mitchell at home."

"Even my go-getters don't like obtaining urine samples from parolees. Disgusting, dangerous—"

"Then you do it! Step in for Nelson. As a former cop, you're licensed to carry—"

"Against the rules for POs here to carry."

"But your union's lobbying to change that...Bend the frickin' rules, Fred! Mitchell bends 'em constantly."

During Fred's uncharacteristic pause, I think, *Can't believe my new self is advocating that someone carry a gun.* "I'm gonna tell Mitchell," Fred says, "there's no chance I'll ever reduce his parole conditions 'til he controls himself, meaning no booze, no travel until his parole's up in thirty-five years."

"Well," I sigh. "Any progress on that ankle monitor?"

"Higher-ups turned me down flat."

"It would've kept him away from us."

"The board agrees monitors are effective, but worries they'll put agents outta business."

"Hate to sound heartless, but that'd be a good thing."

Fred moans.

"Parole's based on the assumption that most prisoners can be trusted, but two-thirds of violent prisoners, and an even larger proportion of drug dealers, get rearrested within three years."

"You got the stats down, Karl."

Feeling I'm getting nowhere, I say, "What I've really got down, Fred, is that Lynn and I will sue you, and the board, if Mitchell assaults us again.."

"Huh?"

"You've been warned!"

****

After meeting with realtors, Lynn and I learn we can't afford the various 'burbs we're interested in unless we buy a fixer-upper or the rare house in a probate sale. Battling Eve taught me about cheap probate sales where out-of-town heirs who want to sell their newly-inherited house frequently don't know local house values or are too busy or grief-stricken to ascertain them properly.

When our realtors find a probate house or gush "charming," "Spanish style," or "fab-floor plan," we drop everything and race across bridges or through tunnels, only to be disappointed. We soon learn to ask a lot of questions before dashing out the door. And, even when we find a winner, we lose out on the house because of bidding wars or because we must first consult flood and quake-fault maps in various city halls.

In short, we kiss a lot of frogs in our effort to find Toad Hall. And because our house hunting's layered atop our jobs, it's additionally stressful. But we try to defuse our stress by communicating our feelings to one another often.

For example, we each share that house hunting energizes us knowing that moving to a new, unknown location may keep Mitchell at bay. We're increasingly clear that the threats he made around Lynn at our home constituted an assault, and that he'll likely escalate his aggression the next visit. For that reason, Lynn proposes she write her mom a letter setting forth clearly what we expect of her now — like blocking Mitchell's mail, stonewalling if he suggests visiting her, Carole — and future consequences if she fails.

When Lynn follows through writing the letter, I tell her I deeply value her efforts to rebuild verbal and behavioral trust between us, asserting it takes just seconds to destroy, but countless hours to rebuild it. She grins coyly, saying that she may've destroyed Carole's trust by writing that she doesn't want Carole living with us after she retires, something Carole's hinted at, being pension-less.

Meanwhile, we're outbid in probate court. Lynn and I return to another probate property we saw earlier. In a hilly town with first-rate schools, it's in a neighborhood of level-lot homes, perfect for children's play and getting to know neighbors. The ranch-style house has a big enough backyard for an addition, and we know this well-off community can afford decent police protection, making our lives, and those of our kids-to-be, safer.

We decide to commit the lion's share of each of our incomes if a bidding war breaks out during the upcoming probate hearing. A speculator, just like Eve and Gayle found, tries to outbid us, but we win the war. Being house-poor now, we each add a vow of poverty to our marriage vow and our vow not to not tell Lynn's family where we're moving.

Unfortunately, our realtor tells us it'll take three months for the paperwork to finish before we can move. Until then, we'll be sitting ducks again in Oakland with Mitchell on the loose.

CHAPTER 37
Collateral Damage from being Mugged by Reality

1985

I'm nervous when I hear Lynn returning from the clinic that tested her for the AIDS virus. She runs up the two sets of concrete stairs to our porch.

"I tested negative," Lynn says breathlessly as she gives me the results sheet.

I feel relief as my neck and shoulders relax while I skim through a lot of disclaimers balanced by assurances and phone numbers to call for support should one test positive. And there it is in writing, she's HIV negative. Lynn says, "I'm not so much happy for myself, but happiest for you, knowing how long you've waited to start a family. As we hug each other, I say, "We can begin now..."

****

Spring has sprung, and we arrive for a family gathering at Lynn's grandmother's house on the hill, above the cottage. Intercepting us on the steps up and blocking our passage, Carole's intent on confronting us. With a fierce stare plus an edge to her voice, she says, "The letter you guys sent really hurt me."

"Didn't intend it to," Lynn says.

"Guess I'm more angry than hurt," Carole responds. "Can't believe, Lynn, that after living in my house for twenty-six years, you won't let me live in yours after I retire."

"Until I turned eighteen, you were legally obligated, as I was your child," Lynn says. "But you weren't really my parent. You didn't protect me...or my sisters."

"But no one protected me," Carole counters, her voice quivering. "My mom didn't protect me."

"What?" Lynn exclaims in a quiet voice, knowing Carole's mom is just inside the doorway.

"I'm sorry to hear that," I say. "What happened?"

"My stepdad took liberties with me, forcibly kissing me while a teen, and my mom did nothing. Before that, she caused my real dad to abandon my sister and me, by kicking him out for having an affair."

"And somehow all this repeated itself in your own life, Carole," I mumble.

"You didn't have to abandon me, Mom, 'cuz you thought you couldn't handle two little ones. You sent me away for months as a toddler. You could've broken that cycle. And today, right now, you can also break the divorce cycle...by honoring my marriage to Karl. And regarding my extra eight years at home, you insisted I stay so I could pay rent since you couldn't make ends meet."

"But we became pals, best friends," she says.

"You shoulda found a boyfriend for that."

****

It's been a while since the faxed threat, so I no longer watch my back for Mitchell at work. But, paradoxically, I now watch for my department chair and some colleagues who periodically hang near my classroom door to overhear my oft-conservative take on some justice issues.

Illustration: In a recent class exchange, a student asks, "Took a course from you years ago, and compared to then, you're sounding like a Reagan Democrat."

Some students laugh nervously, upset that President Reagan's just won reelection.

"Naw. Just evolved from a rabid Democrat to a moderate one, but I'm still more liberal than conservative on most issues. I am fed up, though, with several aspects of the justice system."

"You're evolving," a student ventures, "like social scientists Nathan Glaser and James Q. Wilson."

"Yes, I'm intrigued by both their assessments of knee-jerk progressive liberalism. My current gripe is today's topic: parole."

"Some of our readings," ventures another student, "say parole boards discriminate."

"Yes," I say, "they're often biased in favor of privilege and wealth, which is overlooked since their bias against non-whites is so glaring. Incidentally, judges are guilty of this too."

"What should boards do?" a student wonders.

"Boards should favor fixed, determinate sentences over flexible ones like '7-Up,' which, for 'life,' means 'up for parole after seven years.'"

Another student says, "Not everyone's releasable, even if they claim they're rehabbed, and even if they've served a full sentence."

"Important point," I remark. "Despite guidelines, boards should evaluate every release candidate, even if rehabbed, for any evidence they're likely to relapse, recidivate."

****

Scott and I tighten our shoelaces at Berkeley High, near where he's rented a cottage among a few other detached units, which share possessions as well as produce from a communal garden. Once we start jogging on the school track, he tells me his new job lets him apply his architecture skills to designing affordable housing. I then tell him about the harassment and heart-stopping moments Mitchell has put Lynn and me through lately. When I reveal we're moving to the 'burbs as a result, Scott's loose runner's body stiffens. "You're selling out!" he exclaims.

"You'd leave Oakland too if you cringed every time you saw a stranger near your place or heard your doorbell—"

"You're becoming a law-and-order guy!" he cries.

"I've learned firsthand how antisocial personalities can put one's life into a tailspin."

"Dragon Lady?"

"Yes, manipulators like her, narcissists like Crista, but mostly psychopaths I know who've killed. My life's been a crim-justice lab experiment whose findings have jolted me."

"Oh yeah, heard that that neocon fool Irving Kristol just said 'a neoconservative's a liberal who's been mugged by reality.'"

He's right. I say, "The justice system hasn't protected Lynn or me from a privileged criminal."

"If the system got tougher, it would impact poor, underprivileged criminals even more."

"The poor victimize people too, especially other poor people. You forget that, Scott, when you romanticize poor criminals as revolutionaries." Sidestepping a soccer ball on the track, I say, "You think poor criminals are striking a blow against capitalism?"

"I'm not opposed to capitalism anymore. My trip to Cuba's turned me from a Marxist to a Progressive. Things aren't so great there."

"Even with Soviet subsidies to Cuba?"

"Yes, but back to the 'burbs, Karl. What's scary is you'll become bourgeois being around consumers who insist on luxuries—"

"Not Lynn and me. We just wanna raise kids in a safe place with decent schools."

After our jog, Scott brings up Gayle's request that we each write the mayor of Glendora supporting Aunt Ruth's bid to be its Citizen of the Year. Scott says Ruth's been busy for years developing an organization to help parolees and their families.

I take a deep breath, then say, "Deserving as Ruth is of the award, I'm not writing a letter. Can't support an entity that provides rides, job tips, other things to parolees."

"Don't be a jerk, Karl! Ruth's the only adult on Mom's side who hasn't banished us kids for Mom's suicide."

"Okay, okay. I've thrown the baby out with the bath," I say, patting his arm. "I'll write, praising Ruth for helping underprivileged parolees, like single moms with kids."

****

A month or so later, a mass shooting at a McDonald's in an Hispanic area of San Diego causes me to alter again my approach to guns and gun control. The massacre happens in the San Ysidro district, which sees lots of traffic where I-5 extends to the Mexican border. Late one July afternoon, James Huberty, a gun-collecting former security guard, opens fire for thirty minutes inside and outside the crowded restaurant, killing twenty-one and injuring nineteen before being fatally shot by a SWAT sniper.

Besides a pump-action shotgun, the recently laid-off Huberty used semi-automatics like his Uzi carbine and a high-powered Browning 9mm pistol. So, I resolve to advocate more strongly that civilians be prohibited from possessing any type of semi-automatics, rapid-fire self-loaders, that facilitate mass murder.

But, in a seeming contradiction, the tragedy also causes me to advocate providing American cops more potent ammo and sidearms because standard-issue .38 bullets bounced off the windows at McDonald's rather than piercing them, as .45s would have, allowing cops to neutralize Huberty sooner.

I discuss the mass shooting with Ric as we walk across campus to the library. Ric says, "I read where San Diego SWAT was just patrol officers who got a little extra training and carried a few automatics and semis in their squad cars."

"That's why I predict huge changes in SWAT units, weaponry and training across America. I agree with my cop buddies wanting full-time regional SWAT teams ready to react rapidly anywhere, anytime."

I assure Ric that my new realism about guns is a mixed proposition, not a rigid all-or-nothing ideology.

He responds, "About time you left Gandhi in the dust. We agree that there's an arms race between cops and criminals today. Huberty's a self-proclaimed survivalist, who recently told his wife he sensed himself growing unstable because he wanted to hunt humans."

"Why d'ya think he went ballistic, Ric? Bring your social-psych expertise to bear."

"From what I've read, besides a sullen temperament, he nursed an inferiority complex from a slight limp from childhood polio."

"Ahh," I say, "bet he wanted to be macho, growing up in Canton, Ohio, birthplace of the National Football League and home to its Hall of Fame."

Ric shares that he read that Huberty's mom abandoned his family when he was a preteen and guesses that's why he became a misogynist—beating his wife, terrorizing his daughters, threatening their grade-school girlfriends.

"His mom also role-modeled racism," I say, "and that may be why Huberty targeted and killed Mexican-Americans disproportionately during his rampage. Evidently, he reinforced his racism by believing survivalist rhetoric that the government favored minorities over alleged hard-working, sometimes unlucky, people like him."

As we near the library, Ric describes his diminishing collaboration with the owners of the *Light*. After all the excitement of the Pulitzer for exposing Dederich's psychopathy, they divorced and had to sell their paper. Exacerbating things, a recently aired ABC movie disappointed everyone because Dederich's lawyers significantly changed its storyline.

East Bay Suburb, California – August 22, 1985

Lynn and I congratulate each other for surviving three more months as sitting ducks since Mitchell obtained our address. Our escrow ended, we pack and make multiple trips through nearby Caldecott Tunnel. Our final trip kicks up bittersweet memories of our woodsy yet scary house in Oakland where our phone gadget keeps registering calls from Mitchell.

In the midst of unpacking at our new house, we take a break and Lynn sits while I massage her tight shoulders. A minute into it, she reminds me of our pledge to share more thoughts to keep strengthening the bonds we've forged house-hunting and fending-off Mitchell.

"I'll start," I say. "A few times in the last year, I was scared enough to consider buying a gun."

"You've been against guns forever!"

"Feared Mitchell. Feared for our lives."

Lynn looks up at me and asks, "Scared anymore?"

"No, but we didn't move just to escape. Wanted good schools."

She looks down. "My turn to share. Hmmm. Oh, yeah. I refused to live with Mitchell, not just because of his smoking, but 'cuz he lied about money, alcohol, everything."

"Chronic lying—a key trait and a reason I pegged him as psychopathic early on."

"Habitual lying. Must mean lots have psychopathic traits, not just criminals."

"Yeah. Such traits foster success in many fields."

"Like politics and business?"

"For sure. But they're different from people with dangerous psychopathic traits, like lack of empathy and physical aggressiveness."

****

Lynn and I both breathe easier when the phone installer gives us a new, unlisted number. This, despite an extra monthly surcharge and despite knowing that shutting out Mitchell means shutting out many academic and film-production colleagues too.

However, a news bulletin cuts short our sense of relief. It summarizes Mayor Dianne Feinstein's just-concluded press conference.

"The Night Stalker has reportedly been driving on Dam Road, which connects several East Bay communities. He's already murdered seven, and raped and robbed dozens in L.A. Five days ago, he murdered an accountant in San Francisco and sent his wife to a hospital where she's still fighting to live. He attacks any and all, especially in easily entered homes."

CHAPTER 38
Bring on the Night Stalker

August 23, *1985*

"Holy crap," I shout. I can hear cars driving Dam Road right now. I think, *Out of the frying pan of Oakland into the fire of the 'burbs. Maybe I need a gun after all?*

"You mean the road we use? The one we see from our front yard?" Lynn wails.

"Yes."

I'd just heard from a cop friend about a far-ranging effort by San Francisco detectives to identify whoever murdered a sixtyish accountant as he slept and nearly killed his wife. I figure they must be dismayed that the mayor, who'd taken over after Dan White killed Mayor Moscone, revealed ballistics tests showed the killer to be *the* L.A. Night Stalker. And mad that she disclosed that he wore distinctive shoes and that he'd driven Dam Road several times.

I call my police contacts and learn the Stalker's taken Dam Road to visit friends and gun sellers in the East Bay to avoid major roads with highway patrol officers. He's also left jewelry and $500 he's stolen, his usual objective besides rape, with friends for safekeeping in the East Bay town of San Pablo.

Lynn and I had felt safe enough buying in an upscale area that we didn't mind our house lacked front fences butting up against each of its sides. This allowed easy entry to our backyard, something rare in fenced-for-privacy California neighborhoods. Nor did we mind that the sun porch off the living room and facing the backyard had a few torn screens. Combined, though, this meant now the Stalker could easily access our backyard, reach through torn screens, and remove loose louvered-glass slats to enter our house.

****

Deciding it imperative to act, I tell Lynn we've got to secure the house, now.

I explain that the media should've named the Night Stalker the "Screen Door Killer." His original name in L.A., the "Screen Door Intruder," referred to his MO of entering homes through torn screens. As sweat beads up on Lynn's forehead, I decide to forego explaining that the Stalker also terrorizes hapless victims with sadistic violence inspired by his Satanic studies.

It's my job now to protect her from evil incarnate and to secure the few valuables I own, tools of my trade, like a computer for writing and professional film-production gear.

"No sleeping in the sun porch like last night."

"Okay," Lynn says, "even though it's darn hot, and we don't have air. But what about a gun?"

"No time to buy one," I say, and then suggest she should rush to the local nursery to buy several flats of anything thorny to deter an intruder. Then she should plant them around the perimeter of the sun porch.

Without the conflicted feelings I'd had hardening my Oakland place, I race to the local hardware store to buy, among other things, window screening material and wood-slat-and-wire fencing. Next, I replace the damaged screens and install the fencing on both sides of the house. Then, addressing the front and back door locks, I replace the strike-plate screws on the door jambs with four-inch ones. They screw deeper into the door-frame studs, making it hard for someone to kick in a door. Finally, as the sun goes down, I put new bulbs in the two exterior light fixtures since we'll leave them on all night.

No time to set up our real bed. So, though we're bone tired from moving and securing the premises, we drag our mattress from the sun porch to a bedroom and put a construction crowbar, a gun alternative, under it. Relatedly, we make sure no tools or heavy objects remain outdoors in our yard, providing the Night Stalker a weapon or battering ram.

As I begin to fall asleep in Lynn's arms, I feel I've made peace with a chaotic, crime-filled world. *Just gotta remember to mount a fake alarm-bell box on the front of the house tomorrow. And put extra stickers the Oakland alarm company gave me on our windows. Deception has its place sometimes.*

Happily, nothing but chirping crickets bother us for the next few nights. But we're unnerved to learn police have found the Night Stalker's huge Avia sneakers in the Bay, suggesting he probably tossed his gun too. If so, he may still be driving Dam Road, either to get another gun from a dealer in Moraga, or to break into a home for one or electronics to pawn. Regarding his robbery MO, it's because he also needs to support his drug habit.

After more sleepless nights, we're suddenly deluged with "good" and bad news about the Stalker. According to reports, he left the East Bay to return to southern California, where he broke into a Mission Viejo couple's home through a back door. After shooting the male in the head and raping and sodomizing his fiancée, who happened to be Lynn's age, the Stalker took off with cash and jewelry.

When police found a fingerprint on a stolen vehicle the Stalker abandoned, they finally ID'd him as Richard Ramirez, a twenty-five-year-old drifter from El Paso, Texas. They released a mug shot from one of Ramirez's many prior arrests, and on August 31, a number of residents in East L.A. recognized, chased, and subdued him until the police arrived.

We're happy the alleged Stalker's in custody, but are shocked to learn he had a demonic stare that enabled him to intimidate people immediately. (He scored 31 out of 40 on Hare's scale, making him a full-blown psychopath.) Not surprising, Ramirez' eyes rekindled our worries about Mitchell and his piercing stare. I decide to phone PO Fred Willis.

****

After I've identified myself, Fred jokes, "Hear the Night Stalker slipped through *your*, not my, fingers."

"Be glad he didn't travel north to Portland," I counter. "You Oregonians can't even catch the Green River Killer, and you've got extra detectives and tons of other resources from the state of Washington!"

"Sorry, Karl...How can I help?"

"Well, I do want you to know that my wife's still anxious about Mitchell's terrorizing visit and subsequent phone harassment. The media's coverage of the Night Stalker, and the McDonald's massacre, has compounded her trauma. And I'm exhausted, calming Lynn and looking over my shoulder too for Mitchell. I now experience the anxiety and indirect trauma crime victims endure."

"I'm truly sorry, Karl. Hope you don't transmit your feelings to your crim students."

"I probably do...but, Fred, did you ever determine if Mitchell came down to the Bay Area?"

"No, he denied traveling south."

"Of course he would. Got grad level instruction in crime in prison."

"PO Nelson asked, but Mitchell couldn't account for his whereabouts that day."

"Figures! We're just gonna assume he tried to break into our home."

"Fair assumption."

"Dammit, Fred, you're so matter-of-fact. Don't you see the angst Lynn and I carry, knowing Mitchell could keep harassing and even visit us again? Without an ankle monitor, he's impossible to track, given his common name and use of aliases."

"I'm all over Nelson to make sure Mitchell stays in Portland—"

"Other big question: what've Mitchell's drug tests revealed?"

"He refuses to be tested."

"Pathetic!" I roar.

"I accompanied Nelson on a second try, and when Mitchell refused, I read him the riot act."

"Grounds for revocation."

"Right. But as we'd already filed a petition to revoke parole, the board said we gotta wait to petition again. Anyway, they're not gonna revoke for rule violations, only for another crime."

"Tell that board of progressive liberals—Mitchell, too, if he'll listen—that he's choosing to do coke."

"B-But—"

"Dr. Joel Fort, a psychiatrist I know, just gave a campus lecture, reminding everyone that doing coke's a choice, not a physical addiction."

"I've heard of Fort. Unusual name," Fred says.

"He helped convict a Manson groupie and, later, Patty Hearst by showing they weren't brainwashed."

"Sounds like he thinks for himself."

"Doesn't follow the crim justice herd."

"I'm not the liberal wuss you take me for, Karl. I stand up to the board. Told 'em years ago I didn't want to call my parolees 'clients'—they're ex-cons, fer Chrissake—but the board threatened to fire me."

"Obviously, you wanna keep your job, Fred," I say, anger welling up again in me. "So, you definitely don't want Lynn and me suing you, the board. Keep Mitchell away from us!"

After a hasty and frosty goodbye, I hang up.

Lynn has overheard my threat and says, "Sounds pretty intense."

"I grew up as a dove, a peacemaker. Therapy taught me to confront. Life's taught me to demand."

****

During a discussion at the last session of a summer Crim class, we talk about the final exam and the challenges that continually crop up in the justice system. We talk about the pressures in the implementation of probation and parole, aka community corrections, stemming from increases in caseloads and the seriousness of crime.

We also talk about the challenge posed by permissive sentencing stemming from the '60s and the Supreme Court's focus on offenders at the expense of victims. We eventually get into a discussion of how taxpayers and lawmakers have interests different from both offenders and victims. A student sums up, "Plea-bargained sentences show the conflicting needs of the four interest groups. Too often pleas, pitting defendants against victims, are driven by cost-cutting, led by lawmakers ,to save taxpayers the costs of trials and prisons."

Our last classroom exchange of opinions involves the chances of rehabilitation of various types of murderers. The discussion starts with family-fight murderers who are often rehabbed as soon as the smoke from a gun dissipates, swearing they'll never do wrong again. And it ends with psychopathic killers, like the Night Stalker, whom most agree will never be rehabbed.

"And what sentence should psychopathic killers get?" I ask.

One says life, but others say, "No, that really means 'Release on parole after seven years depending on good behavior.' What's needed is natural life—a sentence without the possibility of parole."

I end the discussion by saying, "It's great that many of you've been doing the recommended readings. You'll ace the final."

****

On the day of the final, I pass out blue books and exam sheets with three questions to answer:

Analyze each of the several tests for sanity used in the U.S. over the last century. Among other things, address deterrence, community safety, and the sense of justice felt by crime survivors.

If you believe there's bias toward privilege in the justice system, give examples of it and show how the system might be reformed to end it. Explain too whether the reform would make the system more responsive and sympathetic to the unique problems women and minorities face in America.

How does each of the following contribute to social control in any society—childhood socialization, teen and adult peer pressure, the criminal justice system, and the incentives of money and maintaining one's reputation?

****

After reminding students they need to cite research studies in their essays, I sit down at the desk in front of the class and reach for a stack of blue books from another class. Before starting to grade them, I smile to myself as I remember Valerie's husband Steve, kidding me recently by asking,

"What sort of sick puppy has three murderers in his circle of acquaintances and friends?"

EPILOGUE

Since the end of the period (1960s through 1980s) covered in this story, I have not compulsively kept track of the privileged psychopathic criminals featured here, who helped change me as a person and a criminologist. I have consulted various databases to see if any of the four men have re-offended, but that's about it. I've also not had contact with any of them.

Nor have I kept track of every misdeed or wrongdoing by two women, who weren't criminals by any means, but whose narcissistic tendencies made my life considerably more challenging. (My apologies for not including Eve in this update, but I felt her manipulative, Machiavellian behavior was well established in the story. She did marry another person like Dad with a generous federal pension.)

For the following six Dark Triad individuals, I include here just what I've learned by chance about each of them over the decades since the end of this cautionary tale. I leave it up to readers as to whether the pictures I've painted of the six adequately justify the narcissist and psychopath labels I've used. Given the many different criteria presented over the years for these DSM behavior disorders, and given various reader sensibilities, I mainly use these labels for simpler, clearer communication. I do respect and honor readers who dispute these labels for any or all of my Dark Triad individuals.

CAROLE CONDE – The Mother-in-Law

1980s

A year after Lynn and I moved from Oakland to a secret location to contend with threats from Mitchell, Lynn gave birth to a baby boy. Mitchell had become mostly an unhappy memory then, and so, after some agonizing, Lynn and I revealed our address to Carole. With my parents deceased and Lynn's father incapable of grandparenting, we wanted at least one grandparent in our baby's life.

During the first year of baby-oriented gatherings, we and Carole danced around to avoid direct confrontations regarding our past battles. Whenever we stumbled by accident into a fight over Mitchell, we realized Carole was incapable of cautious exchanges of feelings and facts. We continued to table any real effort to reconcile at a deep level.

1990s

With her two young sons still at home, Carole manipulated one of the men in her life to marry her. Just like Eve, with whom Scott and I have not reconciled, Carole was ever-mindful of her partners' pensions. (She and Eve had the dark triad tendency to freeload or, to use a likely- sexist verb, gold-dig.) Carole needed to get her two boys through college, so she married a third time despite her new husband being, as she often said, "unreliable, a schmoozer, and a fibber."

Carole's eldest boy eventually graduated Berkeley at twenty-three and followed up with a Wharton MBA from Penn. Carole's youngest, Steven, finished college at twenty-seven and had just started working at Microsoft in 1999 in Seattle, when tragedy struck. He'd gone camping with a friend, and a huge tree limb over their tent broke off and crashed down onto it. Steven died instantly. His friend had just gone to the washroom nearby and was spared.

Carole fell into a depression over Steven's death, and it didn't help that she and her new husband had just separated. Perhaps as a result of this depression, Carole failed to take seriously the asthma she'd begun to develop. Four months after Steven's death, she died of an asthma attack, in large part because she failed to unlock her doors after calling 911. Firefighters had to break into her house and got to her seconds too late.

Regrettably, Lynn and I never had a chance to formally reconcile with Carole and put our battles behind us. When Carole's will was read, she'd left her house in Alameda, a valuable asset her mom had funded, to Lynn's sibs. In a sad parallel to my losing my inheritance to Eve, Carole left Lynn one dollar.

SHARON BELTON – The Ex-Wife

1980s

Sharon married Eduardo Flores—six years her senior, a naturalized citizen, and her illicit lover during our Warehouse days—and soon after, she found herself pregnant. Perhaps manifesting her ambivalence about nurturing kids (due to troubles with bonding and emotional attachment?), she arranged to have her daughter cared for by Eduardo's former wife. So, while she and Eduardo worked together on campus, his ex did a good amount of the childcare of Sharon's daughter and the ex's two sons by Eduardo.

Sharon stayed in touch with me after our divorce but not because she ever felt remorse about lying or coldly ending our relationship. Instead, she just wanted gossip and updates on Einhorn after figuring out that his Holly was the same RISD-bound art student she'd run into at Bryn Mawr College.

Sharon and I talked less and less after Einhorn fled, but at one point, she insisted on meeting Lynn. So when Lynn and I visited Eduardo's place one Saturday, we couldn't believe Sharon was letting her child run around with the sharpened end of a pencil in her mouth. We worried that her child would cleft her palate if she stumbled... and wondered about Sharon's parenting skills.

1990s

During periodic phone calls with Sharon, I'd ask about mutual friends from way-back and relatives of hers I'd gotten to know. More often than not, she told me that she'd ended communication with another of them. I always knew she never had any interest in keeping in touch with our friends from Philly or Berkeley. What surprised me, though, was that she said she'd never ever attend a Palo Alto High School reunion where we had many friends in common. And she never did.

She seemed almost proud that instead of painting, she cooked a lot, mended her family's threadbare clothes (as she termed them), and sewed numerous Halloween costumes.

2000s

I never bumped into Sharon in the East Bay, but haphazard phone conversations indicated that, though she no longer had kids at home to distract her, she still wasn't painting. When I asked if she ever regretted not utilizing the two post-graduate programs in art I paid for, she said no. It made me think of a narcissistic Dark Triad tendency whereby people initiate ambitious plans with others as collaborators, and then on a whim, discard them and move on to other plans that exclude them. Business partners or loved ones who do this to others often leave emotional and financial chaos in their wake.

2010s

Life got busy and I lost complete touch with Sharon. During this period, though, she started a process, unsolicited by me, of slowly mailing me every last photo and travel memento she had from our years together. When I found out she died in 2018, this odd behavior made some sense. However, there were things in her obit that mystified me, and since I was not notified about a memorial service, I never had a chance to get clarity.

Eduardo wrote in Sharon's obit that she died of a congenital heart defect. This shocked me, since she had hardy, long-lived parents and relatives. Moreover, I was the one with the heart defect, and she never shared her condition with me. Still, she may not have known about her heart problem until late in life since she avoided doctors and dentists despite always having robust health insurance.

Eduardo also wrote in Sharon's obit that, as foodies, they had dined at some of the world's finest restaurants. He elaborated saying they'd drunk fine wine and were no strangers to the French

Laundry in Yountville. And if referencing one of America's most expensive restaurants once wasn't enough, Eduardo ended the obit two sentences later with: "A most favored activity for Sharon and me were long, refreshing weekend trips to Point Reyes, Big Sur, Pacific Grove, and especially, our favorite dining locus in Yountville."

So how'd Sharon and Eduardo go from a household needing the mending of well-worn clothes to one frequenting three-star Michelin restaurants? They'd earned middle-class salaries as campus office workers. Further, how'd they buy a second home in the East Bay Hills on a golf course? Not likely inheritance—last I knew, Sharon's parents at least, remained vigorous and alive. A mystery.

PSYCHOPATHS,
Scarier than Dark Triad Narcissists and Machiavellians

Criminologists know that around three percent of Americans sitting alongside us and walking among us, have little conscience and experience feelings minimally. Sure, they may express some feelings and emotions to get by, but these are invariably limited and shallow. Such individuals also don't seem to need other people as a majority of us do.

Psychopaths, those most antisocial of the three dark triad types, tend to dominate others or, if severely disordered, assault them when frustrated. Some psychopaths in my accounting likely continue to do evil today. Sadly, no evidence-based treatment currently exists for psychopaths, considered to have a stable, hard-to-alter personality disorder.

BILL HANSON – The Paper Bag Killer

1970s

I had little contact with the Hanson family after Bill's commitment to Atascadero State Hospital and totally lost touch after my dad died in 1976. Unlike the rules for jails and prisons, privacy rules for mental health incarceration prevented Bill's release date from being made public, yet another perk privileged criminals get if judged insane.

So, like many other hushed-up aspects of Bill's case, it's unclear how long he remained incarcerated. At minimum, he stayed just long enough to be evaluated as sane by Atascadero psychiatrists. At maximum, he stayed by law no longer than the time served by sane offenders sentenced for first-degree murders at the same time he was. Even though most of them received death or natural life sentences in 1974, California voters and courts fought over the length of natural life subsequently, resulting in the parole of many natural lifers.

If I had to guess, Atascadero likely released Bill in 1978, which means he served only one second-degree murder sentence. That's very different from the first-degree-murder and attempted-murder sentences he deserved, given that most Americans wish that such punishment be a combo of incapacitation and repentance to deter others.

1980s

If Bill remained incarcerated into the '80s, he might've been frightened by violent inmates at Atascadero, just like scared, burned-out staff were. Violence escalated because new policies required staff to offer cookies and strolls around the grounds before medicating or restraining violent inmates with wrist or ankle straps. Bill might've also encountered trouble when Atascadero ended centrally dispensed medical and nursing services in favor of treatment customized around an inmate's needs. Many night-shift staff quit over safety concerns, and to lure them back to work Atascadero promised many revisions to safety protocols and salaries.

Bill might've struggled with the untimely death in the mid-eighties of his mother, Myrna, at age sixty-four, from alcoholism. If he did, it's likely his father and his new wife helped him cope.

How Bill initially adjusted to life outside Atascadero depended on whether the hospital achieved its rehab goals with him. As with their other hundred-plus criminally insane inmates, staff probably, besides treating Bill's alleged symptoms, instructed him in anger management and taught him independent-living skills. It's not known whether he benefitted from any of these efforts or from release to a halfway house in L.A. So many records remain sealed in his case that much is still shrouded in secrecy.

1990s

According to public records, Bill, like most ex-offenders, lived in many places—Los Angeles, Glendale, Rosemead, and Capitola. Despite family financial help allowing Bill the luxury of not having to work, he likely found these places inhospitable. Public records don't show Bill committing further crimes, just traffic violations.

After struggling despite his privileges, Bill moved to India for fifteen or so years, and presumably enjoyed life there. He became enamored of the teachings of guru Sathya Sai Baba of Puttaparthi, who claimed to be the reincarnation of a spiritual leader from Shirdi also thought to be god-like. Bill travelled too, putting fifty thousand miles on his motorcycle, exploring the vast and interesting subcontinent.

2000s

Bill married a woman named Nubia, and perhaps they lived in Bangalore, India,— at Guru Sai Baba's summer retreat. He allegedly didn't attend his dad Kent's service in 2005 when he died at ninety-three.

Interestingly, Bill was among relatively few foreigners who followed Sai Baba. Others included Canadian jazz trumpeter Maynard

Ferguson and artist Joan Brown, who taught Sharon at Berkeley. Brown tragically died at Sai Baba's main retreat in Puttaparthi, near Bangalore. Only fifty-two, Brown was installing one of her artistic obelisks in Sai Baba's museum when a concrete floor collapsed, killing her.

Besides everyday Indians, elites, celebs, and politicos joined Sai Baba's cult, thinking it more of a club because its reach extended throughout India, promising access to top jobs business opportunities, and financial funding. Others alleged that the enterprise engaged in murder, kidney-harvesting, money-laundering...and that Sai Baba often molested young boys.

2010s

Bill's guru died in 2011, and outside investigators discovered that his so-called miracles, like pulling wedding rings from mid-air, were sleight-of-hand tricks he'd learned from his magician uncle. Many concluded he was a trickster and a cheat. I thought he resembled Uri Geller, who drew Einhorn, Puharich, and others into his orb of believers in the paranormal and other psychic phenomena.

No doubt Bill found some comfort and happiness with Sai Baba's cult if research into the infamous Rajneesh cult in a small central Oregon town is accurate. One study found serene contentment among the many privileged followers who joined Rajneesh, a holy man who owned endless numbers of Rolls Royce's and was materialistic like Sai Baba.

Somehow, Bill's privilege continues to this day. He's ended up living in a pricey Bay Area suburb. According to one estimate, he's worth over a million dollars.

JED DRELL – The "Psycho"-ologist

1980s

After Jed convinced Angela to reconcile and move to a house not far from where he'd tried to kill her, he remained nonviolent but not rehabbed. His Psych Department colleague Janet Noces alleges he continued to harass women long after being reinstated in 1976. It's sad, but understandable, in this post-Me-Too era that, decades ago, Professor Noces couldn't convince administrators to sanction ex-con Jed for sexual misconduct.

1990s

At some point, Jed stopped talking to all but one of his fellow faculty, not even letting his wife speak to them during a colleague's funeral. This meant he also stopped attending faculty meetings, which may've been a blessing, since he'd advocated splitting the department in two before he'd tried to kill Angela. Jed's estrangement was his own doing: colleagues didn't ostracize him, but eventually, an aura of stigma swirled about him. Like a true psychopath, he carried on as if he'd never been homicidal in the past or predatory in the present, in part because he allegedly expunged student complaints and harassment allegations from his personnel file every five years.

2000s

Jed took several leaves to teach at universities in Canada, England, New Zealand, and Singapore—because he preferred foreign faculty and students. Whether they preferred him remains unclear because locally students often told Professor Noces they thought Jed scary. She still feared him herself. His attorney Lincoln Mintz may've also felt stressed by having to represent Jed. Mintz had begun neglecting his law practice in the late '90s because of stress, and the California Bar stripped him of his license in the 2000s.

2010s

Still a high-functioning academic, Jed managed to keep writing books on drugs, scientific research, and problems in the medical field. However, his comeuppance came in 2013 when he sexually harassed a bright young student. She happened to be a resolute woman whose fiancé and family supported her decision to report Jed to administrators, who took harassment more seriously than their predecessors had.

Since Jed had cyber-harassed the student, among other things, authorities confiscated his computers and found incriminating evidence. They gave him a choice between retiring immediately or having them give the evidence to the police. Jed chose to retire, probably to everyone's mutual relief.

MITCHELL LEWIS – The Executioner

1980s

Soon after Lynn and I moved and I'd threatened to sue Fred Willis and Oregon's parole board, Mitchell stopped stalking us. He got a job as a Portland State janitor and likely augmented his wages by dealing drugs. (Like so many dealers, he'd lived a life on the run, bolting from Florida, then California, and finally from Oregon.)

No surprise then that Portland police arrested Mitchell for three felonies in August 1986! So, less than nine years after his bloody rampage and less than two since his parole, a Portland grand jury indicted Mitchell again. This time, at age thirty-one, for three counts of first-degree grand-theft, which constituted a major violation of his 7-Up parole from his murder sentence. But Mitchell probably sensed before reoffending that his new parole officer, who replaced Grady Nelson, wouldn't revoke his parole since she would anger the progressive-liberal board.

With Mitchell spending but a month in jail, his attorney persuaded a district court judge to release him after paying $1k toward a bail of just $10k. As Mitchell waited for his next hearing, he walked around a free man. Portland State fired him from his job, which he exploited to commit his grand thefts, and booted him from his campus apartment. He moved to a place next door to a church, of all places, and he began work as a construction worker for his brother.

Mitchell's new felonies and the machinations he asked of his new attorney, still taxpayer funded and gratis to still-privileged Mitchell, confirmed Lynn's and my belief that prison never rehabbed him. Once again, he copped a plea by which he withdrew his not guilty pleas and admitted to fewer felonies. In return, a new judge promised not to throw the book at him during sentencing, in return for a lighter sentence.

System indecisiveness (oft-changed entries, incomplete forms) and disorganization stretched out Mitchell's sentencing for nine months. At various times, judges, different from the prior two, considered meting out sentences as disparate as six months in jail, two-years' probation, service at a work-release site, $10k in restitution, time at a halfway house, or combinations of these. Finally, a judge in a specialty court, agonizing about what to do with several temporary and amended judgements, sentenced Mitchell to two years' probation, which constrains and restricts even less restrictive than parole. In short, Mitchell got a slap on the wrist. Justice Lite again.

1990s

When Mitchell got off probation, he likely supplemented the low pay of seasonal construction work with substitute bartending and club gigs. Of course, this courts the danger of dealing relapses and would've troubled victim Cynthia's widower, who continued to own and manage several Portland bars. Paul Gifford remarried, but then divorced: a frequent second tribulation, researchers find, for people intimately touched by murder. This family instability couldn't have helped Cynthia's still-young daughter.

Mitchell's playing with fire may've made him uneasy knowing people in the bar and restaurant business spread stories about him.

But over time, he must've grown most uneasy about conservative Portland and Oregon voters—ticked off with dysfunctional justice systems—who demanded and won: minimums for gun crimes, extra strikes for many offenses, and enhancements for property and drug crimes.

Not a high-functioning psychopath, lacking the strong urges and self-discipline of Ira Einhorn, Mitchell exhibits Cleckley and Newman's hallmark of typical psychopathy where weak urges break through even weaker restraints.

2000s

Mitchell moved to San Francisco in 2004, knowing he could drive from his place on Pine Street to ours in Oakland in twenty minutes. He likely drove by the duplex, and who knows what he would've done if we'd still lived there?

At one point, Mitchell joined his brother and his family in a small town near Yosemite where they'd relocated from Portland. Soon, though his brother and wife separated, perhaps due to the difficulty of living with Mitchell. The two brothers headed by themselves to Billings, Montana.

They spent a year earning money before moving to Hot Springs in northwest Montana, where they purchased land and lived in a Quonset hut while constructing a new house. The tiny town of five hundred, known for its geothermal springs and weekend music festivals, may've provided Mitchell contentment... and freedom. But not freedom from drug abuse. According to his death certificate, he died in 2010 at age fifty-four of chronic alcoholism.

IRA EINHORN – The Unicorn Killer

1980s

The search to find Ira after he'd bolted before his trial in 1981 revealed he'd jumped to Montreal (meeting Seagram heir Bronfman), to London (joining his girlfriend J.M. Morrison), and to Dublin (renting from a professor). Rich DiBenedetto from the Philly DA's Extraditions Office located Ira in Ireland in 1982, and again in 1984 and 1986, but U.S.-Irish treaties prevented Ira's arrest each time. Over time, Ira's petite girlfriend, who'd be helpless like Holly against an irate 220-pound Ira, got Ira to agree to go their separate ways. Morrison returned to the U.S. to her parents' considerable relief and traded immunity from various accessory charges by spilling to DiBenedetto.

Ira remained on the lam, narrowly evading arrest in Stockholm, Sweden, in 1988 and disappearing once more. While lucky to escape, he was unlucky to be exposed that year. A reporter with access to Ira's subpoenaed journals and the names of past girlfriends uncovered damning info about him. His investigation illuminated, like a thunderbolt, the disconnect between Ira's public nonviolent self and a secret violent self, which required a psychopath's cunning and deceptiveness to maintain.

According to the reporter's story, Ira's journals revealed how he equated love with violence, which he seemed to like, in the cases of two women he'd attacked before Holly. The reporter tracked down Rita Siegal, who'd dated Ira after he'd graduated from Penn in 1962. A bright, slightly insecure Long Islander at Vermont's Bennington College, Siegal claimed Ira fabricated their romance in his mind. She said, "The great romance of the century was what was in his head...I got the feeling it was a sick relationship."

And sick it became, when—realizing she really meant it was over six months later—Ira cornered Siegal in her dorm room and approached her. On prior occasions, when he shifted his body in a menacing way, she'd run. A lithe dancer, she could evade him. This time, though, he caught her by the neck and then almost choked her to death. She spent the night in the infirmary but didn't press charges. When she encountered him weeks later at a mutual friend's home, Ira gave her a black eye. With all this, she still managed to leave Ira.

The reporter then found Judy Lewis, who related a similar fantasy relationship during which Ira had decided in 1965 to stop bedding women and focus on her. After a stormy year-long relationship, the tall, attractive Penn student tried repeatedly to end it. Finally, Ira lost control at one point, striking her head with a coke bottle and then strangling her. Ira escaped before Lewis' neighbors rushed to her place, finding her on the floor with blood everywhere. They stayed with her until she regained consciousness, but she never pressed charges.

Amazingly, the handful of people who knew about these two attacks never—effectively, at least—revealed them to authorities. They had ample time during Holly's nineteen-month disappearance until the discovery of her remains, and again, during the twenty-one-month run-up to Ira's trial.

1990s

In exile somewhere in Europe, Ira moved around and lived life freely just as Mitchell and Bill did during the '90s. Meanwhile, Holly Maddux, Cynthia Gifford, Ara Kuznezow, and Lorenzo Carniglia, all murdered around fifteen years earlier, were but photographs hanging on the walls of their loved ones' homes. However, given the shocking revelations of Ira's past violence, Philly authorities decided to try Ira in absentia in 1993. Jurors in a criminal court eventually convicted him of Holly's murder, sentencing him to life in prison without the possibility of parole.

In 1997, DiBenedetto located Ira in a small, picturesque town in France: Champagne-Mouton. French police soon apprehended Ira, living parasitically again, as psychopaths often do, off the wealth of a statuesque Swede, Anika Flodin. Unfortunately, complications involving French and American extradition laws tied up the case in courts for years.

During that time, Holly's family members sued Ira in 1999 in civil court for wrongful death damages. They won a $907-million judgment, ensuring that Ira would never make money off Holly's murder.

2000s

When France's highest court denied Ira's final appeal in a third extradition hearing, he slit his throat and was hospitalized overnight near Champagne-Mouton with non-life-threatening cuts to a couple of veins. Ira's theatrics did help trigger a fourth, and final, hearing. The European Court of Human Rights ruled against him, and authorities flew him back to the U.S. in 2001. He'd been on the lam, living the good life, for twenty years.

Ira immediately had to account for Holly's death in a Philly court. Not surprising, he maintained that the CIA and KGB had framed him, but jury members did not buy it. They found him guilty, and in September 2002, sentenced him to life without parole.

2010s

In April 2016, after Ira had served fourteen years at maximum-security Houtzdale in Pennsylvania, authorities transferred him to Laurel Highlands, a minimum-security prison southeast of Pittsburgh for medical treatment. He lived four years more.

2020s

Ira died April 3, 2020 at age seventy-nine, of natural causes from long-standing cardiac problems, unrelated to the Covid-19 pandemic.

Upon hearing of his death, the prosecutor who convicted him twice said Einhorn died in relative obscurity, which is poetic justice. Being unknown and not being paid attention to was almost the worst kind of punishment for him.

The detective who found Holly's body and arrested Ira in Philly, Michael Chitwood, stated in 2020, "As bad as I feel about anyone dying, I'm not going to lose sleep about his passing." The only thing

Chitwood regretted was that Holly's parents never got closure. Her dad took his own life in 1988, and her mother died two years later of emphysema. They are buried on each side of their daughter's grave in Texas, where all three are at peace, finally free of the Unicorn Killer.

NOTES

To keep this story engaging and readable without compromising facts and people's privacy, I've had to wear alternately the hats of a novelist, a memoirist, a true-crime historian, and a DOJ "witness-protection" specialist. Before elaborating on the last two hats, a SPOILER ALERT: Read these Notes after finishing a given chapter (or even the book) to preserve the suspense I tried to build in wearing the first two hats.

These Notes, and the Bibliography that follows, show how I've tried to anchor my story to historical facts no matter what my recollection of certain facts may have been at the start. Thus, I've augmented my memory via interviews, written accounts, personal journals, and media footage of events–not to mention crime scene photos, court proceedings, and governmental reports.

Several survivors and witnesses I interviewed showed sensitivity to the gravity of the topics discussed and great courage in their honest portrayal of events. Since this story happened relatively recently and these and other key people are still living, I've protected several of them with slightly altered identities and characteristics. And since locations, institutions, and specific dates often reveal identity, I've also engaged in "victim/witness protection" by slightly altering some scenes and places as well as time-shifting a couple of events. In some circumstances, the Notes below reflect this, as in the court-case numbers used, to prevent easy identification of some offenders, victims, and survivors.

A CRIMINOLOGIST'S STORY

p-xvi **accused Abbott of being a sexual psychopath:** According to Webster's Dictionary, sexual psychopathy is "the condition of a psychopathic or sociopathic personality manifested by the commission of sexual crimes." The term _sociopath_ is used to describe what a mental health professional would diagnose as antisocial personality disorder (ASPD). _Psychopaths_ are considered to have a more severe form of ASPD than sociopaths. (More info about psychopaths in text and these Notes, e.g., Ch3.)

p-xvi psychology at Yale, psychiatry at Columbia Med School, and criminology at UPenn: I tend to use social psychology and psychiatry in my criminological work but borrow from the other social sciences when need be. I majored in premed psychology at Yale, which had the foremost Psychology Department in the U.S. at the time. I then studied psychiatry at Columbia's Medical School, tied with Harvard's as the top med school in the US during my time there. Finally, I entered the Sociology PhD program at UPenn in Philadelphia, which is where this story starts, to study first, under the founding dean, and then, second, under the succeeding dean of scientific criminology.

p-xvii When these are extremely _narcissistic_, manipulative: Individuals with a narcissistic personality disorder (NPD) often have a tendency to exploit others and have a sense of excessive entitlement, maybe even demanding special treatment. (See notes for Ch 22, and Epilogue, for more info about narcissists.)

Manipulatives–aka Machiavellians after the author of the first book on manipulating one's way to power–have elements of the antisocial personality disorder (ASPD) and borderline personality disorder (BPD). Although ASPD and BPD are both characterized by manipulative behavior, there're differences in the underlying motivation. Individuals with ASPD manipulate others to reap power, profit, or material gain. Those with BPD, manipulate to gain concern, adulation, or attachment from individuals or caretakers. (Paraphrase of the DSM at psychdb.com/personality/borderline.) Source: American Psychiatric Association. Diagnostic and Statistical Manual of Mental Disorders, 5th ed. (Washington, D.C.: APA, 2022). The DSM is similar to the ICD: World Health Organization, International Classification of Diseases, 11th ed. (Geneva, CH: WHO Press, 2022).

p-xvii **or psychopathic, they're part of what psychologists call the Dark Triad:** I elect to use the terms "Dark Triad" and "psychopath" rather than the strictly clinical ones (e.g. ASPD, etc.) because the former are used in applied criminology, especially by corrections officials Also, it's a convention to do so among true crime authors and many journalists and media writers. They use Dark Triad and psychopath, and so do I in the book, given that readers also use and intuitively understand them. See Robert Hare as well as D.L. Paulhus et al, "Shedding light on the Dark Triad of personality: Narcissism, Machiavellianism, and Psychopathy," (San Antonio, TX, Annual meeting of the Society for Personality and Social Psychology, 2001).

p-xvii **preparation, aspirations, and everyday work of criminologists:** Criminologists study the nature, cause, extent, and control of criminal behavior. Criminalists, by contrast, deal with criminalistics, i.e., forensic evidence like DNA, finger prints, tire and shoe tracks, etc. The first chapter of this book begins with me studying criminology in Philadelphia, where I met my first soon-to-be murderer, Ira Einhorn.

A DETECTIVE'S STORY

p1 **A Detective's Story:** Most of the information and dialogue in this story come from articles and media interviews of Detective Chitwood, as well as from a book written about him: Harold I. Gullan. Tough Cop: Mike Chitwood vs. the Scumbags. (Philadelphia: Camino Books, 2013). While the "omniscient" POV of these couple of pages knows everything about Detective Chitwood–including his thoughts, feelings, actions, and backstory–the account is how I imagine things went down and can't be attributed to an actual interview transcript.

328 • KARL SCHONBORN

CHAPTER 1

p6 **Dubbed the Peace Games:** Twenty people role-played being nonviolent "soldiers" against six soldiers from a fictitious Chinese Communist country called Eurasia, one billion people strong, who were in the process of invading America. Eurasia refused to join the embrace and adoption of nonviolence happening throughout western nations, perhaps because it threatened their authoritarian rule. The Chinese army wanted to preserve the infrastructure of the U.S. and western nations so it used conventional rather than mass-destruction weapons. Presently, Eurasia has taken over most American cities, but the three branches of American government still exist "underground"– fully operational and directing the nonviolent resistance against the Chinese.

p7 **The role-play started:** My depiction of the Peace Games is based on my recollections and on descriptions from Michael Doyle, Radical Chapters: Pacifist Bookseller Roy Kepler and the Paperback Revolution (New York: Columbia University Press, 2012), 249-254. The dialogue I didn't witness while in jail comes from reminiscences by Sharon and others.

p16 **"They can bust me, but they can't pin anything on me:"** Statement based on material in Steven Levy, The Unicorn's Secret (New York: Prentice-Hall Press, 1988), 89. Throughout this book, Ira's words and dialogue with Sharon and me are based on conversations, articles and books dealing with him, and sometimes a combination of all three.

CHAPTER 2

p21 **thesis launched:** Approval to launch a PhD thesis or dissertation comes after a long slog thru proposal, prospectus, and OK for access to needed data. The only mumbo jumbo here is the prospectus. The main purpose of it is to ensure that the dissertation project is "viable" in the sense that (i) it addresses interesting and well-defined question(s), (ii) the proposed methods are appropriate, and (iii) the student has the background and skills to carry out the project. The result of all this, plus blood-sweat-and-tears: Karl Schonborn. Responses to Social Conflict- violent and nonviolent third- party conflict intervention (Ann Arbor, MI: University Microfilms International, 1971).

p25 **would've been good for my conscientious objector's essay:** Source for this, besides my own recollection: Anonymous, "Application Form For C.O. Altered By Draft Board," The Harvard Crimson, 11-12-68.

CHAPTER 3

p31 **Psychopaths ...Often have no friends, even jobs, as a result:** Psychopaths are considered to have a severe form of antisocial personality disorder (APSD). It exists when:

A. There is. a pervasive pattern of disregard for and violation of the rights of others occurring since age 15 years, as indicated by three (or more) of the following:

1. failure to conform to social norms with respect to lawful behaviors as indicated by repeatedly performing acts that are grounds for arrest

2. deceitfulness, as indicated by repeated lying, use of aliases, or conning others for personal profit or pleasure

3. impulsivity or failure to plan ahead

4. irritability and aggressiveness, as indicated by repeated physical fights or assaults

5. reckless disregard for safety of self or others

6. consistent irresponsibility, as indicated by repeated failure to sustain consistent work behavior or honor financial obligations

7. lack of remorse, as indicated by being indifferent to or rationalizing having hurt, mistreated, or stolen from another.

B. The individual is at least age 18 years.

C. There is evidence of conduct disorder with onset before age 15 years.

D. The occurrence of antisocial behavior is not exclusively during the course of schizophrenia or a manic episode.

Source: APA, DSM, 5th ed. Text Revision, 2013, §,301.7.

p32 **But he did reveal his motive:** The absurd motive he cited, in effect to get servants for his rebirth in heaven, is cited in many places, e.g., Michael L. Cole, The Zodiac Revisited: The Facts of the Case. (Cleveland, OH: Twin Prime Publishing, 2021). I've only looked at the first of Cole's three Zodiac books, and despite being "fact-based speculation," it seems better researched and written than Graysmith's popular books on the topic and the basis for the 2007 movie, Zodiac.

CHAPTER 4

p36 **men with that birthday will be drafted immediately:** Based on my memory and historynet.com/live-from-dc-its-lottery-night-1969.

p39 **This is that day:** This account of Ira's speechifying, which went on and off for half an hour, is based on my recollections, newspaper reports, scattered info in Levy's Secret, and from articles written about Ira (e.g., old.poweltonvillage.org/profiles/einhorn1. html).

p40 **from his poem** *Howl*: Allen Ginsberg's poem "Howl," first published in 1956, is one of the most widely read and translated poems of the twentieth century. Many critics consider it a breakthrough in contemporary poetry and a literary masterpiece. Other info at britannica.com/topic/Howl-poem-by-Ginsberg.

CHAPTER 5

p41 **A Slasher's Story** As in "A Detective's Story," most of the information and dialogue in this chapter is based on personal knowledge, articles, books, news accounts, and media footage about the subject. In effect, given the third person POV used, this chapter amounts to a fictional retelling of an event.

CHAPTER 6

p44 **involvement in our grad-student uprising critical, among other things, of Chair Wolfgang's absences:** Jon Snodgrass and others spearhead the revolt, and Mike Hogan and I do as much as we can to get others in the department involved.

CHAPTER 7

p49 I'm Jack Schonborn's boy, Karl: "Besides being a friend of my dad, Bryers was typical of the movers and shakers who would soon sing Ira's praises: "He is of good– excellent – character," exclaimed a corporate attorney with whom he had worked on a fundraising project. "He has the highest level of integrity," remarked an Ivy League lecturer, "a man who is compassionate and loving." A former Wall Street Journal economist. Ranked his reputation as "the finest." And an Episcopalian minister judged him as "a man of nonviolence."(crimelibrary.org/notorious_murders/famous/einhorn/bonded_2.html)

p50 who just got released from prison: "Jim Wood, David Harris," *Marin Magazine*, December 19, 2008, marinmagazine.com/people/david-harris, 68.

p51 Ira at a press conference: Secret, 127.

CHAPTER 8

p59 A Serial Killer's Story: As in the prior "shopping story," most all of the information and dialogue in his story comes from police reports about the bad guy, as well as from newspaper articles and book info about him. In short, the author, knows much about this guy, but this chapter amounts to how I imagined his shopping unfolded.

CHAPTER 9

p65 Manic depressive The current term is bipolar disorder: It causes extreme mood swings that include emotional highs (mania) and lows (depression). Manic episodes may include high energy, reduced need for sleep, reduced inhibitions, etc. Depressive episodes may include flat affect, low energy, low motivation, and loss of interest in daily activities. From Chapter 6 of the DSM.

CHAPTER 10

p74 the Operation Outreach program I've helped implement in Hayward: Karl Schonborn, "Police and Social Workers as Members of New Crisis-Management Teams," The Journal of Sociology and Social Welfare, 3, no. 6 (1976): article 8.

p82 The city feels terrorized.": See Ch8 as well as Henderson and Summerlin, The Super Sleuths (New York: Dodd, Mead, 1976), 269-291.

p77 Can't believe it! In *Cosmopolitan!*": The magazine featured a poster of Scott "nude" as part of O'Breen's ad campaign for her "Men for Women" posters. Cosmopolitan Magazine (New York City: Hearst Corporation, 1972), 225. Newspapers ran stories about O'Breen turning the tables on men's magazines, e.g., Eloise Dungan, "The Male Nudes Women Prefer," S.F. Examiner, August 29, 1972, 21.

p79 Just think of the communists in Burma (now Myanmar)... who couldn't govern and soon relinquished power: For a description, see en.wikipedia.org/wiki/ Communist_insurgency_in_Burma.

p80 a San Francisco law-enforcement official and friend, told me: Officer Chen's comments and information in these passages made up a small part of the totality of what I eventually learned about the Hanson case. I have often edited, rectified, or expanded on them. Like the three other privileged characters in this book, my writing here is a combination of personal knowledge, news accounts, and written materials about the suspect.

p83 Izzy updates me further: See Ch10 above for much of this update. Additionally, the source for "tracking thousands of leads" is Anonymous, "Psychiatrist's Son Arrested for Paper 'Paper bag' Murders," Oakland Tribune, 1-28-74, sec. E, p.3.

p84 So I discuss serial killer stats: An excellent source of info in this regard: Peter Vronsky, Serial Killers: The Method and Madness of Monsters (New York: Berkley Books, 2004).

p86 He sped down the alleyway: Radio report derived from Henderson, Sleuths, 278. **p92 Falzon's investigation revealed:** Ibid., 279, 285.

CHAPTER 11

p89 Izzy tells me: Ibid., 284-5. The next several pages, including dialogue, draw from material written about Hanson in books, news articles, and elsewhere as well as from recollections and conversations with Jack and Eve Schonborn.

p93 According to newspaper accounts: Material presented in the next page and a half, including court dialogue, comes from newspaper accounts of court hearings and proceedings, e.g., newspapers.com, and *The Times Herald* (Port Huron, Michigan, 12-05-76).

p96 takes minimal hits for a few reasons: Here, and later on, I chiefly draw from memory and two books. See Jeffrey Toobin's *American Heiress: The Wild Saga of the Kidnapping* (New York: Anchor, 2017). And see honored true-crime writer Clark Howard's *Zebra:The True Account of the 179 Days of Terror in San Francisco* (New York: Richard Marek Publishers, 1979).

p98 I finally bring up labeling theory: The labeling theoretical tradition in sociology started with social interactionists G.H Mead and Edwin Lemert. Later, Erving Goffman (Stigma), Howard Becker (Outsiders) and David Matza (On Becoming Deviant) popularized it in the '60s. Social psych notions of stereotyping, self-fulfilling prophecies are still relevant in today's debates about crime, gender identity, and mental illness.

p98 checked eight research assistants into twelve psych hospitals across the U.S: For a good description of this type of "field" study, see Erving Goffman, Asylums: Essays on the Social Situation of Mental Patients and Other Inmates (New York: Anchor Books, 1961), p.4.

CHAPTER 12

p100 The judge opens the hearing: I created the account of Bill's sanity hearing chiefly from a) newspapers, b) legal texts re insanity, c) info regarding Bill's Incident Report 73-100684, and d) informant interviews. Examples from these multiple sources include: Anonymous, "Defendant said [to be] Victim of Fantasy," San Rafael Daily Independent Journal, 01-29-74, p.4; Frank Schmalleger, Criminology Today (Upper Saddle River,NJ: Prentice Hall, 2004),189-93; and finally, a source of Judge Convin info: Jay Robert Nash, World Encyclopedia of 20th Century Murder (Saint Paul, MN: Paragon House,1992), 271.

p103 Kent shook their hands, thanking them profusely: Drawn from Henderson, Sleuths, 291.

p104 sentenced forthwith to Atascadero State Hospital for treatment appropriate the criminally insane: Ibid., 290-91.

p111 FBI defines 'em as killers of two or more: The FBI's official definition is: "The unlawful killing of two or more victims by the same offender(s), in separate events."fbi. gov/stats-services/publications/serial-murder#two, p.4.

p108 Bill's an example of their organized killer: The info in this section (e.g., types of serial killers, shrink Joel Fort's take on Bill, Ed Kemper's "insanity") chiefly comes from my basic crim knowledge and from the following sources: Peter Vronsky, Serial Killers (New York: Berkley Books, 2004) and Joel Fort, MD, Alcohol: Our Biggest Drug Problem (New York: McGraw-Hill, 1973).

p109 we drop Ric and Kath off at Synanon: Reports and info about Synanon here and in subsequent chapters come from the author and Ric Orsic's research over time as well as from Lewis Yablonsky, The Tunnel Back (London: Penguin Books, 1967).

p109 Zebra suspects: Numbers, statistics, and descriptive material regarding trials come from Wiki (en.wikipedia.org/wiki/Zebra murders) as well as from Clark Howard's *Zebra*.

CHAPTER 13

p112 found her lying on the floor in a hall: The news accounts here and at the end of the prior chapter come from newspaper accounts such as "Prof held in Stabbing of Wife,"Daily Review, 12-09-74, p8 and "Prof's wife released [from Hospital]," *Berkeley Daily Gazette*, 12-18-74, p17. Generally, for this and subsequent chapters dealing with Jed, statements, information, and created dialogue come from a variety of sources: newspaper articles, conversations and correspondence with Psychology and Sociology department faculty, and interviews with a School Dean (e.g., on 3-7-18, 4-6-17). Additional consulted sources include: university catalogs, Jed's website, his LinkedIn page, and other social media as well as his author profiles on Amazon and elsewhere.

p117 rather than at the tough county jail 26 miles away: Ibid. Examples of judicial and other Jed-related matters (here and in subsequent chapters) which are also drawn from sources noted in Ch13 include: "Judge Sidney Silverman refusing to lower Jed's $50,000 bail, and Jed's various pleadings.

p119 that's why he attacked his wife:" Derived from "Jail Term for Prof in Wife Knifing," *The Montclarion*, 3-28-75, p.37.

CHAPTER 14

p120 Do you so plead now?: Ibid. Ch13 provides the info for statements regarding several rulings, for instance the suspended state prison sentence and the need to prove impoverishment.

p121 couldn't go through the trauma of divorce: These and other confidential statements attributed to Jed come from conversations and interviews with various colleagues and fellow faculty members of Jed's academic department. They became public knowledge too. They were also mentioned in the *The Montclarion* (see Ch13).

p121 It's fourteen years: *Penal Code §217* "Every person who assaults another with intent to commit murder, is punishable by imprisonment in the state prison not less than one nor more than 14 years," according to *Penal Code of California (Peace Officers Abridged Edition)* 4th ed. (Sacramento: Department of General Services, 1971), p.40. Also relevant, "Professor Sentenced for Assault on Wife," *Berkeley Daily Gazette*, 3-27- 75, p14.

p123 Drell's violations of Judge Silverman's orders: A local newspaper wrote about Jed's violations, e.g.,"Prof ordered back to jail," *Berkeley Daily Gazette*, 4-30-75, p12 and again it wrote "A Stunning use of work furlough [an Editorial calling for a grand jury investigation of violations]," *Berkeley Daily Gazette*, 5-06-75, p11.

p123 Jed's applied for a six-figure grant to study the ... inmates with whom he's serving time: "Former prof-felon wants to study Santa Rita, *Berkeley Daily Gazette*, 11-21-75, p.19.

p125 trial of four Death Angel suspects in the Zebra Killings: Passages here based on sources noted at Ch12.

CHAPTER 15

p129 key in the history of both Microsoft and Costco: Founded in 1972, Microsoft moved its HQ to Bellevue, then Redmond, WA, both next to Kirkland in1979. Costco was initially headquartered at its first warehouse in Seattle, but moved its HQ to Kirkland in 1987, naming its signature brand after Kirkland.

p129 he should've ordered bypass surgery for Dad: Autopsy 76-2547274, May 2, 1976, Jack Reiff Schonborn, Jefferson County, WA.

p130 no basis for preventing his permanent return to the psychology department: The radio report of the VP re-instating Jed at the university is derived from Staff Writer, "Convicted professor to resume duties," *Berkeley Daily Gazette*, 6-10-76, p13.

p130 Didn't use all my ammo: The allegations of the next page or so are based on an interview and correspondence with Dr. Janet Noces.

p131 they let slip the rest of the truth:" Source: This comes from specific information, more than speculation, from interviews with Psychology Department colleagues of Jed and a college dean.

p132 I relate Janet's theory: Interview and correspondence with Prof. Janet Noces.

p132 I explain another theory, a Psych prof's, that Jed's got a screw loose: Based on an interview with a faculty member conversant with how department and university decisions were made regarding Jed.

CHAPTER 16

p138 I learn from counseling that losses: Taken from Judith Viorst, *Necessary Losses: The Loves, Illusions, Dependencies, and Impossible Expectations That All of Us Have to Give Up in Order to Grow* (New York: Simon and Schuster, 1998).

CHAPTER 17

p139 the time for a fresh start had come: This statement based on sources noted elsewhere as well as Greg Walter, "Holly," Philadelphia Magazine, pp.12-79.

CHAPTER 18

p141 A Unicorn's Story: As in the prior bad guy "shopping stories," most of the info and dialogue in this chapter is based on articles, books, news accounts, media footage, and personal knowledge of the individual. However, even though I know much about this bad guy— and I've written this chapter from an all-knowing third person POV —it is a fictional retelling of events.

p142 paid extra for a Sunday delivery by two teenagers: This statement is based on articles, books, news accounts, media footage, and personal information about the individual.

p143 books, including ones on the ancient art of mummification: The sources for this sentence and for the two prior paragraphs are noted in Ch18 above. Also key is testimony given at Ira's 2001 trial, namely, "Witness Statements," Action News True Crime, (youtube.com/watch?v=NjLRpvJyLm8) at 15:40 and 15:45, respectively.

CHAPTER 19

p145 foundation which selects the artists for an annual show: The nonprofit, Eyes and Ears Foundation, founded in 1976, called for submissions of ideas and selected a dozen or so artists as winners. Foster and Kleiser, an outdoor advertising company, gave 12' x 24' canvases to Sharon and other winners, and then donated a month of billboard space for the resultant works of art.

CHAPTER 20

p150 An Executioner's Story: Just as in the other three "bad guy shopping stories," most all of the info here is based on extensive information provided in articles, books, news accounts, and court documents. Incidentally, besides it's literary function, this story, like those in the other gun shopping stories, is intended to make real the distressing ease of weapons acquisition in the U.S.

p151 really shoot from a jacket pocket?": It's something that is possible in the right circumstances, but to be done properly, it requires 1) a revolver, 2) a bobbed or hammerless design, and 3) a willingness to have one's pocket and jacket shredded. quora.com/Is-firing-a-pistol-from-inside-a-jacket-pocket-at-close-range-a-feasible-strategy-for-self-defense.

CHAPTER 21

p156 when the O'Neills' *Open Marriage* came out: O'Neill, Nena and George, *Open Marriage: A New Lifestyle for Couples*, (New York: M. Evans 1972.)

CHAPTER 22

p165 Some use the term "narcissist" to describe her: Individuals with a narcissistic personality disorder often have a tendency to exploit others and have a sense of excessive entitlement, maybe demanding special treatment. Other generalities:

-Vulnerability in self-esteem makes individuals with narcissistic personality disorder very sensitive to "injury" from criticism or defeat.

-If their impairment is severe, it may lead to marital problems and interpersonal relationship conflicts.

-Such individuals may face occupational difficulties, and show an unwillingness to take risks in competitive or other situations in which defeat is possible.

-Individuals with narcissistic personality disorder may have more difficulties with the aging process, especially when it comes to new physical and occupational limitations related to ageing and "mid-life crises." (Paraphrase of DSM by psychdb. com/personality/narcissistic.)

p166 An attractive woman doesn't simply disappear. People notice: My sources, besides those listed in the Bibliography for Ira, include numerous news articles by columnists and writers (e.g., AP's writer Ian Phillips) who followed Ira's case as it unfolded over the years. A particularly relevant source for Saul Lapidus and friends is: law.jrank. org/pages/3579/Ira-Einhorn-Trial-1993-An-Abusive-Relationship-Leads- Murder.html.

p166 going to a store to buy tofu and greens for dinner . . . and vanished. Different versions of this explanation by Ira are quoted by several sources, including: R. Kimmie, "Holly Maddux and the Unicorn Killer," (documentingreality.com/forum/f237/holly-maddux-unicorn-killer-149486/), 11-17-14, p.1.

p170 "geographically undesirable" romantic relationships can be difficult: The long distance romantic relationships (LDRRs) that result from GU individuals are particularly prevalent among college students today, constituting 25% to 50% of all relationships according to wiki. With "facetime" and other tech options today, LDRRs may not be as difficult today as in the '70s.

CHAPTER 23

p173 Shocking News and Einhorn's CIA Defense: Almost all of the information and dialogue in this chapter, and others in the book, derives from personal interactions with the man as well as from numerous articles, books, news accounts, and media astories about Ira. Specifically useful for this page, Joe O'Dowd et al, "Skeleton in Trunk Linked to City Guru," *Philadelphia Daily News*, 3-28-79, p.5.

p174 No one would've ever found out: This friend of Ira's, Ehrlich, believed Ira's trunk contained CIA and KGB papers because Ira could've easily disposed of a body anytime. All he'd have to do is ask for Ehrlich's help getting it to one of his dumpsites, and, voila, it would never be found. Levy, *Secret*, 248.

p174 unexplained calamities befalling their colleagues of late: *Secret*, 245, 316.

p176 Puharich, an expert on Soviet psychotronics as mind-control weapons: Ibid., 128-9, 220, 242.

p177 who had an open marriage with his wife. Holly liked Liss a lot: Ibid., 179-82, 191,199.

p178 people get jealous mainly over what matters most to them: Sources: P. Salovey and J. Rodin, "Some antecedents and consequences of social-comparison jealousy." *J of Personality and Soc Psych*, 47, 4 (1984): 780–792; N.T. Feather, "An Attributional and Value Analysis of Deservingness in Success and Failure Situations," *British J of Soc Psychol.* 31 (1992): 125–145; and Sharon Bass, "Connecticut Q & A: Peter Salovey," ow.ly/hXlj50NOAVh, 09-11-88.

p179 **faked hearing voices in his sanity hearing:** Abrahamsen, David, "Psychiatrist's Story: How 'Son of Sam" Faked It," *S.F. Chronicle*, 07-02-79, p.1, 7.

p179 **the CIA framed him because he knows too much about MK-Ultra:** Information about MK-Ultra here and throughout the book is drawn from interviews with Ric Orsic and Colleen Higgins, but chiefly from info provided by Siobhan Barry, "The Psychology of Deception ...and MK-Ultra," ow.ly/gaZB50NFrA1, 05-27-20 and by Anonymous, "CIA files received by the DP," *The Daily Pennsylvanian*, Philadelphia, 09-05-79, p.1.

CHAPTER 24

p182 **She soon moved into 3411 Race Street with him:** This happened after a whirlwind courtship of ten days. Information regarding Holly (and much of it throughout the rest of the book) comes from the same sources noted in Ch22 and Ch23 as well as Walter, "Holly," and AP staff writer, "Key dates in the Ira Einhorn case," *Plainview Herald-(myplainview.com/news/article/Key-dates-in-the-Ira-Einhorn-case-9038216.php)*, 09-22-02.

p183 **Timothy Leary's colleague Richard Alpert, who knows lots about Ultra:** Maia Szalavitz discusses Leary and Alpert's connection to the CIA's effort to weaponize LSD in *Time* healthland.time.com/2012/03/23/the-legacy-of-the-cias-secret-lsd-experiments-on-america.

CHAPTER 25

p191 **put a rattlesnake in the mailbox of an attorney:** Paul Morantz, the attorney, spent time in a hospital, and later wrote about the attack and Dederich's cult (paulmorantz.com/cult/the-history-of-synanon-and-charles-dederich). Dederich and two members of his security force (one, the son of American musician, Stan Kenton) "derattled" the snake before placing it in the mailbox. The sources for other allegations in this chapter (e.g., Dederich was raised in a dysfunctional family group) include: Lewis Yablonsky, *The Tunnel Back*; Dan Casriel, M.D., *So Fair a House*; and Guy Endore, *Synanon*.

p192 On campus, I teach grad students to produce "soc-umentaries: For more about this new film genre, see Nina Alesci, "Soc-umentaries' prove pictures worth a thousand words," *American Sociological Association Footnotes*, Summer 1994, 22, 6, p.7. and "The perspective of a documentary filmmaker and sociologist," *IASSIST Quarterly: Int'l. Assoc. for Soc Sci Info Service and Technology*, 14, 3/4 (1990): 23-27.

Examples of soc-umentaries I've done: "The Guardian Angels—police or vigilantes?"1981;" Gang Signs- are gangs influencing your kids or community," 1997,distributed nationally by Blockbuster Video and Nimco; and "Parenting with the Point System- changing kids' problem behavior," 2000, "Dealing with Sports Fans- the drunks, the disorderly, the rioters." 2006, plus "Alcohol, Disorder and the Police," 2007 – all available from Insight Media (and Alexander Street Press).

p193 "must be understood if we are to survive . . . Peace, Ira Einhorn:" Levy, *Secret*, 244.

CHAPTER 26

p202 coroner's report concludes Holly sustained six blows to her skull: This and other facts about the Einhorn case in this chapter, based on my recollections, journals, interviews, and news clippings, plus Einhorn sources mentioned earlier and herein: Juan Hann Ng, "Peace, Love, and Murder" *CrimeandInvestigation.co.uk*, p.3. Steve Lopez, "The Search for the Unicorn," *Time Magazine* https://content. time.com/time/ nation/article/0,8599,168382,00.html, p.3.

p203 you wouldn't be able to get it all up!: Sources: Stephanie Ramos, "Einhorn on Trial Again for 1977 Murder," *The Daily Pennsylvanian*, ow.ly/C0lj50NNvup, p2; and Levy, Secret, 258.

p203 According to the private investigators: Ibid., 205, 222-227. As the information shared on this page shows, the Madduxes' PI's knew, as retired FBI agents, how to gather intelligence and keep the heat on witnesses and Philly police. Additional source, "Law case summaries,"-(encyclopedia.com/law/law-magazines/ira-einhorn-trial-1993), p. 2.

p203 a rumor that Specter recently tried to get Ira to plead insanity: Information regarding this and the follow-up plea- bargain rumor comes from *Secret*, 250-1. To determine the truth of these two rumors, examine these two articles about the ever- changing, ever-political, Senator Specter: Rich Yeselson, "Arlen Specter," *The American Prospect* (org/health/arlen-specter-poor-man-s-richard-nixon/, 10-16-12; Staff, "The Senator and The Unicorn,"-(nationalreview.com/2004/04/senator-and-unicorn/), 4-08-04,

p204 they sublet their place during summers away from Philly: *Secret*, 230, 241-2.

p206 Since out on bail: Ira's travels to Palo Alto, his new girlfriend, and his preparations for his trial, all come from *Secret*, 252, 254-6, 260-65.

CHAPTER 27

p208 issues a bench warrant for his arrest: The steps taken by Philly authorities as well as the general factors that shaped Ira growing up in this chapter come from all kinds of sources, especially newspaper articles like Bill Collings' "Ira Einhorn: Poet, Wanderer, Hippie, and Now Fugitive," *The Philadelphia Inquirer*, 01-16-81 and online articles like Diana Whitney's "The Killer Who Spared My Mother,"(longreads. com/2018/08/03/ the-killer-who-spared-my-mother), 03-03-18.

p211 New-Age philosopher who promoted himself brilliantly, winning countless admirers: New Age here refers to a range of spiritual-religious practices and beliefs which grew quickly during the early '70s. In the U.S. It arose from influences as diverse as the UFO religions of the '50s, the counterculture of the '60s, and the Human Potential Movement.

p211 he likely scores well into the 30s: Notable evaluations using Hare's system (from en.wikipedia.org/wiki/Psychopathy_Checklist):

Ted Bundy was evaluated as 39 (of 40 possible), Jeffrey Dahmer 23, John Wayne Gacy 27, Gary Ridgway (the Green River Killer) 19, and Aileen Wuornos 32.

p212 reconcile Ira the murderer with Ira the man: A portion of this profile of Ira's upbringing stem from findings in Secret, Chapter 2 and from recollections of Ira's remarks to me.

p213 "...to aid and abet the intellectual development of Ira": Secret, 35.

p213 (he claimed his IQ to be "upwards of 140") would take him far, especially in math and science: Ibid., 33.

CHAPTER 28

p221 Oakland's response to crime during the 1948-78 period, part of a ten city LEAA project.: Our work on the Law Enforcement Assistance Administration grant resulted in a chapter in Anne Heinz et al, eds., *Crime in City Politics* (London: Longman, 1983).

p226 abandoned Leona "fool's gold" mines near their grandmother's house and cottage: Info about crime from interviews and info about Leona rhyolite and fool's gold mines from oaklandgeology. com/2021/05/10/the-pyrite-orebody-of-leona-heights.

CHAPTER 29

p231 being the most common crime in the US: The FBI's Uniform Crime Report (UCR) statistics for "Criminal Victimization in the US" for 1982 and 1983 can be found at ojp.gov/pdffiles1/ Digitization/96580NCJRS.pdf and at ojp.gov/ncjrs/ virtual-library/ abstracts/crime-united-states-1983.

p231 victimized by a so-called opportunity rapist like Val was. For different types of rapists, see Nicholas Groth, *Men Who Rape* (New York: Plenum Press, 1979), p 27.

p232 Harlow's infant monkey studies: These classic wire and cloth "mother" studies hardly need any introduction. They showed that warmth and somatic comfort are as important, if not more so, than food and water. Harlow's studies permanently changed Americans' approach to parenting with regard to socializing, not isolating, infants and children. See Harry F. Harlow, "The nature of love," *American Psychologist* 13 (1958): 673–685.

CHAPTER 30

p238 where Mitchell's on parole: Parole is a term for continued supervision by state or federal agents after an inmate is released *early* before serving a full sentence. If parolees violate conditions of parole they may be returned to prison.

p243 and the manipulative role Carole played: Worth noting, my observations and interviews of Lawson family members are the source of most of what I write about Carole.

CHAPTER 31

p253 see if it clearly favors offenders over victims: Today, one can find such esoterica easily online, e.g., /en.wikisource.org/wiki/ Oregon_Constitution/Article_VII_ (Original). Also *Courts.Oregon.gov* is a useful resource– unavailable, of course, back in the '80s when landline phones were the "information highway." It took some time then, for instance, to discover nuanced differences among district-, circuit-, justice-, and specialty- courts.

CHAPTER 32

p255 A Cold, Calculated *CRIME*: SPOILER ALERT: Read these footnotes after finishing the chapter to preserve the suspense.

I know much about Mitchell Lewis based on interviews noted elsewhere and on impressions growing out of indirect interactions with him. Additionally, I've researched pieces of his life and corroborated the findings using online sources. The most critical piece for this book is Mitchell's crimes. I relied on newspaper stories, of which the following represent but a few bits of the total (headlines only to protect victims and their families): "Robbery try kills owner's wife." *The Oregonian*, p.15. "Man facing murder count in Tavern death," *The Bulletin*, p. 4. "Cynthia Gifford's Funeral," *The Oregonian*, p 79. "Bartender Accused," *Eugene Register-Guard*, p.7.

p254 and forensic techs including the coroner: Based on the sources noted in the prior footnote, I have imagined what words and phrases DA Schrunk used in front of Mitchel's grand jury. I've had to drastically reduce the actual remarks and story of Schrunk's re-creation of Mitchell's crime spree and his speculation regarding Mitchell's thoughts, feelings, and many actions. Know, however, that the fictionalized retelling throughout Part IV of my book is faithful to the facts I gathered, including those contained in the 75 court documents and especially the one entitled: "Grand Jury, Secret # C7X-08-23839 In the District-Circuit Court of the State of Oregon, 1977 Indictment for violation of ORS 163.095, Aggravated Murder + 3 Other Counts."

p256 but can we believe DA Schrunk?: This news story (oregonlive. com/ portland/2023/01/mike-schrunk-multnomah-countys-longest-serving-former-da-dies- at-age-80.html) leaves no doubt regarding Schrunk's reliability and credibility.

CHAPTER 33

p264 I begin going through Mitchell's case file page by page: This chapter is based on 78 court documents, starting with the "Indictment of" and "Warrant of Arrest for [Mitchell Lewis]," entitled *"Secret # C7X-08-23839 In the District/Circuit Court of the State of Oregon for Multnomah County: Count I Aggravated Murder, Count II Robbery in the First Degree, Count III Attempted Murder, Count IV Assault in the Second Degree."*

p264 Carr met alone with Mitchell in his hospital room a week after the murder: See Ch32.

p269 a speedball combo of cocaine uppers with heroin downers:
Cocaine is a powerfully addictive stimulant drug made from the leaves of the coca plant native to South America. Heroin is an opioid drug made from morphine, a natural substance taken from the seed pod of various opium poppy plants (nida.nih.gov/publications/drugfacts/cocaine or /heroin).

CHAPTER 34

p271 Mitchell's case file and make notes. I share them with Lynn:
See Ch33 for explanation of this reconstructed conversation.

p271 powdered coke doesn't addict users the way crack does: For info about what was known about Mitchell's drug use disorder back in the day, see Stanton Peele and Archie Brodsky, *The Truth about Addiction and Recovery* (New York: Simon & Schuster, 1991). Other of Brodsky's many writings are useful (pipatl.org/bibliography/abrodsky. html) as is the US's current take on cocaine (nida.nih.gov/publications/research-reports/ cocaine/what-cocaine).

p274 where the historic Jesus allegedly lived, preached, and died:
See en.wikipedia.org/ wiki/Jerusalem_in_Christianity for why they named their capital Jerusalem.

p275 incarcerated seven years later as a felon for just selling cocaine:
Information about Darnell and Ricardo's cases came from a search of articles in the newspaperarchive.com, which includes *The Oregonian*.

p275 has served more time for nonviolent dealing and using than Mitchell did for his several violent crimes: Ibid.

CHAPTER 35

p279 Uganda's Idi Amin, responsible for the deaths of three hundred thousand, or Cambodia's Pol Pot—behind the killing of two million:
Amin (smithsonianmag. com/history/uganda-the-horror-85439313) and Pol Pot (cla.umn.edu/chgs/holocaust- genocide-education/resource-guides/Cambodia).

p280 predation just beyond the Bay Area: See more about these cases and those cited in the next few paragraphs at murderpedia and (ow. ly/XA5X50NOCJh).

p280 controlled, scientific work. For sure Scott Peck isn't: Re Milgram and Zimbardo's "conforming to do evil" experiments, see Simon A. Haslam and Steve D. Reicher, "Contesting the 'Nature' of Conformity: What Milgram and Zimbardo's Studies Really Show," *PLoS Biology 10*, no. 11 (2012) and e1001426, doi.org/10.1371/journal. pbio.1001426, where they say empirical work and identity theorizing disprove the "shock" and "prison" experiments. Re Peck's '93 book, his only science, and hence proof, is his presentation of incidents he encountered in his psychiatric practice.

CHAPTER 36

p284 "pass" and "cover" using coping strategies: When someone "passes" they strive to completely hide their true identity from those around them as opposed to "covering" where they disclose their identity, but downplay its significance. See Goffman's *Stigma,*especially Chapters 1 and 2, and visit *KarlSchonborn.com* for info about "Stigma" and other soc-umentary topics.

p286 "Put an electronic monitor on his ankle": Developed by two brothers at Harvard in the '60s using military surplus tracking gear, home monitoring began with juvenile offenders in the '70s. (For more, see Lilly and Ball, in their 1987 article at ojp.gov/ ncjrs/virtual-library/ abstracts/brief-history-house-arrest-and-electronic-monitoring.) Judge Jack Love in New Mexico and another judge in Kentucky were among the first to advocate the use of "electronic handcuffs."

p292 get rearrested within three years: S.T. Reid– in her widely adopted textbook, *Crime and Criminology* text (Oxford University Press, 2011)–states that early studies (reported by Reckless in '73 and Allen et al in '81) showed "as many as two-thirds of those released from prison become recidivists." For detailed state and federal "rearrest" rates, including types of parole "crime repeaters," see reports by the Rand Corp, the Council of State Governments, and the U.S. Bureau of Justice Statistics (esp. their'84 report, "Recidivism of Prisoners Released").

p293 the threats he made around Lynn at our home constituted an assault: *Penal Code of California (Peace Officers Abridged Edition)*, 4th ed., Sacramento: Department of General Services, 1971: § 220 Assaults with intent to commit felony other than murder [e.g., rape] § 221 Other Assaults, p.42; §240 Assault defined: "An assault is an unlawful attempt, coupled with a present ability, to commit a violent injury on the person of another." p.43; §459 Burglary [and housebreaking] defined: "Every person who enters any house...with intent to commit grand or petit larceny or any felony is guilty of burglary." p.111.

CHAPTER 37

p299 a mass shooting at a McDonald's in an Hispanic area of San Diego causes me to alter again my approach to guns and gun control: Account and discussion with Ric Orsic are based on my own recollection and news coverage such as that by the *San Diego Union Tribune* (ow.ly/vEqK50NHB7B).

p301 Dianne Feinstein's just-concluded press conference: Words from this radio news update cobbled together from Carlo's book and two archival sources ow.ly/ FPay50NHBHT and ow.ly/ bQrw50NHBEq.

CHAPTER 38

p302 showed the killer to be the L.A. Night Stalker: Ibid. Additionally, this and all other Night Stalker info based on an amalgam of many sources, including britannica. com/biography/ Richard-Ramirez and Michael Newton, *Encyclopedia of Serial killers*, (New York: Facts on File, 2006) pp. 6,104, 218-19, 258, 276.

p306 doing coke's a choice, not a physical addiction.": See Ch34 and Joel Fort, MD, *The Pleasure Seekers: The Drug Crisis, Youth, and Society*.

(New York: Bobbs-Merrill, 1969) and Fort's *Our Biggest Drug Problem* (New York: McGraw-Hill, 1973).

EPILOGUE

p309 Epilogue: Besides drawing on my and others personal recollections, this final chapter draws in part on many of the same sources cited in prior chapters. There are, of course, several other more recent source materials cited the footnotes below because the Epilogue spans several decades beyond the 1960s and 1970s.

p309 whose narcissistic tendencies... manipulative, Machiavellian behavior: I know the history of people with *narcissistic tendencies* has evolved and become more complex since I started following it with "The Desperate Loneliness of Narcissism," *S.F. Chronicle*, May, 12, 1982, p. 37. Currently (according to psychdb.com/personality/narcissistic), it is thought that a person with the DSM's narcissistic personality disorder (NPD):

1. is interpersonally exploitative
2. lacks empathy
3. is often envious of others
4. shows arrogant, haughty behaviors or attitudes.

The DSM's prognosis section hints at other measurable criteria and causes

-vulnerability in self-esteem makes individuals with NPD very sensitive to "injury" from criticism or defeat.

-impairment can be severe, and may include marital problems and interpersonal relationships conflicts

-individuals may face occupational difficulties, and show an unwillingness to take risks in competitive or other situations in which defeat is possible.

Both Carole and Sharon tended toward the vulnerable version of the disorder and also toward the covert (as opposed to overt) entitlement versions of narcissism. I also know the long history of *manipulative behavior*, which was first analyzed by Machiavelli, who taught princes how to gain and hold power in the 16th century. This behavior characterizes Eve, and if interested in more details, see "A Criminologist's Story"and see ow.ly/np6W50NBARH for info about low and high "Machs"and their relationships to APD and BPD persons.

p309 For the following six Dark Triad individuals: I stand behind my use of the labels "psychopath" and "Dark Triad" in this book because it's commonplace for lay authors (e.g., many journalists and true-crime writers) to use these non-clinical terms that readers use and understand intuitively. However, I am not a lay author, being a PhD social-psych-oriented criminologist. As a professor, I've kept up with the literature, done professional research, and written extensively about criminal behavior. I've also kept up with the "applied" branches of criminology and their respective "bibles": forensic psychiatry and its DSM, plus the criminal justice field and its PCR (Hare's Psychopathy Checklist- Revised PCR). This explains the scientific richness of many of the footnotes in this Notes section. So, I've tried to mix lay and professional sensibilities in this book, bringing the best of both worlds to readers.

Carole Conde

p310 She and Eve had the dark triad tendency to freeload or, to use a likely-sexist verb, gold-dig:

Tendencies or traits can be seen in the emotions and interpersonal behaviors of dark triadic narcissists and psychopaths. They can also be seen in their lifestyles, one of which is parasitic relationships. In Natasha Tracy's "20 Signs You're With a Psychopath or You Are a Psychopath,"*HealthyPlace*, 01-28-20, she states that the 9th question professionals ask when using Hare's assessment inventory is "[Are you or] your partner in relationships where he/she uses others (i.e. parasitic relationships)?"

Sharon Belton

p311 RISD-bound art student she'd run into at Bryn Mawr College:
Holly attended the Rhode Island School of Design for only one term

after experiencing an unsettling abortion. She returned to Philly to proofread at *TV Guide*, work at the Philly Zoo, and cohabit with a boyfriend before returning to Bryn Mawr College for her senior year. She graduated in 1971. After time in Europe, work on a kibbutz in Israel, and travel to India–with various short-term relationships along the way–she found herself back in the U.S. and Philly in mid-1972. She would soon meet Ira. (Some info in this summary comes from Secret, Chapter 5.)

p312 discard them and move on to other plans that exclude them: Sharon's growing ambivalence about a painting career did not have to mean discarding and excluding a husband, old friends, and Warehouse artists who all supported her effort to realize her potential.

PSYCHOPATHS

p313 three percent of Americans: I arrived at the 3% figure by averaging a U. of Chicago neuroscientist's estimate of 1% (ow. ly/7IUc50NILmm) with a 4+% estimate by Sanz-Garcia et al in an NIH-cited study (ow.ly/jJFJ50NILkn).

For other sources for references to psychopaths in the rest of the Epilogue, refer to Ch3 of these Notes as well as the Bibliography.

Bill Hanson

p314 Bill's commitment to Atascadero State Hospital (ASH): For a general description of ASH, see ow.ly/Ff1X50NILwT(JCAHO. For a study done at Atascadero around the time Bill was there, see Richard Laws,"The Failure of a Token Economy," *Federal Probation*, 38, (1974), 33.

p314 it's unclear how long he remained incarcerated: Federal and state confidentiality laws strictly limit Atascadero information that can be disclosed. How the California Welfare and Institutions Code 5328 applies is explained here:

dsh.ca.gov/Hospitals/Patient_Information_Requests_FAQs.html.

p314 he might've been frightened by violent inmates at Atascadero: Relevant here is Tonya Strickland's "Safety at Atascadero State Hospital [ASH] is Questioned by Some Employees," *San Luis Obispo Tribune*, 01-29/31-11; Strickland's sources: ASH documents and archives of the *San Luis Obispo Tribune*.

p315 Los Angeles, Glendale, Rosemead, and Capitola: spokeo, peoplefinders, ancestry.

p315 Public records don't show Bill committing further crimes, just traffic violations: spokeo, truthfinder, intelius.

p315 enamored of the teachings of guru Sai Baba: Bill states on his LinkedIn page, "I have been working off and on, on a book detailing some amazing and beautiful experiences with Sathya Sai Baba during my 15 years in India." Info about his guru at en.wikipedia.org/wiki/Sathya_Sai_Baba #cite_366 and about experiences in cults at Epilogue below.

p315 putting fifty thousand miles on his motorcycle: Ibid., Bill Hanson, LinkedIin page.

p315 married a woman named Nubia, and they lived in Bangalore, India: Noted in Anonymous, "Obituary for Karl Hanson, M.D.," *San Francisco Chronicle*, 09-25-05.

p316 installing one of her artistic obelisks in Sai Baba's museum: NYtimes.com/1990/10/30/obituaries/joan-brown-artist-and-profes-sor-52-inspired-by- ancients.html.

p316 Sai Baba often molested young boys: The UK's Guardian rebutted the Sai Organization's denials of molestation by writing, "[T]he U.S. State Department issued a travel warning after reports of 'inappropriate sexual behavior by a prominent local religious leader' which, officials later confirmed was a reference to Sai Baba." (theguardian.com/uk/2006/nov/04/voluntarysector.india).-Other evidence provided by Eamon Hardy and Tanya Datta (2004), *Secret Swami* (Documentary), BBC News.

p316 Many concluded he was a trickster and a cheat: Ibid., Hardy and Datta. Regarding claimed miracles: "Sai Baba: God-man or con man?" BBC News, 12-7-20. Regarding resurrections of the dead: David Lane, *The Mystical: Exploring the Transcendent* (Mt. San Antonio College Press: L.A., 2014) 62–63.

p316 contentment among the many privileged followers who joined Rajneesh: Ibid. Bill Hanson, above. Other sources: Marion Goldman, "I did research at Rajneeshpuram, and here is what I learned," (ow. ly/ZSyf50NCWzy) 04-30-18; Michael Galanter et al, "The Moonies: A Psychological Study..," *Am J Psychiatry.* 1979,136 (2), 165-170.

Be aware that studies of cult impacts are fraught with problems: measurement, definitional (including the words cult, contentment, happiness), and confusion of in/dependent variables with one another. Also fraught is whether the cult appealed to Bill's neediness – whether developmental or situational (lonely, far from home)? Regarding this, see Michael Langone at psychiatrictimes.com/view/clinical-update- cults 6-01-96.

p316 a pricey Bay Area suburb: I've been to Bill's condo development and agree with Trulia's estimate that his condo would sell for a million dollars today. His city is in the 4th wealthiest county in the *US News & World Report*'s rankings, right behind Santa Clara County. (USNWR used median household income to rank).

Jed Drell

p317 not even letting his wife speak to them during a colleague's funeral: This and other information in Jed's section of the Epilogue is based on personal observations, written accounts (e.g., news stories, Psych Department histories), and opinions expressed in several interviews with Jed's colleagues in Psych and in university administration.

p317 because he preferred foreign faculty and students: This allegation based on interviewee statements and on speculation that since his attempt to kill his wife, his local notoriety has made him uncomfortable around university faculty and students.

p317 stripped him of his license in the 2000s: Source for this: sfgate. com/bayarea/article/Oakland-defense-attorney-Lincoln-Mintz-dies-3442750.php.

p318 Jed chose to retire, probably to everyone's mutual relief: The information in this and the prior paragraph comes chiefly from interviews with colleagues of Jed's in the Psych Department.

Mitchell Lewis

p318 arrested Mitchell for three felonies in August 1986: My account in the next few paragraphs is largely drawn from information contained in 26 court documents including "Court Indictment 86-08-26686, In the District/Circuit Court of the State of Oregon (Plaintiff) for the County of Multnomah vs Mitchell Lewis (Defendant), 3 Felony Counts + Parole Violation, 1986."

p319 withdrew his not guilty pleas and admitted to fewer felonies: Ibid. An additional source for this and next paragraph: "Document: Petition to Plead Guilty/No Contest and Waive a Jury Trial."**p325 sentenced Mitchell to two years' probation:** Ibid. Another important document: "Order & Judgment, Amending Judgment of Conviction & Sentence and Transferring Probation."

p319 made him uneasy knowing people in the bar and restaurant business spread stories about him: When Mitchell had murdered his boss, Oregon newspapers covered the case with details of his crimes and headlines like these: "Bartender Accused," "Man facing murder count in tavern death," and "Portlander pleads guilty in murder."

p320 enhancements for property and drug crimes: Oregon voters got tougher on crime (e.g., oregon.public.law/statutes/ors_161.737) and they even began to follow the U.S. Supreme Court's lead in sanctioning capital punishment (e.g., Anonymous, "Supreme Court Upholds Death for Murder," *The Oregonian*, July 3, 1976, p. 1; and Jim

Hall, "Companion Ballot Measures Reinstated Death Penalty," *The Oregonian*, February 15, 1985, p.74.)

p320 from his place on Pine Street to ours in Oakland in twenty minutes: Info in this and the next two paragraphs based on conversations, ancestry, zillow, and spokeo.

p320 died in 2010 at age fifty-four of chronic alcoholism: The source for this is the Montana Death Certificate for Mitchell Lewis (screen shot accessed 2-2-17). Coroner Daniel Bates wrote: "Died [alone] in own residence. Cause of death: chronic alcoholism." Mitchell's brother provided further details for the coroner's report: "Never married. Born in Clearwater, FL." Mitchell's niece posted on Facebook, "Such a shame how he passed away."

Ira Einhorn

p321 to London (joining his girlfriend J.M. Morrison), and to Dublin (renting from professor Weaire): Sources for dates and facts in this and subsequent paragraphs come from various detailed accounts. These tell of of Ira's time on the run, his below- the-radar life married to a wealthy Swede in France, and his two trials: Neil Gordon at salon.com/2002/08/14/einhorn; an Independent writer at ow.ly/ShHE50NIQkj, December 5 1997; Dave Lindorff at salon. com/2002/10/18/einhorn_2/; and a staffer at latimes.com/2002/oct/18/ nation/na-einhorn1823.

p321 uncovered damning info about him: The source for the information in this paragraph and the next four comes from Levy, *Secret*, 278-295. The two women's names, Rita Siegal and Judy Lewis, are pseudonyms for the victims.

p322 try Ira in absentia in 1993: The content here and for the rest of this section is based on: the materials noted at the start of Chapters 7, 18 and 27; the material from twitter.com (/Avi_WA/ status/1405548390415536139/photo/1); and the facts from Peter

Durantine, "Pennsylvania. Senate Approves Bill that Would Give Einhorn a New Trial," *The Philadelphia Inquirer*, 1-21-98.

p323 "...I'm not going to lose sleep about his passing:" Julie Shaw,"'Unicorn Killer' Ira Einhorn, 79, dies in Pennsylvania. prison," The Philadelphia Inquirer, 3-3-20. Here's where Ira's appeal of his verdict and sentence is summarized: casetext.com/case/com-v-einhorn-1.

BIBLIOGRAPHY

This selective bibliography acknowledges the sources which proved to be the most valuable for the writing of this book. In some cases, this meant they gave me guidance and perspective back when I was experiencing the 1968-1986 story told here. Many more sources are cited in the NOTES.

BOOKS & ARTICLES

American Psychiatric Association. *The Diagnostic and Statistical Manual of Mental Disorders*. (5th ed.) Washington, D.C.: APA, 2022.

Baez, Joan. *And a Voice to Sing With: a Memoir*. New York: Summit Books, 1987.

Bartol, Curt R. *Criminal Behavior: A Psychological Approach*. (6th ed.) Upper Saddle River, NJ: Prentice Hall, 2002.

Bentley, Barbara. *A Dance with the Devil*, New York: Penguin, 2008.

Brodeur, Jean-Paul, (ed), *How to Recognize Good Policing: Problems and Issues*, Thousand Oaks, CA: Sage Publications, 1998.

Carlo, Philip. *The Night Stalker: The True Story of America's Most Feared Serial Killer*. Citadel, 2016.

Cole, Michael L. *The Zodiac Revisited: The Facts of the Case*. Cleveland, OH: Twin Prime Publishing, 2021.

Cooper, Becky. *We Keep the Dead Close: A Murder at Harvard and a Half Century of Silence*. New York: Grand Central Pub, 2020.

Doyle, Michael. *Radical Chapters: Pacifist Bookseller Roy Kepler and the Paperback Revolution*. Syracuse: Syracuse U. Press, 2012.

Eisinger, Jesse. *Chickenshit Club: Why the Justice Department Fails to Prosecute Executives*. New York: Simon & Schuster, 2017.

Erikson, Eric. *Gandhi's Truth: The Story of Militant Nonviolence.* New York: Norton Books, 1969.

Goffman, Erving. *Stigma: Notes on the Management of Spoiled Identity.* London: Pelican Books, 1968.

Grann, David. *Killers of the Flower Moon: The Osage Murders and the Birth of the FBI.* New York: Vintage, 2018.

Groth, Nicholas. *Men Who Rape: The Psychology of the Offender.* New York: Plenum Press, 1979.

Gullan, Harold. *Tough Cop: Mike Chitwood vs. the Scumbags.* Philadelphia: Camino Books, Inc, 2013.

Hare, Robert. *Without Conscience: The Disturbing World of the Psychopaths Among Us.* Guilford, CT: The Guilford Press, 1999.

Henderson, Bruce and Sam Summerlin. *Super Sleuths -The World's Greatest Real-Life Detectives and Their Toughest Cases,* New York: Macmillan, 1976.

Jentz, Terri. *Strange Piece of Paradise,* New York: Farrar, Straus & Giroux, 2006.

Junger, Sebastian. *A Death in Belmont.* New York: W.W. Norton, 2006.

Karmen, Andrew. *Crime Victims: An Introduction to Victimology.* (3rd ed.) Boston: Wadsworth, 1984.

Kelling, George and Catherine Coles. *Fixing Broken Windows.* New York: Simon & Schuster, 1996.

Kirn, Walter. *Blood Will Out -The True Story of a Murder, a Mystery, and a Masquerade.* New York: W.W.Norton, 2014.

Larson, Erik. *The Devil in the White City,* New York, Vintage Books, 2003.

Levy, Steven. *The Unicorn's Secret - Murder in the Age of Aquarius.* New York: Prentice Hall Press, 1988.

Marzano-Lesnevich, Alexandria. *The Fact of a Body: A Murder and a Memoir.* New York: Flatiron, 2017.

Nash, Jay Robert . *World Encyclopedia of 20th Century Murder.* New York: Paragon House, 1992.

Nash, Jay Robert . *World Encyclopedia of 20th Century Murder.* New York: Paragon House, 1992.

Olsen, Jack. *Son: A Psychopath and his Victims,* New York: Atheneum Books, 1983.

Olsen, Gregg. *If You Tell: A True Story of Murder.* Seattle: Thomas & Mercer, 2019.

Paulhus, Delroy L and Kevin M. Williams, "The Dark Triad of personality: Narcissism, Machiavellianism, and psychopathy," *Journal of Research in Personality,* 36 (2002) p 556–563.

Schmalleger, Frank. *Criminology Today: An Integrative Introduction.* (3rd ed.) New York: Prentice Hall, 2004.

Schonborn, Karl. *Dealing with Violence: The Challenge Faced by Police and Other Peacekeepers.* Chicago: C.C. Thomas Pubs, 1975.

Schonborn, Karl. *Policing Society: A Comparative Look at Violence, the Use of Force, and Other Issues in the US and the UK.* Dubuque: Kendall-Hunt Publishing, 2001.

Schonborn, Karl, and Robert Harris, assisting Rudolph Moos. "Psychiatric and Staff Reactions to their Physical Environment." *Journal of Clinical Psychology* 25, no. 3 (July 1969).

Sharp, Gene. *Civilian Defense: Civilian-Based Defense.* Princeton, NJ: Princeton U. Press, 1990.

Sides, Hampton. *Hellhound on His Trail.* New York: Anchor Books, 2010.

Stout, Martha. *The Sociopath Next Door.* New York: Harmony Books, 2005.

Vronsky, Peter. *Serial Killers: The Method and Madness of Monsters.* New York: Berkley Books, 2004.

Wambaugh, Joseph. *The Onion Field.* New York: Dell Publishing, 1973.

Wilson, James Q. *Varieties of Police Behavior.* Cambridge: Harvard U. Press, 1968.

Wolfgang, Marvin. *Patterns in Criminal Homicide.* Philadelphia: Science Editions, 1966.

Wolfgang, Marvin, ed. *Studies in Homicide.* New York: Harper & Row, 1967.

COURT DOCUMENTS

"Grand Jury, Indictment of Mitchell Lewis for violation of ORS 163.095 (Aggravated Murder) & 3 Other Counts." Secret # C77-08- 33839 1977. + 77 other court documents

"In the District/Circuit Court of the State of Oregon (Plaintiff) for the County of Multnomah, vs Mitchell Lewis (Defendant), 3 Felony Counts + Parole Violation." Court NBR 86-08-36686, 1986. + 27 other court documents

INTERVIEWS – partial list

Administrators -several faculty of Psychology, Sociology Departments.

Belton, Sharon

Conde, Carole

Crim justice personnel - POs, Chiefs, County Sheriffs, Attorneys, and 11 PD Officers

Dahl, Crista

Hansons - Gwen, Kent, Myrna

Harper, Greg Esq

Holt, Steve

Hooper, Ned

Lawsons - Autumn, Lynn, Valerie

Noces, Janet Orsic, Ric

Schonborns – Eve, Gayle, Jack, Scott

Starkweather, Jerry

NEWSPAPERS

Anonymous, "Jail Term for Prof in Wife Knifing," *The Montclarion*, March 28, 1975, p.37.

Anonymous, "Bill Hanson Case," *Daily Independent Journal*, San Rafael, California, January 28, 1974, p.11

Brill, Steven, Esq,"The Insanity Plea is a Travesty," *S.F, Chronicle*, This World, December 13, 1981.

Special Report, "Stalking the Brown Bag Killer," *S.F. Chronicle*, Nov. 6, 1976, p.13.

ONLINE SOURCES

murderpedia. murderpedia.org/male.H/h/hanson-william.htm

newspaperarchive.com/tags/william-hanson-paper-bag?pr=10&pci=7

psychiatry data base. Psychiatry reference for physicians, residents, and medical students. . . psychdb.com

serial killer crime index. crimezzz.net/serialkiller_index/ serienkiller_h.php

ACKNOWLEDGMENTS

Steve Holt's "sick puppy" witty question at the end of this story suggests, as most of us have heard, that we are often judged by the company we keep. I'm pleased to answer that the many admirable, stand-up people in my life far outnumber the unpleasant ones featured in this book.

It's now my pleasure to mention and thank many of them.

My good friend and consigliere, Dennis Mack, listened and commented astutely for years as I tried to keep my storyline from plunging off trestle tracks into an abyss. So did another good friend, sociologist David Graeven. Others, like seasoned writers Joe DiPrisco, Sheldon Greene, Mary Volmer, and Barbara Schonborn kept the train rolling along so it'd arrive at its destination in a safe and rewarding fashion for readers. My deepest gratitude to them all.

Thanks are in order to several people who braved the disjointed words of the first draft and helped shape the book. Those who gave generous and candid feedback include CBI special criminal investigator, Julio Alfaro; retired corporate writer, Linda Freccia; financial fraud investigator, Jill Bean; and dangerously talented wordsmith, Ron Kalb.

David Ivester from Suncoast Publishing saw something special in my manuscript early on. That has meant the world to me, as has his vast experience in publishing during the long countdown to launch. I greatly appreciate Ivester's hard work and also that of Bef Wilson, Kirsten Barger, Meg Dalton, Maddee Smith, Linda Chernoff, and Karen Frederick. I'm especially lucky to have the best final editor ever, the brilliant and sharp-eyed Beth Lynne. She was unfailingly good at coming up with the perfect word or phrase.

On the academic front, I owe a debt to professors Marvin Wolfgang, Digby Baltzell, and William Evan at UPenn who prepared me for academia, and also a debt to department colleagues and to certain administrators at my university. Likewise, I appreciate the several undergrad, grad, and postgrad students I've known who were part of the *Privileged Killers* story.

And of course, many police departments (PDs) and certain sworn officers deserve a shout out for indispensable help over several decades: NYPD & Deputy Commissioner Wilfred Horne; Philadelphia PD & homicide detective Mike Chitwood; San Leandro PD & officers James Medina and Thomas Hull; San Francisco PD & officers Iggy Chin and Jack Friedman; and countless Oakland PD officers already thanked in previous books.

Members of my extended family provided support and love, especially at critical moments depicted in my story and while writing it. Adam and Steve Horn, as well as Larry and Jerry Plith, need to be singled out in addition to the Meddaugh and Stenerson clans.

Finally, my best friend and the one without whom this book wouldn't have happened, Leslie Schonborn, deserves unending gratitude and love over and beyond what I already owe her as a husband.

ABOUT THE AUTHOR
Karl Schonborn

Schonborn studied psychology as an undergrad, psychiatry in med school, and criminology in a PhD program, all at different Ivy-League universities. After his schooling, he returned home to the San Francisco Bay Area for a university professorship. He has mostly dedicated his teaching and research to finding ways to reduce violent crime and make policing more humanitarian and less authoritarian.

Over the years, Schonborn's research has involved in-the-trenches studies of criminals and police officers, and institutional behavior, as well as a dozen police departments of all sizes. He has studied jails and prisons, and published his insights, resulting in four well-received academic books.

Schonborn's film-making and public service keep him invigorated. One of the many award-winning documentaries he's produced, "Gang Signs," became a "free-rental" nationwide at Blockbuster Video. Other works became featured programs at the Law Enforcement Television Network, LETN.

When not working, Schonborn enjoys painting, traveling abroad with his wife, and visiting their far-flung kids and their respective families.

Discussion questions for Book Clubs and schools
are available at: **KarlSchonborn.com/PrivilegedKillers**

If you've enjoyed this book, please check out the revised edition of *Cleft Heart*, the exciting prequel to *Privileged Killers*. It's the story of Karl Schonborn's triumph over cleft-lip-and-palate bullying and speech challenges.

"A poignant, heartfelt tale of endurance and hope.
Schonborn's story is an inspiration to all who endure physical or mental health challenges and those who care about them."
—John F. Kerry, Senator, Democratic
Nominee for President of the United States 2004,
US Secretary of State

**Cleft Heart: Chasing Normal
by Karl Schonborn
is available through your favorite
bookseller.**

**Suggest that your Public Library
add this title to their
non-fiction collections**

Karl Schonborn's silver tongue is locked away for years by clefts that make his face asymmetrical and his speech unclear. Bullies attack him for being different, an outsider, and for being sidelined from sports due to a medical condition.

Doctors, speech therapists, and his own determination give him a shot at his dream of becoming a debate star and attending an elite college on scholarship. During the turbulence of his youth, Karl's own experiences with violence lead him to study how nonviolence can solve problems in all kinds of situations.

Schonborn's coming-of-age story recounts his friendship with a famous folksinger, his war resistance, two intertwined love stories, and an unexpected around-the-world odyssey. After all this—and an unspeakable tragedy in his family—Schonborn realizes everyone feels like an outsider at some point.

Made in the USA
Middletown, DE
16 March 2024

51028257R00230